2004

KASHMIR

KASHMIR

ROOTS OF CONFLICT,
PATHS TO PEACE

Sumantra Bose

HARVARD UNIVERSITY PRESS

Cambridge, Massachusetts, and London, England

2003

Library of Congress Cataloging-in-Publication Data
Bose, Sumantra, 1968–
Kashmir : roots of conflict, paths to peace / Sumantra Bose.
p. cm.
Includes bibliographical references and index.
ISBN 0-674-01173-2 (alk. paper)
1. Jammu and Kashmir (India)—History—19th century.
2. Jammu and Kashmir (India)—Politics and government—19th century.
3. India—Foreign relations—Pakistan.
4. Pakistan—Foreign relations—India.
I. Title.
DS485.K23B67 2003
954'.6—dc21
2003049919

For the people of Jammu and Kashmir
and in honor of
Subhas Chandra Bose (1897–1945)
Sarat Chandra Bose (1889–1950)
Sisir Kumar Bose (1920–2000)

CONTENTS

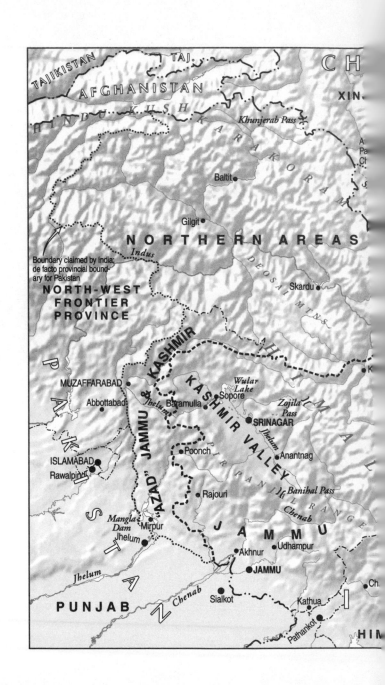

TAJIKISTAN

AFGHANISTAN

TAJ.

CH

XIN·

HINDU KUSH

KARAKORAM

Khunjerab Pass

Baltit•

Gilgit•

NORTHERN AREAS

Indus

DEOSAI MTNS

Skardu•

Boundary claimed by India;
de facto provincial boundary for Pakistan

NORTH-WEST
FRONTIER
PROVINCE

KASHMIR

P

K

MUZAFFARABAD•

Abbottabad•

Jhelum

Baramulla•

Wular
Lake
Sopore•

K

KASHMIR VALLEY

Zojila
Pass

SRINAGAR•

Anantnag•

A

JAMMU &

"AZAD"

Poonch•

Jhelum

K

ISLAMABAD•

Rawalpindi•

Rajouri•

PIR PANJAL RANGE

Banihal Pass

Chenab

S

Mangla
Dam

Mirpur•

JAMMU

T

Jhelum•

Akhnur•

Udhampur•

A

JAMMU•

N

Jhelum

Chenab

Sialkot•

Kathua•

Ch.

I

PUNJAB

Pathankot•

HIM·

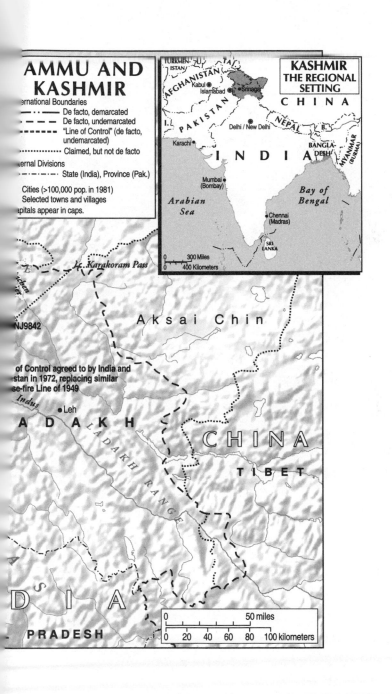

AMMU AND KASHMIR

International Boundaries

- ·— De facto, demarcated
- – – De facto, undemarcated
- -------- "Line of Control" (de facto, undemarcated)
- ············· Claimed, but not de facto

Internal Divisions

- ·—·—·— State (India), Province (Pak.)

● Cities (>100,000 pop. in 1981)
● Selected towns and villages
Capitals appear in caps.

KASHMIR THE REGIONAL SETTING

TURKMEN-ISTAN
TAJ.
AFGHANISTAN
Kabul ●
Islamabad ●
● Srinagar
CHINA
PAKISTAN
I.L.
NEPAL
Delhi / New Delhi ●
B.
Karachi ●
BANGLA-DESH
I N D I A
MYANMAR (BURMA)
Mumbai ● (Bombay)
Arabian Sea
Bay of Bengal
Chennai ● (Madras)
SRI LANKA

0   300 Miles
0   400 Kilometers

Karakoram Pass

Aksai Chin

NJ9842

of Control agreed to by India and
istan in 1972, replacing similar
se-fire Line of 1949

Indus
● Leh
A D A K H
LADAKH RANGE

C H I N A

T I B E T

D I A

PRADESH

0   50 miles
0   20   40   60   80   100 kilometers

THE KASHMIR VALLEY AND CONTIGUOUS REGIONS

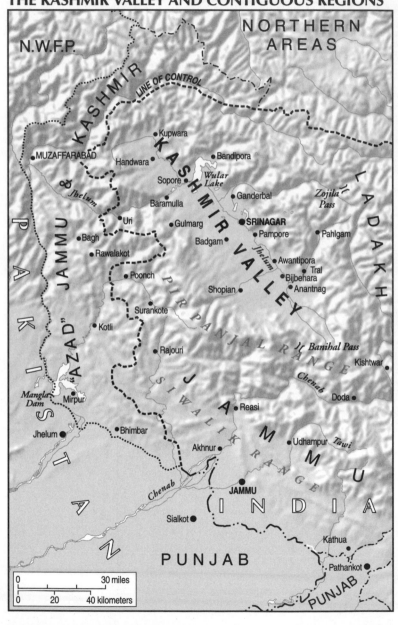

NORTHERN AREAS

N.W.F.P.

KASHMIR

LINE OF CONTROL

Kupwara
MUZAFFARABAD
Handwara
Bandipora
Sopore
Wular Lake
Zojila Pass
Ganderbal
Baramulla
KASHMIR VALLEY
Jhelum
Uri
Gulmarg
SRINAGAR
Pampore
Pahlgam
Bagh
Badgam
Jhelum
Rawalakot
Awantipora
Tral
Poonch
Bijbehara
Shopian
Anantnag
JAMMU &
PIR PANJAL RANGE
Surankote
Banihal Pass
Kotli
Kishtwar
"AZAD"
Rajouri
Chenab
SIWALIK RANGE
Doda
PAKISTAN
Mangla Dam
Mirpur
JAMMU
Reasi
Jhelum
Bhimbar
Udhampur
Tawi
Akhnur
JAMMU
Chenab
JAMMU
INDIA
Sialkot
LADAKH

PUNJAB

Kathua
Pathankot
PUNJAB

0   30 miles
0   20   40 kilometers

KASHMIR

INTRODUCTION

In our search for a lasting solution to the Kashmir problem, both in its external and internal dimensions, we shall not traverse solely on the beaten track of the past. Mindsets will have to be altered and historical baggage jettisoned.

—ATAL BEHARI VAJPAYEE,
prime minister of India, January 2002

If we want to normalize relations between Pakistan and India and bring harmony to the region, the Kashmir dispute will have to be resolved peacefully through a dialogue, on the basis of the aspirations of the Kashmiri people. Solving the Kashmir issue is the joint responsibility of our two countries . . . Mr Vajpayee, . . . I take you up on this offer. Let us start talking in this spirit.

—GENERAL PERVEZ MUSHARRAF,
president of Pakistan, January 2002

 DURING THE FIRST HALF of 2002, India and Pakistan mobilized their armed forces in apparent preparation for war, sparking concern in Western capitals and in the international media that a potentially catastrophic conflict was imminent between two countries armed with huge conventional arsenals and some nuclear weapons. The confrontation focused worldwide attention on the dispute between India and Pakistan over the territory of Jammu and Kashmir (J&K), often called simply Kashmir. The dispute is as old as the two states themselves, dating back to the circumstances of their independence from Britain and the partition of the subcontinent in 1947. Since the end of the first India-Pakistan war over Kashmir in January 1949, the territory has been divided into Indian-controlled Jammu and Kashmir (IJK, comprising the regions of the Kashmir Valley, Jammu, and Ladakh), with approximately 10 million people, and a smaller area under Pakistani control ("Azad" Jammu and Kashmir, or AJK, plus sparsely populated regions in the high Himalayas known as Pakistan's Northern Areas), with perhaps 3 million.

The dividing line between IJK and AJK–Northern Areas, which originated as a ceasefire line in 1949 and was marginally altered during India-Pakistan wars in 1965 and 1971, was renamed the Line of Control (LOC) by India-Pakistan agreement in July 1972. During the summer of 1999 a limited war between Indian and Pakistani forces occurred along a particularly mountainous stretch of the LOC after units of the Pakistani army crossed the line and occupied strategic heights on the Indian side. After two months of fierce combat and some gradual gains by India, the Pakistanis reluctantly withdrew after an agreement to that effect between U.S. President Bill Clinton and Pakistani Prime Minister Nawaz Sharif.[1]

A major change differentiated 1972 from 1999, however. As a publication of the Carnegie Endowment for International Peace put it in 1995: "Before 1989, India and Pakistan fought over Kashmir. Since late 1989, it is Kashmiris who have done [much of] the fighting"—and most of the dying.[2] In early 1990 a group of young men in the Kashmir Valley launched a guerrilla revolt against Indian rule under the banner of a movement calling itself the Jammu and Kashmir Liberation Front (JKLF). The JKLF's stated objective was to liberate IJK and reunite it with Pakistani Kashmir as a single independent state. The JKLF nucleus in IJK had received weapons and training from a JKLF organization located across the border in AJK, as well as from Pakistani military agencies. They were stunned by the enthusiastic popular response their makeshift insurrection received from the people of the Kashmir Valley. The militants were aware of widespread, deep-rooted grievance against India, but they were still taken by surprise by the intensity of mass support for *azaadi* (freedom), expressed in huge pro-independence demonstrations in the Valley during 1990.[3] The guerrilla war rapidly intensified, to a significant degree because of an Indian response of repression and reprisal targeted not just against armed militants but frequently also against "disloyal" civilian communities that aided and sheltered the rebels. The independentist, Muslim but secularist JKLF's dominance of the uprising yielded by 1992–1993 to the rise of a pro-Pakistan, moderate Islamist guerrilla group called Hizb-ul Mujahideen, strongly promoted by Pakistani military authorities.

The struggle continued to evolve. By the mid-1990s the intensity of local support for the insurgency had waned to some extent, and in the second half of the decade pan-Islamist fighters, primarily from Pakistan, infiltrated into IJK in significant numbers, adding a supra-local, strongly Islamist flavor to the conflict. In the India-Pakistan wars of 1947–1948, 1965, and 1971, sizeable numbers of J&K residents had fought on the Kashmir fronts as soldiers and auxiliaries for both armies. But protracted "low-intensity" warfare in the interior of IJK between thousands of guerrillas and hundreds of thousands of Indian security forces signaled a great transformation in the military and political character of the Kashmir conflict, marking its transition from a stubborn dispute over real estate between two adversarial neighbors to a much more complex, multidimensional problem.

From 1989 to 2002, between 40,000 (official Indian estimates) and 80,000 (claimed by the Hurriyat Conference, a coalition of pro-independence and pro-Pakistan groups) civilians, guerrilla fighters, and Indian security personnel died in violence that gradually spread beyond the Kashmir Valley to affect most of Jammu, IJK's other populous region. According to Indian counterinsurgency sources, in this period, more than 4,600 security personnel were killed, along with about 13,500 civilians (the vast majority Muslims) and 15,937 "militants" (the term for guerrilla fighters) including approximately 3,000 from outside IJK, "mostly Pakistanis and some Afghans." Also in this period, 55,538 incidents of violence were recorded and Indian forces engaged in counterinsurgency operations captured around 40,000 firearms, 150,000 explosive devices, and over 6 million rounds of assorted ammunition.[4]

Statistics, even as remarkable as these, cannot adequately portray the trauma and tragedy that have overwhelmed Kashmir, once a prime tourist destination because of its temperate Himalayan climate and scenic beauty. Life in a society under daily siege is powerfully expressed in the tortured works of a new generation of Kashmir's writers. Shakeel Shan writes about a friend who went missing in the Valley one night, abducted, in a routine occurrence, by unidentified gunmen:

> Who knows where my friend is?
> Who knows where my friend is hiding?
> Who knows whether he is scared of the dark night?
> Who knows whether he is hungry and unable to stand
>   on his feet?
> Who knows whether the place where he sits is not
>   damp?

Bashir Manzar writes about the fear that grips a society in the throes of protracted warfare:

> Break the pen, spill the ink, burn the paper
> Lock your lips, be silent, shhh . . .
> Say "I saw nothing" even if you did
> Or else have your eyes gouged out
> Keep humming eulogies, be silent
> It is the season of burying the truth . . .

Another young writer, who prefers to remain anonymous for his own safety, expresses himself as follows:

> I can't drink water because I feel it is mixed with the blood of young men who die up in the mountains. I can't look at the sky because it is no longer blue, it is painted red. I can't listen to the roar of the gushing stream, it reminds me of the wailing mother next to the bullet-riddled body of her only son. I can't listen to the thunder of the clouds, it reminds me of a bomb blast. I feel the green of my garden has faded, perhaps it too

mourns. The sparrow and cuckoo are silent, perhaps
they too are sad.

Kashmir's best-known contemporary poet, Agha Shahid Ali, who
died as an expatriate in the United States in 2001, expressed a little
more hope from his deathbed, in a poem dedicated to a Kashmiri
Hindu friend:

> We shall meet again, in Srinagar
> By the gates of the Villa of Peace
> Our hands blossoming into fists
> Till the soldiers return the keys
> And disappear.[5]

The dual purpose of this book is to explain how the Kashmir conflict has come to present such a grave threat to South Asia's peace
and to global security in the early twenty-first century, and to shed
light on what can be done about this situation. I intentionally
move beyond a preoccupation with the origins of the Kashmir
conflict and its inter-state territorial dimension, topics that have
been the focus of most literature on Kashmir over the past fifty
years. I do not argue that the genesis of the conflict is unimpor-
tant, nor do I deny that the dispute between India and Pakistan
over the contested territory is the crux of the problem. I do argue,
however, that the contemporary Kashmir conflict—particularly
the strife in IJK, the central aspect of the problem and the primary
focus of this book—has much more to do with events that have
unfolded in the decades *since* 1947 than with those of 1947 itself. I
also argue that an adequate understanding of the Kashmir conflict
must widen its focus beyond the inter-state territorial dispute to

take account of the great diversity and complexity of society and politics *within* Jammu and Kashmir.

To convey the essence and the complexity of the conflict as effectively as possible, I try (especially in Chapter 3) to tell the story from the vantage point of those on the ground in Jammu and Kashmir. To do so, I draw on my personal experience over the past decade in numerous localities and frontiers of armed conflict in the three regions of IJK, and on interviews I conducted during my visits there.

The book is structured around three key points and emphases. First, I stress that the roots of the crisis that erupted in 1989–1990 lie in a post-1947 history of denial of democratic rights and institutions to the people of J&K, particularly those of IJK. This is not simply an academic point. Reframing the Kashmir question as a challenge for *democratic* politics and statecraft implies that real and relevant methods of democratic institutionalization and conflict resolution can potentially be brought into play, and that Kashmir is not inevitably doomed to remain trapped in a zero-sum conflict of antagonistic nationalisms.

In other words, a subtly different definition of "self-determination," one that downgrades the fulfillment of national(ist) claims and destinies and upgrades the right of people to live and be governed in accordance with democratic norms, can potentially provide the space for the negotiation of an institutional design which is a compromise between rival, maximalist conceptions of self-determination. In 1929 it was observed that "the Jammu and Kashmir State is laboring under many disadvantages, with a large Mohameddan population . . . practically governed like dumb-driven cattle. There is no touch between the Government and the people, no suitable opportunity for representing grievances, and the administrative machinery itself requires overhauling from top to bottom . . . It has at present little or no sympathy with the people's wants and grievances."[6] Thus the slogan of the first organized political movement in modern Kashmir, which emerged during the 1930s in response to this state of affairs, was "Responsible Government": government accountable to and in the interests of the citizenry. As we shall see, that agenda of institutionalizing "responsible government" remains unrealized seven decades later, and Kashmir's people have not yet made the transition from being subjects to being citizens. The only way to enable them to make this transition is to make up the democratic deficit.

My second point is one of caution and circumspection: achieving a lasting democratic solution is obviously far easier said than done. This is, first, because India and Pakistan have chosen since 1947 to make possession of Kashmir the cornerstone of their respective identities as states. Indian official ideology has claimed that India's identity as an inclusive, secular state would be grievously damaged without IJK, the only Muslim-majority unit of the Indian Union. Why retention of Kashmir, apparently by any means necessary, should be indispensable to the validation of India's tolerant, civic credentials is not clear, since nearly 150 million Muslims live in India *outside* IJK, and their status and treatment could equally serve to validate those credentials (or otherwise). Pakistan was conceived as a homeland for the Muslims of the subcontinent, and from its inception Pakistani nationalism has been firmly based on the notion that Pakistan is territorially and ideologically incomplete without Kashmir. Once again, the premise itself is dubious: Pakistan's disintegration along its main ethnoregional fault line in 1971, when eastern Pakistan became Bangladesh, exposed the limitations of the concept of an overarching Pakistan. But the abiding power of both of these flawed constructions to influence minds and policy is a reality. One of the most important Kashmiri writer-activists of the twentieth century, Prem Nath Bazaz, noted that the conflict between India and Pakistan over Kashmir is "primarily . . . an ideological war," in which the elites of both countries have perceived foundational, nonnegotiable principles of statehood to be at stake.[7] In the maximalist versions, Kashmir is claimed to be India's *atoot ang* (integral part) and Pakistan's *shah rag* (jugular vein). A territory that has only one percent of India and Pakistan's total population has thus been transformed symbolically into the cornerstone of the nationhood of both countries.

The maximalist positions of the Indian and Pakistani ideologies are, however, only one dimension of the Kashmir problem. More than eighty years ago, C. E. Tyndale Biscoe, a British missionary worker who made a significant contribution to education in Kashmir, observed: "To write about the character of the Kashmiris is not easy, as the country of Kashmir, including the province of Jammu, is large and contains many races of people. Then again, these various countries included under the name of Kashmir are separated the one from the other by high mountain passes, so that the people of these various states differ considerably the one from the other in features, manner, customs, language, character and religion."[8]

The missionary was right about the cultural and social multiplicity of J&K. The 5 million residents of the Kashmir Valley are overwhelmingly Muslim (primarily Sunni, with a sizeable Shia minority), inheritors of a distinct regional culture built on mystic Sufi traditions, and mostly Kashmiri-speaking. But the Valley is only one of IJK's three regions, and one of five in J&K as a whole.

To the south of the Valley in IJK lies the sprawling Jammu region, inhabited by about 4.5 million people. Jammu is topographically a formidable mix of plains, low-lying hills, and rugged mountain ranges, and socially a mosaic of religious, ethnic, linguistic, and caste groups. Muslims make up one-third of its population overall, but they are a majority in the three most mountainous of its six districts; Hindus, plus a noticeable sprinkling of Sikhs, dominate the less mountainous and hence more populated areas. The Valley's kind of ethnolinguistic Kashmiri community is found only in one Jammu district and pockets of two others. Most Muslims in the Jammu region belong to other ethnic and linguistic categories: Gujjars and Bakerwals, traditionally mountain pastoralists and herdsmen and speakers of Gojri and Pahadi (a dialect of Punjabi), are a very sizeable component; Rajputs (high-caste Hindu converts to Islam) are another. Jammu's overall Hindu majority is also differentiated along lines of ethnicity, language, caste, and locality. In other words, while the Jammu region as a whole is very different from the Valley, it does not have a unitary regional personality because of its internal heterogeneity.

Ladakh, the third IJK region, covers a huge land mass but is thinly populated because of its harsh terrain and climatic conditions. Even here, however, there is diversity—Buddhists of Tibetan ethnic stock dominate one of Ladakh's two districts, while the other has a strong Shia Muslim majority. Across the LOC, the Pakistani-controlled AJK districts are predominantly Punjabi-speaking and very different in sociocultural terms from the Valley.

It is very important to appreciate that J&K's *social* heterogeneity is reflected in a high degree of *political* fragmentation and complexity. The most basic political cleavage in J&K is constituted not by party loyalties but by much more fundamental fault lines—conflicting national identities and state allegiances. In IJK, three orientations of this type exist: (1) Kashmiri proto-national identity, pro-independence for Kashmir; (2) Indian national identity, pro-India; and (3) Pakistani national identity, pro-Pakistan. The first and third orientations are also present acroos the LOC in AJK. In the first, the legitimate sovereign unit is Jammu and Kashmir, separate from both India and Pakistan. In the second, India, *including* J&K, is the legitimate sovereign unit. For adherents of the third orientation, the legitimate sovereign unit is Pakistan, including J&K. The sovereignty dispute that is central to the international, India-Pakistan conflict over Kashmir is thus mirrored within the society and political space of the contested territory.

In short, there are three political segments in J&K professing rival notions of national self-determination. It has been pointed out that such conflicting preferences regarding the legitimate boundaries of sovereignty, governance, and citizenship tend to generate "the most intractable and bitter political conflicts." The political scientist Robert Dahl has noted that "we cannot solve the question of the proper domain" of sovereignty from within the framework of liberal democracy, since any democratic process, such as competitive elections, presumes "the rightfulness of the unit," which is precisely the crux of disagreement in cases such as Kashmir. Dahl has observed that "a crisp, unimpeachable solution" to this conundrum "would be a marvellous achievement of democratic theory and practice . . . [but] alas, no altogether satisfactory solution seems to exist."[9]

It is possible to make some plausible predictions regarding the relationship between social elements of identity and political preference. For example, it is probable that the non-Muslim minorities—Hindus, Sikhs, and Buddhists—who total about 35 percent of IJK's population adhere nearly unanimously to an Indian national identity and wish to live under Indian sovereignty, a preference overriding the social diversity and lower-order political conflicts within these groups. In the Kashmir Valley, historically a stronghold of Kashmiri regional patriotism and aspirations to political self-rule, the pro-independence segment is very far ahead of its two competitors, but even in the Valley, committed support to Pakistan and India, in that order, exists among much smaller segments. The Jammu region predictably presents a more ambiguous picture, and the relative strengths of the segments are likely to vary significantly in different parts of this diverse region.

Nor is there any clear-cut link between social alignments/cleavages and political alignments/cleavages. The small Hindu minority indigenous to the Kashmir Valley, known as Kashmiri Pandits, share a history, a locality, and a culture with the Muslim majority of the Valley, but are resolutely loyal to India and hostile to the dominant pro-independence sentiment. In AJK, pro-independence sentiments are especially prevalent in and around a southern town called Mirpur, which is geographically and culturally distant from the Valley but adjacent and culturally similar to contiguous areas of Pakistani Punjab. The internal social and political context of IJK, and of J&K as a whole, thus resembles the Russian *matryoshka* doll—layers of complexity which render easy "solutions" such as plebiscite or partition impracticable if not dangerous, and which call for a more sophisticated approach.[10]

My third key point in this book is that the configuration of the Kashmir problem—a sovereignty dispute between two states over a territory whose population is itself fractured in its political preferences—is not unique. In fact, cases with similar configurations and circumstances exist in our contemporary world. There is much to be learned from comparing Kashmir with such cases, both to illuminate the obstacles to constructive statecraft inherent in conflicts defined by interlocking, mutually reinforcing "internal" and "international" disagreements over the legitimate unit of sovereignty and the meaning of self-determination, and to identify pathways to peace in such contexts. An observer of the conflict in and over Cyprus has commented: "The political stance of both sides has been one of mutual self-justification and mutual grievance, repeating incompatible narratives of wrongs and tragedies with scripts learned in the 1960s and 1970s . . . while the world has moved on."[11] This description could easily apply to the Kashmir conflict, except that the scripts were learned even earlier, in the 1940s and 1950s.

In Chapters 4 and 5 I compare Kashmir with the cases of Bosnia and Herzegovina and, especially, Northern Ireland. This comparative approach helps identify critical shortcomings of prescriptions frequently advanced for the Kashmir conflict, such as plebiscite / referendum on the one hand and partition on the other. It also helps me build a case for working toward a (tacitly) multinational political settlement in Jammu and Kashmir, a settlement that recognizes the reality of multiple national identities (and quasi-national identities, such as Kashmiri-independentist) within that territory while respecting the core concerns of the Indian and Pakistani states and their elites regarding sovereignty and territorial integrity. Zero-sum conflicts over sovereignty and self-determination are very difficult challenges for those who seek democratic political solutions, but they are not fated to remain utterly intractable. In this book I propose a multidimensional framework for peace, to cope with a problem defined by multiple but intersecting sources of conflict. Such a framework, I argue, is the only viable strategy for converting a stalemated zero-sum conflict into a positive-sum scenario for *all* sides.

1

ORIGINS OF THE CONFLICT

It is an irony of history that by a combination of fortuitous circumstances a tiny nation of Kashmiris has been placed in a position of great importance, where it can be instrumental in making or marring the future of so many.

—PREM NATH BAZAZ,
Kashmiri writer and political activist, 1967

IN 1947 JAMMU AND KASHMIR was among the largest of 562 so-called princely states in the Indian subcontinent. These were nominally self-governing units, ranging in size from tiny principalities to sprawling fiefs, ruled by Hindu, Muslim, and Sikh feudal potentates with pretensions to royal status. Collectively, the princely states covered 45 percent of the land mass of the subcontinent. These vassal statelets constituted a major pillar of the British concept of "indirect rule" in India. Their rulers, a colorful assortment of maharajas and nawabs, were permitted to administer their holdings as personal and dynastic fiefdoms in exchange for acknowledging the "paramountcy" of British power, while the British directly controlled and administered the rest of the subcontinent. Typically, British overseers known as "residents" were stationed in the capitals of the larger princely states, but by and large the Indian rulers were left to their own devices.[1]

The ruling family of Jammu and Kashmir were ethnic Dogras, upper-caste Hindus from the Jammu region. The founder of the lineage was a man called Gulab Singh, one of many local princes in the court of Ranjit Singh, a Sikh warrior who established a mini-empire in northern and northwestern India in the early nineteenth century with its capital in the Punjab city of Lahore (in Pakistan post-1947). After Ranjit Singh's death in 1839, Gulab Singh began to collude with British schemes to undermine and eventually eliminate Sikh power. During the 1820s and 1830s Gulab Singh gradually expanded his own dominion from his base in the southern reaches of the Jammu region, first over mountainous areas in the Jammu interior and then over the even more remote Himalayan regions of Ladakh and Baltistan. The ascendancy of the new dynasty was consolidated with Gulab Singh's acquisition of the Valley of Kashmir from British control in 1846, under a British-Dogra pact signed in the Punjab city of Amritsar (in India post-1947). The Treaty of Amritsar stipulated that "the British Government transfers and makes over, for ever, in independent possession, to Maharaja Gulab Singh and the heirs male of his body" the Kashmir Valley as well as the area of Gilgit to the north. In return, the Dogra king agreed to pay a substantial sum of money and to lend his military forces to the British when required. He also acknowledged "the supremacy of the British Government" and undertook, "in token of such supremacy, to present annually to the British Government one horse, twelve perfect shawl goats of approved breed (six male and six female), and three pairs of Kashmir shawls."[2]

The princely state of Jammu and Kashmir, a sprawling, polyglot entity of diverse regions and peoples, was born through this agreement. The eternal jurisdiction promised to the Dogra elite in the Treaty of Amritsar lasted exactly a century, until the moment of decolonization and partition in 1947. In that year Gulab Singh's last heir, Maharaja Hari Singh, presided over a territory where the "state subjects" were, according to the British census of 1941, 77 percent Muslim, 20 percent Hindu, and 3 percent other (mostly Sikhs, with a sprinkling of Buddhists). J&K was not the only princely state in which rulers and elites belonged to one religion and the majority of subjects to another. For example, in the large kingdom of Hyderabad, in southern India, and in the principality of Junagadh, in western India, Muslim ruling families presided over predominantly Hindu populations. In J&K, however, the distance between the privileged Hindu elite centered on the ruling family and their large majority of Muslim subjects was particularly vast. In 1941 Prem Nath Bazaz, a prominent Kashmiri Pandit journalist and political activist, reported: "The poverty of the Muslim masses is appalling. Dressed in rags and barefoot, a Muslim peasant presents the appearance of a starving beggar . . . Most are landless laborers, working as serfs for absentee [Hindu] landlords . . . Almost the whole brunt of official corruption is borne by the Muslim masses . . . Rural indebtedness [to Hindu landlords and moneylenders] is staggering."[3]

Practically all accounts of J&K in the late nineteenth and early twentieth centuries paint a grim picture of a self-absorbed, hopelessly incompetent regime and a Muslim subject population living in medieval conditions of poverty and oppression. In 1889 a visiting British dignitary, Walter Lawrence, commented on the *begar* (indentured labor) system prevalent in the Kashmir Valley, under which Muslim serfs were forced to work without compensation for a small Pandit landed elite and state officials. This feudal sys-

tem endured well into the twentieth century. In a book published
in 1924, a Pandit writer, Gawasha Lal Kaul, painted a Dickensian
picture of the city of Srinagar in the early 1920s. Prostitution,
theft, begging, and disease were apparently rife. C. E. Tyndale
Biscoe's narrative of life in the Kashmir Valley in the early twentieth century is full of anecdotes about Muslim peasants living in
virtual enslavement in the scenic countryside, and about the Muslim neighborhoods of Srinagar—a city situated in a beautiful natural setting of lakes and mountains—as filthy, fetid places populated by illiterate people with no conception of rights. "It is quite
possible," Tyndale Biscoe wrote sympathetically,

> that if we Britishers had to undergo what the Kashmiris
> have suffered, we might also have lost our manhood.
> But thank God, it has been otherwise with us and other
> Western nations, for to us instead has been given the
> opportunity of helping some of the weaker peoples of
> the world, the Kashmiri among them. May we ever be
> true to our trust. Gradually are the Kashmiris rising
> from slavery to manhood. Though the growth is natu-
> rally very slow at present, they are on the upward road.
> I trust that they will become once more a brave people,
> as they were in the days of old when their own kings
> led them into battle.[4]

Muslims were generally not permitted to become officers in the
state's military, which was led by Sikhs and Hindu "martial" castes
such as Dogras and Rajputs, and were virtually unrepresented in
the state's civil administration. Until 1924 "there was not a single
newspaper printed or published in the State of Jammu and Kashmir."[5] Apart from the mass illiteracy due to a paucity of even primary education for Muslims, the maharaja's government regarded

any semblance of a free press and public opinion as subversive, and regularly tried to prevent newspapers and journals published in Lahore by émigré Kashmiris from reaching the kingdom. Underscoring the Hindu character of the state, until 1920 a death sentence was mandatory for any subject who slaughtered a cow; this was generously reduced to ten years in prison after 1920 and subsequently to seven years.

Until the end of the 1920s, the absence of popular protest against this state of affairs was typically attributed to what the British scholar Alastair Lamb described as "the exceptionally docile nature of the peasantry in the Vale"[6]—a view consistent with Tyndale Biscoe's theory of a people whose "manhood" had been crushed by exploitation. In the 1930s, however, the era of popular politics in Kashmir arrived. Kashmir émigrés living in the Punjab had established a forum called the All-India Kashmir Muslim Conference, based in Lahore, which started to offer scholarship grants to enable talented young Muslims from J&K to acquire university education in India proper. The nucleus of a new generation of political leaders emerged through this scheme, usually after training at the Aligarh Muslim University, a celebrated institution of learning in northern India. This generation of pioneer activists was headed by a schoolteacher called Sheikh Mohammad Abdullah, born in 1905 in Soura, then a village near Srinagar and now a suburb of the city. In 1930 Abdullah and a few friends established a Reading Room Association in Srinagar to discuss questions of social and political change, while a similar group, the Young Men's Muslim Association, was formed in the southern city of Jammu. (Srinagar and Jammu are J&K's two capital cities: by long-established tradition, the state's administration is based in Srinagar during the summer months and in Jammu during the winter.) In July 1931 an attempt by young Muslims to organize a deputation to present a list of grievances to the maharaja ended in a riot on the streets of downtown Srinagar; twenty-one persons were killed when the maharaja's police opened fire on protesters.

This event marked a turning point in the history of political mobilization in Kashmir. In the words of the Kashmiri historian Mohammad Ishaq Khan: "13 July 1931 was a historic day in the annals of Srinagar. The 'dumb-driven cattle' raised the standard of revolt. The people were never to be cowed again by punitive police action. Even the women joined the struggle and to them belongs the honor of facing cavalry charges in Srinagar's Maisuma bazaar." Indeed, as the human rights activist Rita Manchanda writes, Maisuma, then as now "a rough lower middle-class warren of a neighborhood in the heart of Srinagar," emerged as "the center of support for Sheikh Abdullah's campaign to free Jammu and Kashmir from Dogra rule," and "Maisuma women were in the forefront of demonstrations." (Almost six decades later, in 1989–1990, the winding lanes of Maisuma would once again be a stronghold of political agitation, as hundreds of women demonstrated their solidarity with the Jammu and Kashmir Liberation Front's armed campaign to free J&K from Indian rule.)[7]

The events of 13 July, which have since achieved near-mythological status in Kashmir's political folklore, had an impact on the regime as well as in the sphere of grassroots politics. In November 1931 the maharaja's government agreed to the formation of a commission headed by B. J. Glancy, an official of the foreign and political department of the British government of India, to inquire into the causes of unrest and propose a strategy of reforms. The Glancy commission did suggest, in April 1932, a series of reforms to the administrative structure and the systems of education, land tenure, and taxation in order to make life somewhat more bearable for the Muslim masses and provide opportunities to the small but increasingly vocal stratum of educated, angry young men who were advancing demands on their behalf. The commission also urged that minimal freedoms of the press and public expression should be tolerated. Some limited, halting action on the Glancy proposals was undertaken in the following years. But through the 1930s and 1940s it became increasingly clear that the autocratic regime could not be reformed to the extent demanded by an increasingly mobilized, politically conscious population.

J&K's first political party, the All–Jammu and Kashmir Muslim Conference (MC), was founded in October 1932 to direct the nascent but growing movement for social and political change. Its principal leaders were Sheikh Abdullah from the Valley and Chaudhary Ghulam Abbas from the Jammu region. In 1938 the MC published a manifesto entitled "National Demand," calling for the implementation of substantive reforms to bring about a "Responsible Government" in the state, albeit "under the aegis of the Maharaja." The token concession to the maharaja proved insufficient to avert "mass arrests of the party leaders . . . and a policy of total repression by the Government."[8] In 1938 the MC, after considerable internal debate, decided to redefine the basis of its politics. Primarily at the behest of the Abdullah group, which included a handful of progressive Pandits and Sikhs, the party declared its intent to "end communalism by ceasing to think in terms of Muslims and non-Muslims" and invited "all Hindus and Sikhs who believe in the freedom of their country from the shackles of an irresponsible rule" to participate in the popular struggle.[9]

At the party's annual convention in 1939, the MC was accordingly renamed the All–Jammu and Kashmir National Conference (NC). Of the 176 delegates present, 173 voted to ratify the change, although "some Muslim members expressed misgivings that a secular organization would gravitate towards the Indian National Congress," the party leading India's independence movement, and "that the Hindu-Sikh element in the party would undermine the movement because of their vested interests in Dogra rule." These fears, voiced in 1939 mainly by Ghulam Abbas and his followers but initially, in 1938, also by some of Abdullah's close colleagues, "were allayed by an off-the-record understanding that the movement would steer clear of both the Congress and the All-India Muslim League,"[10] the party that passed the "Pakistan Resolution" a year later in 1940 and then led a campaign culminating in the creation of Pakistan in 1947. The religious and social conservatives in the NC fold were, however, rapidly alienated from the reoriented party by a combination of factors, including personal and factional conflict, ideological disagreement, and interregional differences. The predominantly Valley-based group led by the charismatic Abdullah was, in the perception of Abbas and his largely Jammu-based faction, developing unacceptable leftist and socially radical tendencies and moving steadily closer to left-wing nationalists in the Congress, thus violating the off-the-record agreement. Abbas's loyalists in Jammu districts, together with a small anti-Abdullah faction in the Valley, split from the NC in 1941 and revived the Muslim Conference. From then on, the NC would be identified with the personality and politics of Sheikh Abdullah, who came to be known as the *Sher-é-Kashmir* (Lion of Kashmir).

The reservations of Abdullah's critics were not baseless. In 1940 Abdullah invited Jawaharlal Nehru, then a top Congress leader and subsequently independent India's prime minister from 1947 until his death in 1964, to visit the Kashmir Valley. Among Congress leaders, Nehru, a man of sternly anti-feudal, anti-monarchist convictions, took a special interest in Kashmir because his family were Kashmiri Pandits who had migrated from the Valley to the plains of north India. The visit was a great success and marked the beginning of a tortured personal and political relationship between Nehru and Abdullah. In August 1942, at the height of World War II, the Congress launched a direct-action movement calling on the British to "Quit India." The movement, which spread like wildfire across non-princely India and assumed the form of armed resistance to British authority in some parts of the country, was put down by means of mass arrests of Congress organizers and brutal violence against rank-and-file Congress activists. The Muslim League, the colonial government's collaborator at the time, condemned the Quit India movement as "not directed for securing the independence of all constituent elements in the life of the country, but to establish Hindu *raj* [rule] and deal a death-blow to the Muslim goal of Pakistan," and the J&K Muslim Conference's stance was similar. The NC, however, passed a resolution sharply condemning the repression unleashed by the British government in India proper.[11]

In 1944 it was the turn of the Muslim League's leader, Mohammed Ali Jinnah, to visit Kashmir. Although the NC and the MC competed with each other to organize a grand welcome for him, Jinnah chose to address the annual gathering of the MC and certified the MC as the representative organization of "99 percent" of J&K Muslims. After this rebuff, Abdullah had no alternative but to cultivate closer links with the Congress leadership, particularly Nehru. In 1945 the NC's annual gathering was attended not only by Nehru but by two other Congress leaders, Maulana Abul Kalam Azad and Khan Abdul Ghaffar Khan, the latter known as "Frontier Gandhi" because of the influence of his pacifist movement in the North-West Frontier Province (NWFP), which borders both J&K and Afghanistan. In 1946, as the NC's campaign against the autocracy entered a climactic phase and was met with severe repression by the regime, Nehru entered J&K in a show of solidarity with the NC's struggle and was promptly arrested by the authorities.

Despite these personal links and a certain ideological affinity—socially leftist republicanism—with a section of the Congress, the J&K National Conference was not reduced to a satellite or surrogate of India's Congress movement. Maintaining an entirely separate and independent organizational existence, the NC during the 1940s gradually acquired the dimensions of a mass movement, especially in its center of activity, the Kashmir Valley. Writing a tumultuous decade later, Josef Korbel, the Czech chairman of the United Nations Commission for India and Pakistan (UNCIP), recorded the mass support the NC and Sheikh Abdullah himself enjoyed across most of what had by then become Indian-controlled Jammu and Kashmir (IJK)—separated from "Azad" (Free) Jammu and Kashmir (AJK) and erstwhile Muslim Conference strongholds by the ceasefire line—although he noted a distinct dilution of support for the NC beyond the Kashmir Valley.[12] The movement's growing strength owed much to the popularity of Abdullah, then already on the way to becoming a legend in Kashmir, but even more to the remarkable organizational abilities of his talented young lieutenants—Mirza Afzal Beg, G. M. Sadiq, Bakshi Ghulam Mohammed, Ghulam Mohiuddin Karra, and Syed Mir Qasim, among others.

Two very important core characteristics distinguished the NC in this mobilizational phase from its Congress counterpart in India proper. First, the NC's ideology was specifically directed to the emancipation of J&K from the post-1846 dispensation, and was based ideologically on a deep sense of regional patriotism, centered on the Kashmir Valley. In this conception, Kashmir and India were fraternal but ultimately separate entities, whose relations ought to be governed by equality and mutual respect. Second, despite its declared secularism, embodied in the 1939 decision to include non-Muslims, the NC movement never abandoned its Kashmiri Muslim heritage.

To some extent the NC's Muslim orientation was inevitable—the movement was directed against a corrupt, repressive, and Hindu ruling hierarchy, J&K's population had a Muslim majority of 77 percent, and the Kashmir Valley was even more overwhelmingly Muslim. But the movement's inclusive, left-leaning, yet decisively Muslim character was not simply an effect of religious demography or the nature of the 1846–1947 regime. The NC's ideology and mobilization strategies were, from its inception and during the dynamic 1940s, steeped in a distinctly Muslim ethos, shaped above all by the Valley's history, culture, and traditions. Sheikh Abdullah's popularity with the masses owed much to the fact that he excelled in reciting beautifully from the Quran. His power base in the Valley was rooted in his and his associates' control of most of its mosques, acquired at the expense of religious preachers of the more traditional variety. During the cataclysmic events of 1946 and 1947, he established his political and militia headquarters on the premises of Hazratbal, a beautiful, gleaming white shrine on the shores of the Nageen Lake on the outskirts of Srinagar, where a hair of the Prophet Mohammad is preserved as a relic.[13] The general secretary of the NC and editor of the party's paper *Khidmat* was a prominent cleric, Maulana Mohammed Sayyid Masoodi, "highly respected by the people for the depth of his views and the sobriety of his judgment."[14]

In the years leading up to 1947 the National Conference proved to be a remarkably dynamic agent of political mobilization. The party's defining traits—the charismatic leader, the solid organizational network of talented and committed young men, the assertion of a proud regional patriotism rooted in a shared Muslim identity, and the promise of progressive social change—were a beacon of hope for an impoverished, politically disenfranchised population. Meeting in the northern Valley town of Sopore in September 1944, party delegates adopted a manifesto entitled "Naya Kashmir" (New Kashmir), an ambitious program for J&K's future under a democratic regime.

The Naya Kashmir manifesto is the most important political document in modern Kashmir's history. It has three sections. The first lays out the party's conception of the state's future constitutional framework. At the apex, it visualizes a representative legislature called the National Assembly and a cabinet government, and it calls for decentralized governance based on devolution of decisionmaking and administrative responsibilities to districts, *tehsils* (subdivisions of districts), towns, and villages. The monarch is reduced to a titular, figurehead role. Recognizing the multilingual character of J&K—Kashmiri being the dominant tongue only in the Valley and a few areas in Jammu, while Dogri is dominant only in the Jammu plains—the manifesto designates Urdu as the official lingua franca. Kashmiri, Dogri, Punjabi, Hindi, Balti, and Dardi are all given the status of national languages. The second section, on the economy, is heavily socialist in tone— communist sympathizers such as G. M. Sadiq, the party's main ideologue, were prominent in the NC leadership at the time.[15] There is a heavy rhetorical emphasis on state-led, planned industrialization. The more significant content of this section, given the reality of a predominantly peasant society, relates to the agrarian economy. The manifesto called for the abolition of parasitic landlordism without compensation, transfer of land to the tillers, and establishment of cooperative associations. The final section elaborates social and educational schemes for various "down-trodden" sections of Kashmir's population, including a charter of rights for women.[16]

Almost six decades later, Naya Kashmir is a very distant memory for people in Kashmir. In June 2002 a third-generation Abdullah, the sheikh's grandson Omar, formally took over as president of the NC—a party that retains the name but is in every other sense a debased, skeletal version of the historic National Conference—from his father, the sheikh's elder son, Farooq Abdullah. The ceremony was held in Srinagar, amid tight security and orchestrated sycophancy of the Abdullah family, including ritual invocations of the unfinished Naya Kashmir agenda, by "a few thousand men . . . escorted to the venue" in typical rent-a-crowd fashion. A sixty-five-year-old veteran NC worker noted the contrast with the era when the NC was truly a popular movement. In those days, he recalled, "the Sher-é-Kashmir's National Conference and Kashmir were synonymous. Today I had to fight with my son, who is vehemently against my participation in this program. Kashmir has changed and so have its people."[17] (On this transformation see Chapters 2 and 3.)

Two elements of the Naya Kashmir manifesto deserve to be highlighted, since both were central to the politics of Kashmir after 1947. First, the manifesto was clearly based on a Jacobin conception of popular sovereignty, augmented by a generous dollop of Bolshevism—ideas inspired by the Soviet model—in the socio-economic parts of the program. In April 1946, launching the Quit Kashmir movement, an all-out mass agitation against the regime, Abdullah declared: "The time has come to tear up the Treaty of Amritsar . . . Sovereignty is not the birthright of Maharaja Hari Singh. Quit Kashmir is not a question of revolt. It is a matter of

right."[18] This conception of popular sovereignty is perfectly understandable in the context of struggle against a narrowly based, autocratic system which systematically denied the most basic rights
and representation to the vast majority of people. It is also democratic in that it reflects a genuine, broadly based popular movement for a more inclusive and responsive system of government.
However, like the ideology of the original Jacobins of revolutionary France and that of many other twentieth-century "third
world" movements inspired or influenced by the Jacobin model,
this sort of conception tends to be in tension with *liberal*-demo-
cratic norms of political pluralism, accountability of those in
power, and tolerance of dissent and opposition. The deeply authoritarian streak in the NC's emancipation movement rapidly became evident after 1947 and made its own contribution to the subversion and retardation of democratic development in Kashmir.

Nonetheless, for the peasant masses in IJK after 1947, the arro-
gance and authoritarianism of the new ruling elite—the revolutionaries of the NC-led movement—were compensated for by the
rapid fulfillment of a key point of the Naya Kashmir program.
"On 13 July 1950 the Kashmir Government," with Sheikh Abdullah
at its helm, "introduced the most sweeping land reform in the entire subcontinent." Prior to this, almost all of Jammu and Kashmir's arable area of 2.2 million acres had been owned by 396 big
landlords and 2,347 intermediate landlords, "who rented to peasants under medieval conditions of exploitation."[19] Between 1950
and 1952, 700,000 landless peasants, mostly Muslims in the Valley
but including 250,000 lower-caste Hindus in the Jammu region, became peasant-proprietors as over a million acres were directly
transferred to them, while another sizeable chunk of land passed
to government-run collective farms. By the early 1960s, 2.8 million

acres of farmland (rice being the principal crop in the Valley) and fruit orchards were under cultivation, worked by 2.8 million smallholding peasant-proprietor households.

Visiting J&K in the mid-1950s, Daniel Thorner, an agrarian historian and economist, found that despite some "defects in implementation, many tillers have become landowners and some land has even gone to the landless. The peasantry of the Valley were not long ago fearful and submissive. No one who has spent time with Kashmiri villagers will say the same today." Another expert, Wolf Ladjensky, observed that "whereas virtually all land reforms in India lay stress on elimination of the *zamindari* [large estates] system with compensation, or rent reduction and security of tenure [for tillers], the Kashmir reforms call for distribution of land among tenants without compensation to the erstwhile proprietors . . . [and] whereas land reform enforcement in most of India is not so effective, in Kashmir enforcement is unmistakably rigorous."[20]

The transformation of rural Kashmir had far-reaching political consequences. Hundreds of thousands of newly empowered peasant families would henceforth regard Sheikh Mohammad Abdullah, seen as the principal agent of this transformation, as a messiah. The NC's flag, depicting a plow, the farmer's key implement, set in yellow against a red background, aptly reflected this bedrock support among masses of emancipated serfs. However, in parts of the Jammu region the imposition of land reform catalyzed a tenacious movement of social and political reaction, which persists to this day. The "majority of landlords and moneylenders were Hindus, and the axe naturally fell on them."[21] The Hindu population was numerically dominant in large tracts of southern and southeastern Jammu, especially after the expulsion and flight of large numbers of Muslims from this area to AJK and

Pakistan amid large-scale communal (sectarian religious) violence in late 1947. Dispossessed landlords and former officials in the Dogra administration regrouped after 1947 principally in this area, and began to vent their class and communal grievances in the form of regionalist opposition to the political supremacy of the new elite of Valley-based Muslims.

The Quit Kashmir movement of May–June 1946 was a landmark in the history of political mobilization in Kashmir. The Muslim Conference leader, Ghulam Abbas, speaking in Lahore, condemned the movement as "an agitation started at the behest of Hindu leaders," in a tone and phrase strikingly reminiscent of the Muslim League's denunciation of Congress's Quit India agitation in 1942. But mass protests spread in response to the NC's call for a revolutionary overthrow of the regime, particularly in the party's Valley strongholds, and were contained after several weeks only by means of mass arrests of leaders, including Abdullah, and brutal police action against the rank and file. The agitation wilted under intense repression, but "the Dogra military excesses in the Valley caused tremendous commotion, leaving bitter memories of cruelties firmly implanted in the minds of the normally peaceful Kashmiris."[22] In late 1946 the Muslim Conference, in a strategy strikingly similar to that used by the Muslim League in India proper after the Congress's Quit India movement was crushed, attempted to exploit the political vacuum in the Valley caused by the incarceration of many NC leaders and the flight of those who had managed to evade detention. This attempt backfired. After Jammu-based MC leaders made speeches critical of the regime in front of a Friday prayer congregation at Srinagar's Jama Masjid (Big Mosque), they were arrested and detained indefinitely. As the momentous year 1947 dawned on the subcontinent, members of

J&K's political class were either imprisoned or in hiding, the regime was enjoying its temporary upper hand, and the population was sullenly recuperating from the repression of 1946.

Two independent "Dominions," India and Pakistan, were born on 14–15 August 1947. The princely states were a peculiar issue in the decolonization process. With the lapse of British "paramountcy" over them, they were technically free to accede to either Dominion, or to become independent states. Addressing a large gathering of princes and their representatives in Delhi in late July 1947, however, Lord Mountbatten, the last British administrator of India, was unequivocal that the third was merely a theoretical option. He urged them to make a decision to accede to one or the other Dominion, before 15 August if possible, after evaluating two criteria: geographical embeddedness in or contiguity to India or Pakistan, and the wishes of their population of subjects.

Under these criteria, the accession of the vast majority of princely states to India was a certainty. Only a handful of statelets—such as Bahawalpur, a large principality in southern Punjab—lay within the borders of Pakistan. A sizeable minority of units within India had Muslim rulers, but their future was sealed by territorial location as well as by the fact of a majority of Hindu subjects. Only two of these states, Junagadh (80 percent Hindu) and Hyderabad (87 percent Hindu) would pose any problem at all, because of the recalcitrance of their rulers. In Junagadh, in western India, the ruler acceded to and then fled to Pakistan. In Hyderabad, southern India, the ruler stalled on a decision for a year, until the Indian army invaded in September 1948 and settled the matter. Nonetheless, Congress leaders were deeply concerned to ensure rapid and orderly integration of the

princely states into the Indian Union. In early July 1947 the Congress set up a special department, headed by independent India's
first interior minister, Sardar Vallabhbhai Patel, a Gujarati Congress leader known for his right-wing pro-Hindu leanings, to organize and supervise the transition.

For the Pakistanis, far less was at stake. Thus Mohammed Ali
Jinnah, by profession a constitutional lawyer, adopted the tactical
stance that the princely states would become "autonomous and
sovereign states on the termination of paramountcy" and free to
choose any of the three options before them (the phrase "autonomous and sovereign" was identical to the wording of the Pakistan
Resolution of 1940, which called for the creation of autonomous
and sovereign states in Muslim-majority regions of northwestern
and eastern India once the British withdrew).

The choice was straightforward for practically all princely
states—except Jammu and Kashmir. J&K was territorially contiguous to both India and Pakistan, although its contiguity to two Pakistani provinces, (western) Punjab and the NWFP, was far more
pronounced than its territorial link to Indian eastern Punjab. The
princely state also had close trade, transport, and commercial
links with contiguous areas of western Punjab and the NWFP,
and many émigrés of Kashmiri origin were settled in west Punjab.
The population of J&K was 77 percent Muslim, reinforcing the
case for accession to Pakistan. However, this case was complicated
by two factors specific to J&K. The first was the predominance of
the NC, a Kashmiri regionalist movement with ties to left-wing,
republican elements in the Indian National Congress, in the Kashmir Valley and Kashmiri-speaking Muslim enclaves in the Jammu
region. The Hindus, Sikhs, and Buddhists who made up 23 percent of J&K's population were almost certain to favor India, and
the Muslim Conference's following in the Jammu region, Pakistan.

But the NC's mass base remained an indeterminate factor, albeit potentially tilted toward India because of its leaders' ideological affinities and personal relationships. The second factor was the unique situation of a Hindu autocrat who ruled a Muslim-majority population, but who nonetheless was the legal authority to decide the issue of accession.

The lull in Kashmir was broken in the spring of 1947, when an uprising against the maharaja broke out in Poonch, an area in northwestern Jammu sandwiched between the Kashmir Valley to the east and Rawalpindi division of northwestern Punjab to the west. Poonch had been an autonomous principality within the state of J&K, and ruled by its own raja, until World War II, when the local ruler was deposed by the Dogra kingship. The maharaja's administration then started levying punitive taxes on Poonch's Muslim peasantry. The local revolt began in protest against this taxation policy, and the regime's Sikh and Dogra troops reacted with severe reprisals against the population. This was a grave error. Poonch, along with neighboring west Punjab and NWFP districts, was a prime recruiting ground for soldiers of imperial Britain's Indian army. Indeed, of a total of 71,667 men from J&K who had served in British forces during World War II, 60,402 were Poonchi Muslims.[23] The area was thus full of recently demobilized soldiers, who responded to the reprisals by evacuating their families to west Punjab areas beyond the boundaries of the princely state, then returning to confront the regime's forces. The revolt was renewed in the aftermath of partition in August, this time with a definite pro-Pakistan character. By early October the rebels had gained control of almost the entire Poonch district except the town of Poonch, garrisoned by a government force. Flush with success in the Poonch fighting, the pro-Pakistan chieftains of western Jammu districts—Muzaffarabad,

Poonch, Mirpur proclaimed the formation of a provisional "Azad" Jammu and Kashmir government in Rawalpindi, Pakistan, on 3 October 1947.

On 15 August 1947, meanwhile, the maharaja's regime had concluded a so-called standstill agreement—normally the precursor to accession—with the government of Pakistan. Under this agreement, the Pakistani government assumed charge of J&K's post and telegraph system and undertook to supply the state with foodstuffs and other essential commodities. This strange entente between a ruler and regime with manifestly anti-Muslim policies and the new Muslim state in the subcontinent was the result of compulsions and calculations on both sides. The Pakistanis knew that geographical contiguity and religious demography favored J&K's accession to Pakistan. However, the maharaja was still the authority empowered to sign a legally binding accession, and they decided to court his cooperation. The maharaja's overriding priority was maintaining his throne and privileges, and he and his advisers thought it was worth negotiating with the Muslim League's Pakistan on this, given Congress's well-known aversion to the feudal, autocratic nature of princely rule and the Congress connections of J&K's largest organized political movement, the NC.

The Poonch uprising upset this delicate flirtation. To make matters worse, Punjab and the NWFP were convulsed with violence in August–September 1947, communal massacres were taking place amid a collapse of civil order and traditional neighborly relations, and armed brigandage was rife. In early September armed groups from Pakistan began infiltrating J&K from west Punjab, especially the Rawalpindi zone, looting and attacking Hindu and Sikh minorities. By early October the J&K government complained to Pakistan's foreign ministry that cross-border attacks were being conducted across several hundred kilometers of the

Jammu border, from Rawalpindi in the north to Sialkot in the south. In language that was to be echoed by Indian protests against "Pakistan-sponsored cross-border terrorism" in Kashmir several decades later, the J&K government demanded that Pakistani authorities put a stop to the infiltrations if intergovernmental dialogue was to continue. The government of Pakistan, again in language reminiscent of Pakistan's typical response to India's accusations decades later, denied that the infiltrations were systematic and called attention to terror and atrocities perpetrated by J&K forces against the Muslim population of Poonch—atrocities which, it suggested, were provoking spontaneous reactions both within J&K and from ethnic and religious kin across the border.

In the first half of October the relationship between the two governments disintegrated. On 3 October, the day the "Azad" Kashmir government was proclaimed in Rawalpindi, the J&K government cabled Pakistan's foreign ministry in Karachi, charging Pakistan with violation of its obligations under the standstill agreement and with complicity in cross-border raids. On 18 October an even more acrimonious cable on the same lines, alleging attempted economic strangulation as a pressure tactic, was sent to Pakistan's prime minister, Liaquat Ali Khan, and its governor-general, M. A. Jinnah, signaling a breakdown of relations. In response, Pakistani officials called for talks to relieve cross-border tensions and noted with disapproval the J&K government's decision to release Sheikh Abdullah on 29 September 1947 while continuing the incarceration of leading pro-Pakistan figures. Emerging from sixteen months of imprisonment, Abdullah delivered a typically populist speech at a huge public meeting at Hazratbal on 5 October, in which he declared the accession issue to be secondary to the establishment of a popular government.

Pakistan's diplomatic strategy in Kashmir had clearly unraveled by mid-October, and its economic blockade of J&K had backfired. On 21 October the climactic episode in the unfolding drama began. On that day several thousand Pashtun tribesmen, known then as now for their impressive if unruly warrior tradition, began an offensive into J&K from the sprawling Hazara district of the NWFP, located north and northwest of the princely state. The fact that these "tribal" areas largely lay (then as now) beyond the writ of established government enabled Pakistan's prime minister to claim on 4 November that Indian attempts to portray "the rebellion of an enslaved people" against the maharaja's "illegal and immoral" regime as "an invasion from outside, just because some outsiders have shown active sympathy with it," amounted to "a dishonest rewriting of history."[24]

The incursion showed clear signs of organization and planning, however. Although many of the raiders were motivated by the prospect of loot and rape, they were "led by experienced military leaders familiar with the terrain and equipped with modern arms, [and] they poured down in numbers estimated at 5,000-strong initially, with a fleet of transport vehicles numbering about 300 trucks."[25] It soon became clear that the attack had precise strategic aims. After taking the town of Muzaffarabad (later the capital of AJK) on the Pakistan-J&K border, the raiders headed straight for the heart of the Kashmir Valley. Meeting almost no resistance from the maharaja's crumbling forces as they advanced into the northern part of the Valley, they rapidly captured the town of Baramulla, just twenty miles northwest of Srinagar. On 24 October the maharaja's administration sent an urgent request to New Delhi for military assistance to repulse the raiders.

After a quick assessment of the crisis, the top Indian leaders were more than willing to oblige. However, Nehru, Patel, and others were advised by Mountbatten, governor-general of the Indian Dominion, not to send in troops without first securing the accession of Jammu and Kashmir to India, since military intervention prior to accession would in legal terms be an Indian invasion of a neutral territory. Accordingly, the beleaguered maharaja signed the formal "Instrument of Accession" to India—ceding to the federal government, as per normal practice, jurisdiction over defense, foreign affairs, and communications—and handed it over to an emissary of the Indian government in Jammu city, who flew back to Delhi with the all-important document. The following day, 27 October, Mountbatten replied to the maharaja accepting accession, but noted that once law and order had been restored and the "invader" expelled the accession should be ratified by "a reference to the people."

Abdullah had arrived in Delhi from Srinagar on the evening of 25 October and was there on 26–27 October—indeed he was staying at Prime Minister Nehru's residence—reinforcing bitter Pakistani suspicions of an Indian-Abdullah conspiracy, abetted by Mountbatten, which had turned the tables in the struggle for Kashmir. On 27 October Abdullah told an Indian newspaper, the *Times of India,* that the "tribal invasion" had to be resisted because it represented an attempt to coercively absorb Kashmir into Pakistan. Indeed, a veteran political commentator in IJK has written that many Kashmiris were "outraged" by the Pakistani attempt to first secure accession by wooing the hated maharaja, and after that failed, "to decide the issue by force."[26] On the morning of 27 October 1947, the first Indian airborne units landed at Srinagar's airport and were warmly greeted by top NC leaders. On hearing of India's military intervention, Jinnah immediately asked the British general commanding the Pakistani army to deploy regular Pakistani troops in Kashmir, only to be told by the general's counsel that since the territory was now legally and constitutionally part of India, such a deployment would amount to a declaration of war on India, inviting a broader India-Pakistan war.

The Indians arrived to find that raiding units had penetrated the outskirts of Srinagar. Much like Indian forces in the Kargil conflict of 1999, they also rapidly "discovered that they were dealing with an organized body of men armed with medium and light machine-guns and mortars, and led by commanders thoroughly conversant with modern tactics and use of ground" and possessing "considerable engineering skill."[27] The Indians fought a defensive, holding operation to prevent Srinagar from being overrun in the first week of the operation, but subsequently they regained the initiative, primarily because of two factors. First, some of the raiders had engaged in looting, rape, and murder against the overwhelmingly Muslim population during their advance, spoiling any possibility of goodwill and support from the co-religionists they had ostensibly come to liberate. The town of Baramulla, for example, had been pillaged, and brutal acts against local civilians in general and women in particular had occurred in other north Kashmir towns taken by the raiders, such as Handwara. Second, the existence and cooperation of a well-honed NC organization throughout the Valley was invaluable to the Indians. While signing the accession to India, the maharaja appointed his bête noire, Sheikh Abdullah, to head an interim administration. In Srinagar the NC soon emerged as the de facto government. Thousands of volunteers enrolled in the NC's "National Militia," quickly organized by the sheikh's top aides like Bakshi Ghulam Mohammed and G. M. Sadiq, which included a women's unit.

Fortified by this formidable support on the ground, Indian troops, reinforced by armored cars which had arrived by road via Jammu and the Banihal Pass, first pushed the raiders out of the vicinity of Srinagar, eliminating a threat to the city's airfield. They then retook Baramulla on 8 November and Uri, a town farther west which has straddled IJK's border with AJK ever since, on 14 November. The Pakistani leadership explicitly held the NC's collaboration with the Indians responsible for this dramatic reversal of the military situation. Prime Minister Liaquat Ali Khan said in late November 1947: "Sheikh Abdullah has been a paid agent of Congress for the last two decades and with the exception of some gangsters he has purchased with Congress money, he has no following among the Muslim masses. It is astonishing that Pandit Nehru should proclaim this Quisling to be the acknowledged leader of the Muslims of Kashmir." On 2 November 1947, as fighting raged on the ground, Nehru declared his government's "pledge," given "not only to the people of Kashmir but to the world," to "hold a referendum under international auspices such as the United Nations" to determine whether the people of J&K ultimately preferred India or Pakistan. Nehru reiterated this commitment numerous times over the next few years at press conferences, public meetings, and international forums. In August 1952, for example, he told India's Parliament that he wanted "no forced unions," and that if the people of Jammu and Kashmir decided "to part company with us, they can go their way and we shall go our way."[28]

This was also the stance of the United Nations. In January 1948, in response to an Indian complaint about Pakistan-sponsored aggression in a territory which had acceded to India, the U.N.'s Security Council established the United Nations Commission for India and Pakistan (UNCIP) to play a mediating role in Kashmir. In April 1948, as winter snows melted and fighting resumed on several fronts in J&K, the Security Council adopted a detailed resolution "instruct[ing] the Commission to proceed at once to the Indian subcontinent and there place its good offices and mediation at the disposal of the Governments of India and Pakistan with a view to facilitating the necessary measures by the two Governments, both with respect to the restoration of peace and order and the holding of a plebiscite, acting in cooperation with one another and with the Commission."

This resolution urged the government of Pakistan "to use its best endeavors" to "secure the withdrawal from the State of Jammu and Kashmir of tribesmen and Pakistani nationals not normally resident therein who have entered the State for the purpose of fighting." Once UNCIP was satisfied that such a withdrawal was taking place, the government of India was urged to "put into operation in consultation with the Commission a plan for withdrawing their own forces from Jammu and Kashmir and reducing them progressively to the minimum strength required for the support of civil power in the maintenance of law and order." Once this was achieved, the resolution said that "the Government of India should undertake that there will be established in Jammu and Kashmir a Plebiscite Administration to hold a plebiscite as soon as possible on the question of the accession of the State to India or Pakistan."[29]

In August 1948 UNCIP adopted a resolution calling on India and Pakistan to reach a ceasefire agreement in Kashmir, following which an internationally supervised process could be set in motion whereby "the future status of the State of Jammu and Kashmir shall be determined in accordance with the will of the people."[30] After such a ceasefire finally came into effect on 1 January 1949, UNCIP adopted another resolution on 5 January, announcing that "the Secretary-General of the United Nations will, in agreement with the Commission, nominate a Plebiscite Administrator who shall be a person of high international standing."[31]

That the plebiscite was never held is regarded by Pakistanis, and by pro-Pakistan as well as pro-independence people in J&K, as proof of Indian perfidy. The typical Indian rejoinder is that since Pakistani forces never vacated the areas of J&K under their control, the first condition specified by the United Nations for holding the plebiscite was not fulfilled, and the blame lies with Pakistan.

This hiatus between the efforts and prescriptions of international organizations and officials on the one hand, and the actual evolution of a conflict on the ground on the other, is not at all unusual, as for example demonstrated throughout the 1990s by the succession of wars in former Yugoslavia. On the ground in Kashmir, prospects for any kind of negotiated settlement had been severely undermined in late 1947, not just by the fighting in the Kashmir Valley, but by an orgy of mass killing and expulsion in the Jammu region between October and December. Because of its location, after partition the Jammu region became a transit point for huge numbers of refugees in both directions—traumatized, terrorized Hindus and Sikhs fleeing to India from Pakistani Punjab and the NWFP, and traumatized, terrorized Muslims fleeing to Pakistan from Indian Punjab—both sides with harrowing experiences of slaughter and atrocities. This destabilizing influx combined with rising tensions within the region to set off further carnage. The entire Hindu and Sikh populations of Muslim-majority districts in western Jammu like Muzaffarabad, Bagh, Rawalakot (western Poonch), Kotli, Mirpur, and Bhimbar were killed or expelled. Mass murder and expulsion of Muslims occurred in Hindu-dominant eastern Jammu districts—Udhampur, Kathua, and Jammu city and its environs.

The front lines remained static over the winter of 1947–1948 because of the combination of harsh weather and hilly terrain, but hostilities resumed with a vengeance with the onset of spring. In

April May 1948 the Indian army made further gains, retaking the strategic town of Rajouri on the Jammu front and expanding Indian-controlled territory farther north in the Valley. At this point the regular Pakistani army entered the fray, and the fighting stalemated. The final act of the first India-Pakistan war over Kashmir occurred when Pakistani forces launched a thrust toward the Valley from the mountainous areas of Gilgit and Skardu to the north. The drive was repulsed by Indian light tanks at the Zojila Pass, which marks the boundary between the Valley and the huge, sparsely populated region of Ladakh, and the Indians consolidated their position by capturing the Ladakh towns of Dras and Kargil in November 1948, establishing in the process a strategic road link between Srinagar and Leh, the center of Buddhist-dominated eastern Ladakh.

The truce of January 1949 came into effect only because each side was exhausted and convinced that it could no longer make significant territorial gains against the other. The ceasefire line left the Indians with the bulk of Jammu and Kashmir's territory (139,000 of 223,000 square kilometers, approximately 63 percent) and population. The Indians had gained the prize piece of real estate, the Kashmir Valley, and they also controlled most of the Jammu and Ladakh regions. These areas became Indian Jammu and Kashmir (IJK). The Pakistanis were left with a long strip of land running on a north-south axis in western J&K, mostly Jammu districts bordering Pakistani Punjab and the NWFP (these districts constitute AJK), a slice of Ladakh (Skardu), and the remote mountain zones of Gilgit and Baltistan (the Northern Areas). The Kashmir dispute had been born.

This original dividing line—called the ceasefire line (CFL) until it was renamed the Line of Control (LOC) in 1972—has changed only marginally since the end of 1948 in subsequent military conflicts between India and Pakistan, notably in December 1971. Since this de facto border drawn in blood clearly favors India in territorial terms, India has been the status quo power in the South Asian conflict over Kashmir. As late as mid-1954, Nehru was asserting that "India still stands by her international commitments [to a plebiscite] on Kashmir."[32] However, in April 1956 the Indian leader disclosed that in May 1955 he had asked his Pakistani counterpart to consider settling the dispute by converting the CFL into the permanent international boundary between the two countries. The Pakistani prime minister, Mohammed Ali Bogra, confirmed that the offer had been made—and immediately rejected, not surprisingly, given Pakistan's persistent stance as the revisionist power in the dispute. Bogra added that Nehru had first broached the idea as early as October 1948 to Pakistan's first prime minister, Liaquat Ali Khan.[33] The reaction to India's rigid determination to maintain the status quo has been the entrenchment of an equally tenacious revisionism and irredentism in Pakistan—manifested in Pakistani military incursions into IJK in 1965 and 1999—and this clash between defense of the status quo and revisionism has defined the interstate territorial dimension of the dispute over Kashmir.

That has been a stalemated conflict. Pakistani leaders from Liaquat Ali Khan to Pervez Musharraf have consistently rejected India's preferred status quo "solution" as unacceptable, while India has countered Pakistan's attempts, renewed in 1965 and then in Kargil in 1999, to challenge the status quo through military means.[34] The nature of the international conflict over Kashmir has thus remained essentially unchanged—indeed, static and frozen—over the fifty-six years that have passed since its genesis. Even the adversarial rhetoric used by both countries, for their domestic audiences as well as in international settings, has stayed remarkably similar in tone and content over this span of time. The real change in the Kashmir conflict has occurred in its "internal" dimension—specifically, through the evolution of the relationship between Kashmir and India in the decades since 1947. That relationship has been deeply ruptured since 1989–1990, and the rupture has refocused attention on Kashmir as a problem for the subcontinent and the world.

2

THE KASHMIR-INDIA DEBACLE

India is a bouquet. Kashmir is the rose in the bouquet.

—Indian army billboards on roads in the Kashmir Valley

Hum kya chahtey? Azaadi! (What do we want? Freedom!)

—Popular slogan in the Kashmir Valley

KASHMIR WAS INTENDED to be the centerpiece of India's bouquet of democratic diversity. Instead, it became the thorn in the bouquet. Tracing the reasons for the rupture between India and Kashmir, which has engulfed most areas of Indian Jammu and Kashmir (IJK) in guerrilla warfare and counterinsurgency since 1990, is crucial to understanding the contemporary Kashmir conflict and to identifying what needs to be done about it. As we shall see, the rupture has very largely been caused by consistently anti-democratic, authoritarian policies of successive New Delhi governments toward IJK.

In November 1951 Sheikh Abdullah addressed the opening session of his hand-picked Jammu and Kashmir Constituent Assembly in these terms: "The real character of a state is revealed in its Constitution. The Indian Constitution [enacted in January 1950] has set before the country the goal of secular democracy based on justice, freedom and equality for all without distinction . . . The national movement in our State [Jammu and Kashmir] naturally gravitates towards these principles of secular democracy . . . This affinity in political principles, as well as past associations and our common path of suffering in the cause of freedom, must be weighed properly while deciding the future of the State."[1]

In August 1952 Abdullah repeated the same theme while informing the assembly that negotiations with Prime Minister Nehru had reaffirmed IJK's autonomous status within the Indian Union: "The supreme guarantee of our relationship with India is the identity of democratic and secular aspirations, which have guided the people of India as well as those of Jammu and Kashmir in their struggle for emancipation, and before which all constitutional safeguards [Article 370 of the Indian constitution, the autonomy statute for IJK] will take a secondary position."[2] Abdullah did add a note of caution, as well as a thinly veiled warning, in the same speech: "I would like to make it clear that any suggestion of arbitrarily altering this basis of our relationship with India would not only constitute a breach of the spirit and letter of the Constitution, but might invite serious consequences for a harmonious association of our State with India."[3]

In 1968, during a brief interlude of liberty from twenty-two years (1953–1975) of almost continuous incarceration in Indian prisons, Abdullah said: "The fact remains that Indian democracy stops short at Pathankot [the last major town in Indian eastern Punjab before the Jammu region of IJK]. Between Pathankot and the Banihal [a mountain pass that connects the Jammu region with the Kashmir Valley] you may have some measure of democracy, but beyond Banihal there is none. What we have in Kashmir bears some of the worst characteristics of colonial rule." In a message to the people of India on the occasion of India's Republic Day on 26 January 1968, the Kashmiri leader added:

> Respect for the rule of law, the independence of the judiciary, the integrity of the electoral process—are all sought to be guaranteed by the Indian constitution. It is not surprising that many other countries have drawn upon this constitution, particularly the chapter on fundamental rights. Yet it must at all times be remembered that the constitution provides the framework, and it is for the men who work it to give it life and meaning. In many ways the provisions of the constitution have been flagrantly violated in recent years [in Kashmir] and the ideals it enshrines completely forgotten. Forces have arisen which threaten to carry this saddening and destructive process further still.[4]

Abdullah was no paragon of liberal democracy. Indeed, as noted in Chapter 1, his movement had deeply authoritarian traits. These were latent during the phase of mass mobilization until 1947, but became manifest as soon as the National Conference (NC) became effectively the government of IJK after late 1947. Between 1948 and 1953, as head of this government, Abdullah—with Nehru and New Delhi's essential support—ran IJK as a party-state fiefdom of the NC, and the Lion of Kashmir's founding contribution to the entrenchment and perpetuation of anti-democratic politics in IJK is beyond dispute. As Benedict Anderson has put it:

> The model of "official nationalism" assumes relevance, above all, at the moment when revolutionaries success-

fully take control of the state, and are for the first time
in a position to use state power in pursuit of their visions . . . Even the most radical revolutionaries always,
to some degree, inherit the state from the fallen regime
. . . Like the complex electrical system in a large man-
sion where the owner has fled, the state awaits the new
owner's hand at the switch to be very much its old bril-
liant self again. One should therefore not be much surprised as revolutionary leaderships come to play lord of
the manor . . . The more the ancient dynastic state is
neutralized, the more its antique finery can be wrapped
around revolutionary shoulders.[5]

Nonetheless, Abdullah's bitter reassessment of India's democracy in its relationship to Kashmir was powerfully accurate. His
words capture with chilling eloquence the root cause of the Kashmir conflict as it exists in the early twenty-first century. His prognosis for the future—that the "saddening and destructive process"
of New Delhi–sponsored subversion of democratic rights, processes, and institutions in Kashmir would continue—also proved
prophetic.

It is March 1987. Almost two decades have passed since Sheikh
Abdullah spoke his mind with such clarity and conviction. Elections are being held in IJK to constitute a legislative assembly and
government. Two men are competing to win a seat in this assembly from Amirakadal, a congested district in the heart of Srinagar,
capital city of the Kashmir Valley. One, Ghulam Mohiuddin Shah,
is the candidate of the National Conference, led since the sheikh's
death in 1982 by his elder son, Farooq Abdullah. The NC, by
now far removed from its popular base and very much the tool of

the vested interests of a narrow political elite, has allied in this election with Congress, India's ruling party. Ghulam Mohiuddin Shah's opponent, Mohammad Yusuf Shah, is representing a polyglot coalition of anti-establishment groups calling itself the Muslim United Front (MUF).

As an Indian newsmagazine observes during the campaign, the MUF is an improvised "ad hoc bloc" of diverse groups with "no real unifying ideology," consisting of "educated youth, illiterate working-class people and farmers who express their anger at the Abdullahs' family rule, government corruption and lack of economic development." However, its emergence means that "the Valley is sharply divided between the party machine that brings out the traditional vote for the NC, and hundreds of thousands who have entered politics as participants for the first time under the umbrella provided by the MUF." Khemlata Wakhloo, a Kashmiri Pandit who was at that time a prominent member of the NC, has written subsequently of a "wave" of popular support for the MUF in the Valley and contiguous enclaves of Kashmiri-speaking Muslims in the Jammu region. In her words, in 1987 "there was only one voice on the lips of the people, that in a democracy we would bring the party of our choice to power, a party that will meet the aspirations of the people and heed their grievances." Indeed, the MUF's message of Kashmiri regional pride and its call for responsible government has attracted a huge army of Kashmiri youth as volunteer workers. For the first time in IJK's political history, it seems that a popularly based but *constitutionally bound and sanctioned* opposition to traditional, New Delhi–backed ruling coteries may be taking shape in the Valley and its environs.[6]

Turnout is heavy. As counting of ballots begins, it becomes clear that the MUF's Yusuf Shah, a member of a conservative religious party called the Jama'at-i-Islami, is winning by a landslide. This is his third attempt to be elected to the IJK assembly, and finally the public seems to be en masse on his side. The other Shah, routed in the contest, leaves the counting center in a visibly dejected mood and goes home. But he is summoned back— to be declared the winner by presiding officials. As the crowd protests, police arrive in strength and summarily arrest the MUF candidate and his supporters, including his election manager, Mohammad Yasin Malik, a twenty-one-year-old resident of the adjoining lowermiddle-class Maisuma neighborhood. Both candidate and manager are imprisoned until the end of 1987, without any formal charge or court appearance, let alone a trial.

The fate of Yusuf Shah's third and final attempt to become a legislator in India's Kashmir assembly is replicated throughout the Valley and some parts of the Jammu region. The Indian newsmagazine mentioned above recorded what happened in Kashmir in spring 1987. Its eyewitness report speaks of a pattern of "rigging and strong-arm tactics all over the Valley," of "massive boothcapturing [forcible takeover of polling stations] by gangs," of "entire ballot-boxes pre-stamped in favour of NC," of numerous citizens "simply not being allowed to vote," and of government-nominated supervisors "stopping the counting as soon as they saw opposition candidates taking a lead." Meanwhile, the bureaucrats and clerks administering the process "worked blatantly in favour of the NC-Congress alliance," and "the police refused to listen to any complaint." In an anticlimactic outcome, MUF won just four of seventy-six seats in the IJK assembly (although even according to the official count it won 32 percent of the vote). The NC-Congress alliance took an overwhelming majority—sixty-two seats—and formed the government.[7]

As we shall see, this atrocious episode of denial and subversion of democratic rights, processes, and institutions was no aberration: it was entirely consistent with Kashmir's political fate in India's democracy over the preceding forty years. More than sixteen years after that tragic farce, both Shahs who contested that race in 1987 are still active in politics. Ghulam Mohiuddin Shah, loser turned victor, was compelled to flee his homeland in early 1990, as popular uprising and guerrilla war overwhelmed the Valley. But he resurfaced in 1996 as a senior minister in an Indian-sponsored IJK government revived after dubious "elections," and he continued in that position until 2002. However, it is his challenger, Yusuf Shah, who has really emerged from relative obscurity since 1987—but not under that name. Yusuf Shah now goes by his *nom de guerre*, Syed Salahuddin (Salahuddin was a legendary Muslim warrior who fought against the Christian Crusaders). As Salahuddin, Yusuf Shah has since the early 1990s been commander in chief of Hizb-ul Mujahideen (HM), the largest guerrilla force fighting Indian control of IJK. In 1992 he told an Indian interviewer that he had chosen to fight for the cause of Pakistan in Kashmir because experience had convinced him that "slaves have no vote in the so-called democratic set-up of India."[8]

As Yusuf Shah metamorphosed into Salahuddin, his young campaign manager of 1987, Yasin Malik, also made a personal choice and a political transition. In 1989 Malik returned to the Valley from Pakistani-controlled "Azad" Jammu and Kashmir (AJK), where he had procured weapons and trained in their use, and became a core member of the Jammu and Kashmir Liberation Front (JKLF) group that launched insurrection in the Valley. Unlike his former candidate, Malik rejected the option of supporting Pakistan and remained committed to the goal of an independent, sovereign Jammu and Kashmir encompassing—at least at the level of JKLF rhetoric—the entire territory of the princely state as it existed in 1947. In May 1989 Malik, by then an underground militant, discussed his months in captivity in 1987 with an Indian interviewer:

"They called me a Pakistani bastard. I told them I wanted my rights, my vote was stolen. I am not pro-Pakistan but have lost faith in India."[9]

The Kashmir conflict is driven by a complex of multiple, intersecting sources, and the Kashmir problem is, consequently, defined by multiple, interlocking dimensions. Nonetheless, the ruptured relationship between the majority of IJK's people—especially its Kashmiri-speaking Muslim population—and the Indian Union is the core of the contemporary problem. The guerrilla war in IJK has passed through a number of phases since 1990, but the gap between democratic aspirations and a repressive reality remains wide in India's Kashmir.

Handwara is a town located in the northwestern part of the Kashmir Valley, in the frontier district of Kupwara close to the Line of Control (LOC) with AJK. The town was taken and briefly held by tribal raiders from Pakistan in late 1947. On 1 October 1990 the town's bazaar—the center of life in all Kashmir towns—was burned down and a number of civilians were killed by Indian security forces after a guerrilla attack. Since then, the town itself—heavily garrisoned and guarded by Indian police and military units—has been largely quiet, although on 6 August 2002 two guerrillas and an Indian soldier were killed when the guerrillas tried to storm the main security post in the center of town, a mini-complex of bunkers and improvised firing positions festooned with Indian flags and Indian nationalist slogans. But the calm has always been deceptive and deeply uneasy. Kupwara's Handwara *tehsil* (administrative subdivision), named after the town, has been a major theater of the guerrilla war since 1990. The dozens of villages in the *tehsil* have produced hundreds if not thousands of "militants" (guerrilla fighters)—and, of course, "martyrs"—over the years, and Kupwara's extensive tracts of forested hills have been a sanctuary and base for the militants' war against the Indian army, which is heavily deployed in the *tehsil* and throughout the district.

When I spent a few days in Handwara in late April and early May of 2002, there was an unusual air of excitement in the town. An election was about to take place to select a president for the traders' federation, the town's guild and chamber of commerce. The electorate comprised 899 shopkeepers and traders operating in the town. The bazaar (rebuilt since 1990) was abuzz, especially because the contest reflected a larger political conflict. One of the two candidates, Ghulam Din Banday, was an associate of Chaudhary Mohammed Ramzan, then the town's NC legislator and a senior minister in the Srinagar government. His rival, Ghulam Mohiuddin Sofi, belonged to a local family with strong ties to the All-Parties Hurriyat Conference (APHC), the coalition of groups favoring self-determination descended from the MUF of 1987 (the Arabic word *hurriyat* means freedom). Sofi himself was affiliated with an APHC constituent called the People's Conference (PC), a local party very popular in Kupwara and pockets of the neighboring Baramulla district, founded and led by a veteran Kashmiri politician, Abdul Ghani Lone, a Handwara native. (Lone was assassinated in Srinagar, in an unrelated development, on 21 May 2002.) One of Sofi's younger brothers, Imtiyaz, a lawyer practicing in the high court in Srinagar, is a senior member of the independentist JKLF.

When the votes were counted, Sofi had won by forty-five votes. The local police pronounced the process transparent. "We thought it is such a small affair so let us try to have an absolutely free and fair election," said an officer, adding that "this was the first such democratic process, even if at such a local level, happening after so many years." But the NC's hierarchy refused to accept the outcome. First the two local police officers who had worked to ensure a fair poll were transferred out of the area, "in the public interest." Then local bureaucrats were pressured to annul the result. When this failed, the defeated candidate declared the election invalid and formed his own, parallel "traders' and shopkeepers' association" with the support of the Srinagar authorities. Sofi reacted with weary disgust, recalling the elections of 1983, when Lone, the PC's candidate for an assembly seat, had been first declared the loser and later the winner; and 1987, when Lone had been ruled the loser although according to local people he had in fact won with a huge majority, like Yusuf Shah in central Srinagar. "Fraud is the NC's habit," Sofi said. "They did it in 1983 when they announced that we had lost the Assembly election by seven votes. Then they did it again in 1987. I was Mr Lone's counting agent then, so I was picked up from the counting center and taken to Srinagar central jail . . . We don't want to repeat it ever. We neither trust them nor their elections."[10]

The narrative of politics in Amirakadal, Srinagar, in 1987 offers a compelling insight into Kashmir's descent into violence. The narrative of Handwara, north Kashmir, in 2002 provides an equally compelling insight into why the conflict drags on, sixteen years and tens of thousands of violent deaths later. Unfortunately, the purposeful denial of democratic rights has been the defining theme of democratic India's policy toward Kashmir consistently since 1947.

Sheikh Abdullah was IJK's prime minister from March 1948 to August 1953. His crowning achievement during those years was the implementation of land reform (described in Chapter 1), which consolidated mass support for the NC and for Abdullah himself. Besides abolishing the feudal system in agrarian Kashmir,

Abdullah also eliminated the hereditary monarchy, which had in any event become inconsequential after October 1947. By 1952 the Dogra monarchy was formally abolished, IJK proclaimed a "republic," and the last king's son, the erstwhile heir-apparent Karan Singh, relegated to a largely ceremonial position styled Sadr-e-Riyasat (Head of State).

As noted in Chapter 1, the NC-led movement's conception of politics was built on a Jacobin vision of popular sovereignty. The tension between this ideology and core principles of a liberal-democratic polity remained latent during the mass mobilization phase of the 1930s and 1940s, but rapidly became overt once the movement's leaders seized power. In early 1951 the NC government began preparations to convene a Constituent Assembly in Srinagar. An alarmed Pakistan immediately raised the matter at the United Nations, where the Security Council responded with a resolution, passed in late March 1951, "reminding the Governments and Authorities concerned of the principle embodied in the Security Council resolutions of 21 April 1948, 3 June 1948 and 14 March 1950, and United Nations Commission for India and Pakistan resolutions of 13 August 1948 and 5 January 1949, that the final disposition of the State of Jammu and Kashmir will be made in accordance with the will of the people, expressed through the democratic method of a free and impartial plebiscite conducted under the auspices of the United Nations." The resolution further warned that "the convening of a Constituent Assembly as recommended by the general council of the 'All Jammu and Kashmir National Conference,' and any action that Assembly might attempt to take to determine the future shape and affiliation of the entire State, or any part thereof, would not constitute a disposition of the State in accordance with the above principle."[11]

Abdullah and his colleagues went ahead nonetheless, and a

Constituent Assembly of seventy five deputies was elected, theo-
retically on the basis of universal adult franchise and secret ballot,
in the autumn of 1951. This assembly comprised forty-three representatives from the Kashmir Valley, thirty from the Jammu region,
and two from Ladakh. Twenty-five additional seats were left vacant for the areas of Pakistan-controlled Kashmir, making a nominal total of one hundred. The manner in which this election was
conducted made a mockery of any pretence of a democratic process, and set a grim precedent for future "free and fair elections"
in IJK.

In the Kashmir Valley and Ladakh, forty-three NC candidates
were "returned unopposed" one week prior to the election. Non-
NC candidates who had filed nomination papers for the other
two seats "withdrew under pressure subsequently," according to
Joseph Korbel of the United Nations Commission for India and
Pakistan. Muslim opposition to Abdullah's regime had been
eviscerated by the division of Jammu and Kashmir. The Muslim
Conference's following was largely concentrated in the western
Jammu districts making up AJK, safely beyond the ceasefire line,
and MC supporters from IJK's Jammu districts had fled to AJK.
Leaders of the minority pro-Pakistan opinion in the Kashmir Valley, opposed to the NC, were also in exile in Pakistani-controlled
territory. However, a non-Muslim opposition to the new dispensation was present in the Hindu-dominated southern and southeastern districts of the Jammu region. Led mostly by officials in the
former maharaja's administration and subsequently also by Hindu
landlords dispossessed by the NC regime's land reforms, these elements had organized a party called the Praja Parishad (literally,
Subjects' Forum) in late 1947 and had been locked in confrontation with Abdullah's government since 1949. The Parishad decided
to flex its muscles by contesting twenty-eight of thirty seats in

the Jammu region, although its base was limited to a segment of the Hindu population in parts of Jammu. Thirteen Parishad candidates were arbitrarily disqualified before the election—in official parlance, their nomination papers were rejected because of irregularities—the first use of a common method by which oppositions in IJK were to be neutered in years and decades to come. In protest, and in anticipation of a completely rigged election that was pointless to contest, the Parishad announced an eleventh-hour boycott and pulled out its other fifteen nominees. Non-NC candidates in the remaining two Jammu seats also dropped out, giving the NC a clean sweep before any votes had been cast.

The circumstances of formation of the Constituent Assembly revealed that the NC elite wished to govern Kashmir as a party-state, in which they would have a monopoly on political power. Indeed, the NC's slogan was "One Leader, One Party, One Programme"—meaning Abdullah, the National Conference, and the 1944 Naya Kashmir agenda. In fact, fragments of opposition to the Abdullah regime existed even in the Valley, where the NC was overwhelmingly popular as the agent of opposition to the Dogra autocracy before 1947 and of land reform after 1947. Ghulam Mohiuddin Karra, formerly chief of the NC organization in Srinagar district and a moving force of the Quit Kashmir movement in 1946, had fallen out with the party leadership after 1947. Purged, he formed a group called the Jammu and Kashmir Political Conference. As Abdullah consolidated his absolute power, Balraj Puri, a political activist in Jammu, met with Prime Minister Nehru in Delhi and appealed to him to ensure that Karra's group be allowed to function as a democratic opposition in the Valley, on the grounds that one-party rule was antithetical to India's commitment to a liberal-democratic polity. Nehru, Puri later recalled, conceded "the theoretical soundness of my argument, but maintained that India's Kashmir policy revolved around Abdullah, and therefore nothing should be done to weaken him." In June 1952 Nehru told a press conference in India: "When the Constituent Assembly met in Kashmir for the first time I might inform you that it was its intention to pass forthwith a resolution confirming the State's accession to India. We asked it not to do so as not to be embarrassed before the United Nations."[12]

The Praja Parishad would probably have won a few seats in the Constituent Assembly had a free election been tolerated in Jammu. It would then have functioned as a small opposition group in the house, a potentially troublesome presence the NC leadership was not willing to risk. Denied institutional representation, the Parishad took to the streets to press its case for "full integration of Jammu and Kashmir State with the rest of India like other acceding [princely] States and [to] safeguard the legitimate democratic rights of the people of Jammu from the communist-dominated anti-Dogra government of Sheikh Abdullah."[13] Its rallying cry was *Ek Vidhan, Ek Nishan, Ek Pradhan* (one constitution, one flag, one premier) for all of India—a direct attack on Abdullah's "prime minister" title, on the adoption in late 1949 of the NC's party flag as the IJK state flag, and above all, on the constitution-making mandate of the IJK Constituent Assembly. The Parishad's strategy of direct action and civil disobedience had extremely disruptive consequences for IJK's fragile political order. The protest campaign intensified through 1952 and the first half of 1953 in areas of southern Jammu where the Parishad had influence. The agitation received support from the spiritual and political leader of Ladakh's Tibetan Buddhists, who disliked the meteoric ascendancy of the new Kashmiri Muslim ruling elite and particularly feared the implications of its land reform policies for the Buddhist clergy's immense private landholdings in Ladakh.

The government's response was reminiscent of the former Dogra regime's tactics—police action against agitators and mass arrests of the organizers, most of whom had been imprisoned for the first time as soon as the Parishad raised its voice in 1949. The agitating Jammu and Ladakh factions represented social and political reaction, but they also reflected the social and political plurality of IJK. It was ultimately the new regime's intolerance of that plural character, first of any opposition within the legislature and then of dissent on the streets, that drove the crisis. The confrontation did not remain confined to IJK. From mid-1952 onward, India's Hindu nationalist parties began, inside and outside India's Parliament, to draw attention to the issue and pressure Nehru's Congress government to intervene. In May 1953 a prominent Hindu nationalist politician entered IJK to support the Parishad's campaign and was arrested—much as Nehru had courted arrest in support of the NC's campaigns in the 1940s—and the situation soured further when he died, of natural causes, while imprisoned in the Kashmir Valley. The ultimate aim of the supporters of "full integration" was to eliminate the political autonomy given to IJK under India's constitutional provisions. In the Hindu nationalists' unitary conception of sovereignty, IJK should not have the trappings of a state within a state—including a prime minister, a flag, and a constitution. The autonomy issue lay at the heart of the relationship between India and Kashmir and would determine its future.

The maharaja's accession to India in October 1947 had limited the jurisdiction of India's central government to three categories of subjects: defense, foreign affairs, and communications. This was standard practice for rulers of princely states signing accession statements, and normally did not preempt or preclude further integration of acceding entities into the political framework of India or Pakistan. Jammu and Kashmir, however, was an exceptional case among former princely states, in that there was an international dispute over its status and U.N. resolutions existed calling for settlement of the question through a plebiscite. There was also an important "internal" political reality that India's leaders had to take into account—the existence in IJK of a well-organized regionalist popular movement, the NC. In October 1949 India's Constituent Assembly inserted Article 306A in India's constitution, affirming that New Delhi's jurisdiction in IJK would remain limited to the three categories of subjects specified in the Instrument of Accession. This was qualified at the time as a provisional measure, pending final settlement of the Kashmir dispute. After India became a republic in January 1950, Article 306A became the basis of Article 370 of the Indian constitution, which asserts Jammu and Kashmir's—for practical purposes, IJK's—autonomy within the Indian Union. Under Article 370's provisions, India's federal government can legislate even on the three categories of subjects within its competence only "in consultation with the Government of Jammu and Kashmir State," and on other subjects in the Union List only with "the final concurrence of the Jammu and Kashmir Assembly."[14]

We saw at the outset of this chapter that during key points of his five and a half years in office Sheikh Abdullah repeatedly justified his movement's decision to side with India in the ringing rhetoric of ideological and programmatic affinity. In his opening address to the IJK Constituent Assembly in November 1951, for example, he praised India's democratic and secular credentials, derided Pakistan as a landlord-ridden country without a written constitution, and dismissed full independence for Kashmir as a utopian idea. There are indications, nonetheless, that the sheikh privately viewed the association with India in far more contingent terms, as a strategic necessity given the circumstances and the alignment of political forces in 1947, and that he retained a subliminal attachment to the idea of a sovereign Kashmir.

In April 1949, shortly after the cessation of fourteen months of fighting between India and Pakistan in and over Kashmir, Abdullah spoke candidly in an interview with a British newspaper, the London *Observer*. He lamented not only the division of Jammu and Kashmir through war but the prospect, unacceptable to a Kashmiri patriot, that the territory would remain indefinitely trapped in the vortex of a bitter feud between the two countries. The people of the contested territory would never enjoy either peace or prosperity in such a context, since because of its location as well as its fractured internal politics, J&K needed the goodwill, the tourists, and the markets of *both* countries for its stability. The only way out, he reflected, would be for J&K to have a neutral and friendly status vis-à-vis both India and Pakistan. However, since the "Punjabis of Poonch" and the "Pathans of Gilgit" favored Pakistan, while the Hindus of Jammu were loyal to India, an independent state's territorial integrity would need to be recognized and guaranteed not only by India and Pakistan but by world powers and the United Nations. Abdullah's remarks raised great alarm in the Indian capital. Nehru's deputy prime minister Vallabhbhai Patel, a hard-line right-wing Indian nationalist, apparently took particular objection, and Abdullah recanted in an interview with a major Indian newspaper, *The Hindu,* a month later in May 1949.[15]

Three years after that, in April 1952, Abdullah was in his populist element again. In response to the Praja Parishad agitation for abolition of IJK's autonomous regime, he delivered a combative speech in the town of Ranbirsinghpura, near the southern city of Jammu. The venue was perhaps deliberately chosen: Ranbirsinghpura is on the border of Indian Jammu and Pakistani

Punjab, it has been a predominantly Hindu area since 1947, and it derives its name from one of the kings of the Dogra dynasty. In this Praja Parishad heartland, Abdullah attacked what he described as the insidious influence of Hindu majoritarian ideas in the Congress party and the central government, and referred to the "full integration" movement as "unrealistic, childish and savoring of lunacy."[16] His speech was widely reported in the Indian press and deepened the controversy. To calm the first crisis of Kashmir-India relations, negotiations were held in Delhi in June and July 1952 between a delegation of the IJK government led by Abdullah and his cabinet minister Mirza Afzal Beg and Indian government representatives headed by Nehru.

The talks resulted in an unwritten modus vivendi known as the Delhi Agreement, whose contents were reported to India's Parliament by Nehru on 24 July 1952, and to IJK's Constituent Assembly by Abdullah on 11 August. The agreement largely preserved the status quo on IJK's autonomous status. In his 11 August speech, Abdullah was explicit that his aim had been to preserve "maximum autonomy for the local organs of state power, while discharging obligations as a unit of the [Indian] Union."[17] It was agreed that the IJK flag and India's national flag would fly side by side in IJK, with the latter in the "supremely distinctive" position. Otherwise, the Kashmiri delegation made only one substantive concession, enabling extension of the Indian supreme court's arbitrating jurisdiction to IJK in case of disputes between the federal center and the state (IJK) or between IJK and another unit of the Union.

Even here, however, IJK negotiators blocked an attempt by the New Delhi team to extend the Indian supreme court's purview to IJK as the ultimate court of appeal for all civil and criminal cases before IJK courts. The IJK team also managed to stall on two other matters under negotiation: financial and fiscal integration of IJK with the Union, and the extension of the Indian constitution's fundamental rights to the territory and people of IJK. During discussions on the latter issue, the IJK delegation objected citing possible implications for their land reform program, which had dispossessed the landowning class without any right to claim compensation. On more general principles of the Kashmir-India relationship, it was agreed that residual powers of legislation would be vested in the IJK assembly, in contrast to the arrangement elsewhere in India's relatively centralized federation, which vests such powers in the center.

Superficially, the Delhi Agreement appeared to be a victory for the Abdullah government's resolute defense of IJK's asymmetrical autonomy within the Indian Union. In his confident report of the outcome of the Delhi talks to his hand-picked legislature, Abdullah, as noted earlier, adopted his typical twin tactics of celebrating the ideological affinity of India and Kashmir in glowing terms while ominously warning the Indian government against unilateral attempts at centralization and integration. But over the following year it became clear that the NC government had merely managed to negotiate a temporary, uneasy truce in an unresolved tussle with New Delhi in which anti-autonomy factions in Jammu and Ladakh continued to be an important factor. The anti-autonomy, pro-integration agitations intensified in the first half of 1953, and India's Hindu nationalist parties directly entered the fray.

In April 1953 Abdullah appeared to be looking for a compromise solution to the crisis. In that month the Constituent Assembly's basic principles committee proposed a scheme for devolution of authority to regions within IJK. Under the plan, the Kashmir Valley and Jammu regions would each have elected assemblies

with competence to legislate on specified subjects of local governance, as well as separate councils of ministers for regional affairs.
(Ladakh, with its sparse population, would have a lesser degree
of internal autonomy, exercised by an elected district council.)
This formula of multi-tiered autonomy clearly aimed at a cre-
ative mutual accommodation—preserving IJK's autonomous regime while devolving powers within that regime to placate the
groups in Jammu (and Ladakh) opposed to that regime. Indeed,
the committee proposed an eventual union of five units—including "Poonch" ("Azad" Jammu and Kashmir) and "Gilgit" (the
Northern Areas) across the LOC—and suggested changing the
name of the interim three-unit entity to "Autonomous Federated
Unit of the Republic of India," terminology borrowed from the
Soviet Union's model of multi-tiered ethno-territorial federalism.
Fifty years later, these ideas remain relevant to dealing with the internal complexity of the Kashmir problem, although, in 2003 as in
1953, an essential prerequisite is the democratization of IJK's political life to guarantee civil liberties and rights of participation and
representation to all segments of the territory's rainbow spectrum
of political opinion and allegiance.

The compromise scheme rapidly foundered on the treacherous
internal shoals of IJK politics. The sectarian Jammu and Ladakh
factions—and their external supporters and advisers—were inter-
ested in nothing short of total overthrow of the autonomous
regime and a settling of scores with Abdullah and company. They
refused the bait. The picture was further complicated by the
matryoshka-doll character of IJK society and politics. A huge portion of Indian Jammu's land area—11,500 of 26,293 square kilometers—consists of a mountain district called Doda, which has three
tehsils—Doda, Kishtwar, and Bhaderwah. The Doda district has a
Muslim majority (57 percent in 1981) of mainly Kashmiri-speakers,

an ethno-cultural and political spillover from the Kashmir Valley to the immediate north. These Kashmiri-speaking Muslims, largely adherents of the NC, refused to be part of an autonomous Hindu-majority Jammu region and declared their unbreakable identity with the Valley. From the 1960s to the present day, sectarian Hindu political groups in the Jammu region have intermittently agitated for totally detaching the Indian Jammu region— which has an overall Hindu majority, concentrated in its southern districts—from the Kashmir Valley. It was pointed out as early as the mid-1960s that this demand is blind to the social and political complexities of the Jammu region. Specifically, the three Muslim-majority districts—Doda, Rajouri, and Poonch—of Indian Jammu's six districts would, then as now, "almost certainly refuse to be bracketed with Dogra Hindus and prefer to stay with the Valley Muslims."[18]

In May 1953 Sheikh Abdullah switched from compromise to confrontation. The NC's highest policymaking body, its working committee, appointed a subcommittee to examine constitutional options for IJK, and for J&K as a whole. The subcommittee had eight members—five Muslims from the Kashmir Valley including Abdullah, a Kashmiri Pandit, a Sikh, and a Dogra from Jammu (thus, counting the Pandit representative, six members were from the Valley, the party's stronghold). On 9 June the special committee put forward four possible options for Kashmir's future, all involving a plebiscite and/or independence for part or whole of the disputed territory. The first and favored option called for a plebiscite in the entire territory to determine the core issue of legitimate sovereignty. Unlike the U.N. resolutions, which expressly limited the choice to India or Pakistan, the subcommittee unanimously recommended, on the suggestion of the NC's general secretary, Maulana Masoodi, that the J&K electorate be offered a third option—full independence. Abdullah refused to soften this stance during July, in correspondence with Nehru and India's education minister, Abul Kalam Azad. Instead, he decided to summon the NC's working committee and general council in late August to ratify the new line, and planned to go public with his stance on 21 August, the day of a major Muslim religious celebration.

The summer of 1953 was a decisive and fateful time for Kashmir. In early August a major rift appeared within the top NC leadership. The rift divided Abdullah's five-member cabinet, with Abdullah and his loyalist Mirza Afzal Beg outnumbered by the dissident faction comprising Shyamlal Saraf (a Kashmiri Pandit), Giridharilal Dogra (a Jammu Hindu), and significantly, Bakshi Ghulam Mohammed, Abdullah's deputy prime minister and a Valley Muslim. The power struggle tilted against Abdullah when the pro-communist bloc within the NC joined with the dissident ministers in rejecting Abdullah's confrontational, pro-independence strategy. This group, led by the Constituent Assembly speaker G. M. Sadiq and including D. P. Dhar, a Pandit deputy minister of interior, was influenced by the Soviet Union's shifting posture on the Kashmir dispute. In 1948 the Soviet propaganda organ *New Times* had hailed Abdullah as the leader of "a progressive and democratic mass movement" and condemned the alleged interference of "Indian reactionaries" in Kashmir. By 1953 the same paper was calling the Kashmir question an "internal affair" of India and decrying alleged "imperialist [American-led] efforts to turn the Valley into a strategic bridgehead."[19] Bakshi Ghulam Mohammed seems to have been motivated primarily by personal ambition, above all the prospect of displacing the Lion of Kashmir as leader of Kashmir. For Hindu NC leaders—Saraf, Dogra, and possibly Dhar—allegiance to India appears to have been the deciding factor.

The outcome of the power struggle shaped New Delhi–Srinagar relations, and the pattern of politics within IJK, for the next three and a half decades. On 9 August 1953 Sheikh Abdullah was dismissed as prime minister by the nominal head of state, Karan Singh, and arrested by police under a law called the Public Security Act, used until then to persecute the sheikh's opponents. He would remain incarcerated for the next twenty-two years, until 1975, barring brief spells out of prison in 1958, 1964–1965, and 1968. Bakshi Ghulam Mohammed took over as prime minister at the head of a government purged of Abdullah loyalists. On 9–10 August, 33 other NC leaders, including the former cabinet minister Afzal Beg, were also arrested under the Public Security Act. By October 1953 large majorities of Constituent Assembly delegates (60 of 75) and members of the NC general council (90 of 110) formally ratified the new leadership in specially convened sessions. Maulana Masoodi, the respected cleric who held the post of party general secretary, was summarily removed for continuing to support Abdullah.

Despite appearances, these events bore telltale signs of a putsch, executed at the behest of New Delhi—whose government was the sovereign authority in IJK, at least according to the Instrument of Accession—by a clique of NC leaders. On 10 August Bakshi Ghulam Mohammed issued his first statement as prime minister, denouncing Abdullah as an oppressive leader who had become a tool of foreign conspiracies designed to undermine Kashmir's indissoluble ties with India. In September 1953 Nehru justified Abdullah's eviction from office before India's Parliament on the grounds that he had lost the confidence of the majority of his cabinet and by his actions caused "distress to the people." However, there was no convincing "democratic" justification for Abdullah's arrest (and prolonged imprisonment in a Jammu jail). Curiously, Nehru had agreed with the Pakistani government in

August 1953 to set up a joint Indian-Pakistani committee of civilian and military experts to hold preliminary discussions on organizing a Kashmir plebiscite—the same month Abdullah was removed for resurrecting the plebiscite demand. Abdullah's detention, accompanied by mass arrests of key members of the NC organization, purges, and unconvincing, possibly stage-managed shows of loyalty to the new leadership, revealed the change of regime in Kashmir to be a narrowly based coup that needed to resort to such measures in order to succeed.

One senior member of the NC old guard, aligned with the "leftist" group in the party, who sided with the putschists and immediately became a cabinet minister in the new government, was Syed Mir Qasim. In his memoirs, published in 1992, Qasim recorded massive popular protests that swept the Valley after the sheikh's overthrow and the brutal police methods used to suppress the disturbances. Qasim's candid account suggests that the Indian-sponsored regime would have collapsed like a house of cards had the sheikh been allowed to remain at liberty to organize and lead a mass movement against it.[20]

The second half of 1953 signaled a decisive turning point in the basis and nature of the relationship between Kashmir and India. The old NC conception had viewed that relationship as an honorable partnership of equals. After 1953 this conception became history. From August 1953 onward, any defiance of New Delhi's absolute supremacy in the relationship guaranteed not only a swift passage to political oblivion but criminalization as an enemy of the state. The fate suffered by a leader of Sheikh Abdullah's stature sent out a very powerful—and unambiguous—message. Only those who unequivocally agreed to follow the Indian state's agenda in Kashmir could aspire to office, or indeed, could play any sort of role in institutionally sanctioned politics.

The problem was that this situation could be effected only at the expense of the consent of a large proportion of the governed. Sheikh Abdullah's tenure was unmistakably authoritarian, his policies were somewhat divisive, and his decision to challenge New Delhi's supremacy—whether for tactical purposes or otherwise—was possibly a reckless move by an overconfident populist politician. But his "Kashmir first" line nonetheless struck a chord among people in IJK, particularly in the Valley. That "patriotic" stance, combined with the successful delivery of land reforms in the rural sector, invested the charismatic sheikh with almost saintly status in the eyes of many ordinary people, especially in the Valley, and gave his authoritarian, dispute-prone regime more than a critical mass of popular support. The post-1953 New Delhi–approved successor governments in IJK would be at least as authoritarian and considerably more corrupt, and they would lack the significant popular base that the sheikh, despite all his flaws, enjoyed.

Bakshi Ghulam Mohammed's term in office lasted a full decade, until October 1963. The sequence of events during that decade strongly suggests a contractual relationship between Bakshi and the government of India, whereby he would be allowed to run an unrepresentative, unaccountable government in Srinagar in return for facilitating IJK's "integration" with India on New Delhi's terms. The result was twofold: a crippling of rule of law and democratic institutions in IJK; and an erosion of IJK's autonomy, achieved (as required by Article 370) with the "concurrence" of IJK's government—which consisted of a motley clique of New Delhi's client politicians.

IJK's statutory autonomy had been proclaimed in 1950 by a constitutional order formally issued in the name of the president of India. In May 1954 another constitutional order was issued superseding the previous proclamation. The new communiqué extended the central government's right to legislate in IJK to the majority of subjects on the Union List. IJK's financial and fiscal relations with New Delhi were placed on the same footing as those of other, undisputed units of the Indian Union. The Indian supreme court now had full jurisdiction in IJK. The fundamental rights of citizens guaranteed by India's constitution were to apply in IJK, but with a crucial caveat: these civil liberties could be suspended at any time at the discretion of IJK authorities in the interest of "security," and no judicial reviews of the suspensions would be allowed. In effect, this was carte blanche for the operation of a draconian police state in IJK. The only concession to popular sentiment in the constitutional order was that it upheld the deposed IJK government's policy of land reform without compensation. Bakshi Ghulam Mohammed's government and legislature eagerly consented, in February 1954, to the proposed roster of integrative measures, as was legally and constitutionally necessary for their validation. Bakshi informed the Constituent Assembly—in the absence of a dogged minority of pro-Abdullah deputies—that Kashmir had "irrevocably acceded to India more than six years ago and today we are fulfilling the formalities of our unbreakable bonds with India." On the floor of India's Parliament, Prime Minister Nehru "welcomed the decision of the Constituent Assembly of Kashmir as representing the wishes of the people of Kashmir." He added that India's "international commitments" on Kashmir were still valid and that the Indian government planned "to proceed with them in due course in consultation with the Government of Kashmir . . . unless something else happened."[21]

The developments of 1954 were the beginning of the end for Article 370, which has effectively been dead in letter and in spirit since that time. Strangely, the autonomy clause formally remains in India's constitution. Between the 1950s and the 1990s, successive

Congress governments in New Delhi rejected demands by opposition Hindu nationalists for its formal removal from the constitution (Hindu nationalist ideology regards the existence of Article 370 as implying favoritism and special treatment for India's sole Muslim-majority state). However, when Hindu nationalists assumed power in India in the late 1990s, their governments continued the Congress practice of paying lip service to Article 370, repudiating calls from their own extreme right wing for its elimination. This is understandable from the viewpoint of practical politics. Article 370 has been a cipher for decades and its formal retention is an irrelevance.

In the mid-1950s, developments in international politics facilitated the Indian government's emerging Kashmir strategy. In the late 1940s and early 1950s, Stalin's Soviet Union was in a radical ideological phase and derided India's new democracy as a bourgeois hoax. By 1953—the year of Stalin's death—the USSR had changed its strategy. The emphasis was now on courting India as a major Asian country whose foreign policy showed signs that it might remain at least neutral, or "non-aligned," in the Cold War. The Soviet stance on Kashmir shifted accordingly, and the shift was reinforced by Pakistan's gradual gravitation toward regional security alliances fostered across Asia by the United States to "contain" the Soviet Union.

Nehru's February 1954 speech to India's Parliament on Kashmir anticipated that "something else" might "happen" to influence India's Kashmir policy, and noted explicitly that India's international commitments on Kashmir were "subject to changes which might come about because of other events."[22] In fact, the Indian prime minister had already written to his Pakistani counterpart, Mohammed Ali Bogra, in November 1953, expressing grave concern over Pakistan's reported moves toward joining U.S.-sponsored regional military alliances in exchange for American military assistance which could be used against India, including in Kashmir, and warning him that if Pakistan went ahead repercussions would ensue for "every question pending" between the two countries. Between April and September 1954 Pakistan formally entered the American orbit. A military aid agreement providing for sending American military equipment to Pakistan was signed in Karachi in May 1954, and Pakistan joined the South-East Asian Treaty Organization (SEATO, also known as the Manila Pact) in September 1954. It became a member of the Turkish-Iraqi mutual cooperation pact (also known as the Baghdad Pact, and later as the Central Treaty Organization or CENTO) in September 1955.

Pakistan's alignment with the United States encouraged the Soviet Union's emerging pro-India posture on Kashmir. In December 1955 the Soviet leaders Khrushchev and Bulganin visited India and traveled to Srinagar. In Srinagar, Premier Khrushchev informed his audience: "The people of Jammu and Kashmir want to work for the well-being of their beloved country—the Republic of India. The people of Kashmir do not want to become toys in the hands of imperialist powers. This is exactly what some powers are trying to do by supporting Pakistan on the so-called Kashmir question. It made us very sad when imperialist powers succeeded in bringing about the partition of India [in 1947] . . . That Kashmir is one of the States of the Republic of India has already been decided by the people of Kashmir." Marshal Bulganin referred to Kashmir as "this northern part of India" and to its population as "part of the Indian people," who, he discerned, felt "deep joy" at being included in India.[23]

Three months after this visit, in March 1956, Nehru told India's Parliament that a plebiscite in Kashmir was "beside the point" and emphasized "Pakistani aggression in Kashmir and the legality of

Kashmir's [1947] accession to India," which, he claimed, had been ratified by the IJK Constituent Assembly in 1954. Nehru publicly said in April that he had offered Pakistan's prime minister a permanent, de jure division of Jammu and Kashmir along the existing CFL a year earlier, in May 1955. Pakistani leaders rejected Nehru's "strange logic" in linking the matter of Kashmir with Pakistan's military alliances, and characterized the Soviet leaders' statements as "extraordinary." But the die had been cast. In February 1957 the USSR exercised its U.N. Security Council veto for the first time during a discussion of Kashmir convened at Pakistan's initiative. This became a regular occurrence thereafter.[24]

Inside IJK, Bakshi's regime rapidly became notorious for its two salient attributes: rampant corruption, with officials looting the exchequer at will; and Mafia-style authoritarianism, marked by liberal use of police and gangs of professional thugs against any sign of opposition. In Delhi, Balraj Puri, the activist from Jammu, once again met with Nehru to apprise him of this oppressive situation and ask him to ensure that pro-Abdullah elements be allowed some political space to operate in the Valley. Nehru, Puri recalls, agreed that Bakshi Ghulam Mohammed was an extremely unsavory individual, but "argued that India's case [on Kashmir] now revolved around him and so despite all its shortcomings, the Bakshi government had to be strengthened." Puri quotes Nehru as saying that Kashmir's politics "revolved around personalities" and hence "there was no material for democracy there." In 1954 an attempt by a left-wing all-India party, the Praja Socialist Party (PSP), to set up a branch office in Srinagar was disrupted by a gang of regime-sponsored hooligans. Nehru's reaction was to accuse the PSP of "joining hands with the enemies of the country."[25]

Despite incessant harassment by the police state, efforts to organize a political opposition continued. In October 1954 four members of the Constituent Assembly formed an opposition group in the legislature. This expanded within months to a caucus of eight legislators. On 10 August 1955 this group, along with a nominated Kashmiri representative in India's Parliament, launched a political movement calling itself the Jammu and Kashmir Plebiscite Front (PF). Mirza Afzal Beg, Abdullah's loyal lieutenant, who had been temporarily released from prison, became its first president. The PF stood for "self-determination through a plebiscite under UN auspices, withdrawal of the armed forces of both nations from Kashmir, and restoration of civil liberties and free elections." On 23 August the IJK government banned public meetings, "to prevent clashes between supporters and opponents of the Government," and all top leaders of the PF and its allied organizations were subsequently arrested. Indeed, "between 19 November 1955 and 29 September 1956 four presidents of the Plebiscite Front were arrested," one after another, in a relentless cycle of repression.[26]

This intensified repression was related not only to changing international alignments on the Kashmir dispute, described earlier, but to moves inside the Constituent Assembly. In October–November 1956 the Constituent Assembly was presented with a draft constitution for IJK, which was rapidly approved by sixty-seven of its seventy-five members—"the remaining members were either in gaol or had withdrawn from the proceedings." This document started from the premise that "the State of Jammu and Kashmir is and shall be an integral part of the Union of India."[27] The expression "integral part," with its implications of finality, was subsequently made into a central maxim of the Indian state. Any "reference to the people" was now, as Nehru had said in March 1956, entirely "beside the point." From prison, Sheikh Abdullah wrote protest letters to G. M. Sadiq, his former colleague and the procommunist speaker of the Assembly, and to Nehru. He received no replies. Only four opposition deputies were not in prison when the draft constitution was placed before the house. They decided to boycott the proceedings, "but when Mirza Afzal Beg was released on 19 October they changed their mind and participated in the discussion. On 22 October Beg moved a motion of adjournment for two weeks to enable Sheikh Abdullah to be present. Sadiq [presiding] ruled the motion out of order whereupon Beg and his followers [again] boycotted the proceedings . . . On 25 October Beg was re-arrested."[28]

In a symbolic gesture of allegiance, IJK's new constitution—which supposedly applies to the whole of J&K, including Pakistani-controlled areas—came into effect on 26 January 1957, the seventh anniversary of the proclamation of the Republic of India. On 24 January 1957, at Pakistan's initiative, the U.N. Security Council passed a resolution in response to these developments. It reiterated its 1948–1951 resolutions calling for a final settlement "in accordance with the will of the people expressed through the democratic method of a free and impartial plebiscite conducted under the auspices of the United Nations." It further reiterated "the affirmation in its resolution of 30 March 1951 . . . that the convening of a Constituent Assembly as recommended by the general council of the 'All Jammu and Kashmir National Conference' and any action the Assembly may have taken or might attempt to take to determine the future shape and affiliation of the entire State or any part thereof, or action by the parties concerned [India and Pakistan] in support of any such action by the Assembly, would not constitute a disposition of the State in accordance with the above principle." The resolution concludes with the assertion that "the Security Council . . . decides to continue its consideration of the dispute."[29]

The international status of the Kashmir question was—and is—

quite clear. But the United Nations was powerless to prevent developments in IJK from taking their course. After adopting the constitution, the Constituent Assembly dissolved itself and fresh elections were ordered to constitute a new IJK Legislative Assembly. In June 1957 the election process was completed. At first glance, the outcome appeared to represent a marginal improvement over the Constituent Assembly "election" of autumn 1951, in which Abdullah's National Conference had secured 100 percent of the 75 seats at stake. This time Bakshi Ghulam Mohammed's NC obtained 69 seats—92 percent of the total. However, only 28 seats were filled after any kind of contest (and balloting). Of 43 Kashmir Valley seats, 35 were "won" by official NC candidates without any contest. Across IJK, 30 NC candidates, including Bakshi Ghulam Mohammed, were "returned unopposed" and another 10 NC candidates were elected after nomination papers filed by opposing candidates were declared invalid. The official in charge of deciding whether nomination papers were valid or not was Abdul Khaleq Malik, a Bakshi henchman. Of 8 seats in the Valley where a nominal contest took place, 7 were won by NC candidates against politically unknown persons standing in token opposition, while the last was taken by a disgruntled Bakshi man standing against the official candidate. Twenty of the Jammu region's 30 seats witnessed a contest—here the NC won 14 seats, the Praja Parishad elected 5, and a candidate representing a party of "low-caste" Hindus bagged one seat. There was thus a small representation of opposition Hindu groups in the legislature, but representation of the majority Muslim population was effectively monopolized by the New Delhi–sponsored establishment faction. The 25 additional seats reserved for Pakistan-controlled Kashmir of course remained vacant.

Bakshi Ghulam Mohammed was "elected unopposed" as head

of the NC legislature party and hence as prime minister. Membership of the legislature's unelected, consultative upper house, called the legislative council, was also monopolized by nominees of the official clique. In 1958 the Legislative Assembly gave its concurrence, after due consultation with New Delhi, to the deployment of Indian staff from outside IJK in IJK's administration. Three decades later, in 1989, IJK's population was 65 percent Muslim, but of 22 senior-level officers in the IJK branch of India's professional civil service, only five were Kashmiri-speaking Muslims, and the Valley's tiny Pandit minority was hugely overrepresented in IJK's own civil service and among officers in its banking system.[30]

IJK's next elections were held in 1962. The intervening years were notable for China's entry into the international politics of the Kashmir conflict. China's relations with India deteriorated precipitously after the Chinese annexation of Tibet in 1959, and rising tensions flared into a military conflict in late 1962 at a number of disputed border flashpoints stretching in an east-west arc along the Himalayan ranges, including a desolate area called Aksai Chin on Ladakh's frontier with Tibet and China's Xinjiang province. Indian forces were routed in the fighting, and India immediately began a massive program of expansion, reorganization, and rearmament of its military.[31] Since communist China was at the time viewed as a major threat by the Western allies, the United States began to supply some weapons and equipment to India's armed forces. This deeply offended Pakistan, which started to cultivate diplomatic and military ties with China in response.

In March 1963 the Chinese government signed an agreement with the military regime then in power in Pakistan on "delimitation" of the boundary between Pakistan's Northern Areas in J&K and China's Xinjiang province (which has a large Muslim population and a history of political unrest). Under this agreement, the Pakistanis ceded a sizeable chunk of territory in this remote region to China, exacerbating Indian fears of the emergence of a Sino-Pakistani alliance against India. Article 6 of the boundary agreement cleverly dealt with the unresolved international status of the Kashmir question by specifying that "after the settlement of the Kashmir dispute between Pakistan and India, the sovereign authority concerned will reopen negotiations with the Government of the People's Republic of China . . . so as to sign a boundary treaty to replace the present agreement . . . In the event of that sovereign authority being Pakistan, the provisions of this agreement shall be maintained."[32]

In IJK, the major development during these years was an internal schism in the ruling coterie. The split developed when Bakshi Ghulam Mohammed failed to appoint any members of the pro-Soviet leftist faction to the cabinet he constituted after the 1957 elections. This group, led by G. M. Sadiq, then formed a separate party called the Democratic National Conference and was joined by fifteen legislators. In late 1960 a reconciliation was mediated by New Delhi—ostensibly to close ranks against the Chinese threat—and Sadiq and his followers were once again accommodated in the government. In elections held in 1962, the happily reunited government party won 68 of 74 seats in IJK's Legislative Assembly (the Praja Parishad got 3, and another 3 went to independents, including the chief Buddhist Lama of Ladakh). Of 43 constituencies in the Kashmir Valley, 32 were decided without a contest. In 20 of these seats no other candidates filed papers, in 8 electoral districts non-official candidates who had filed papers withdrew before the polling date, and in another 4 the papers of non-official candidates were declared invalid. Bakshi and his cabinet colleagues Sadiq, Mir Qasim, and Khwaja Shamsuddin were all returned unopposed to the Assembly. The NC secured 41 of 43 seats in the Kashmir Valley and also won 27 of 30 seats from the Jammu region, including 2 unopposed seats. In protest against massive malpractices and a farcical process, "a mass demonstration" was held in Jammu city, jointly organized by a diverse spectrum of parties including the Praja Parishad, the socialist PSP, and Akali Dal, a Sikh group. However, "the prime minister of Kashmir dismissed their complaints as frivolous."[33]

The years 1963–1965 were a volatile period in Kashmir. In October 1963 Bakshi Ghulam Mohammed reluctantly stepped down as prime minister—apparently at the behest of his patrons in New Delhi, where he was increasingly regarded as an embarrassment who had outlived his usefulness. Before the 1962 elections, Nehru urged the PSP—the leftist India-wide opposition party whose members he had described as enemies of the state in 1954 because they opposed Bakshi's strong-arm tactics—to field candidates because recurrent unopposed elections in IJK were earning India's democracy "a bad reputation." After the elections, Nehru wrote to Bakshi that "it would strengthen your position much more if you lost a few seats to bonafide opponents." Bakshi was replaced as premier by one of his more obscure cabinet ministers, Khwaja Shamsuddin. Bakshi, although ousted, still commanded the loyalty of the majority of party legislators and managed to fend off the New Delhi-backed candidacy of his principal rival for the coveted post, G. M. Sadiq. The new government subsequently formed by Shamsuddin once again excluded Sadiq and his group from ministerial appointments.[34]

In late December 1963 more than a decade of pent-up resentment finally exploded in the Kashmir Valley. The spark was provided by the theft of a religious relic, said to be a hair from the head of the Prophet Mohammed, from Srinagar's Hazratbal shrine which had been the NC-led movement's headquarters in 1946–1947. In a peculiar turn of events, the holy hair reappeared in the shrine on 3 January 1964, but "in the meantime a central action committee led by Maulana Masoodi, the former general secretary of the National Conference had been formed for recovery of the relic, and it had taken control of the city in the wake of a mass upsurge." Other leaders of this committee were G. M. Karra, who had been Srinagar district chief of the NC in the 1940s, and Maulvi Farooq, a *mirwaiz* (religious figure) of pro-Pakistan inclinations.[35]

The crisis was compounded by an outbreak of sectarian rioting in the province of Bengal, more than three thousand kilometers away in eastern India. During January–February 1964 the violence claimed the lives of hundreds of minority Hindus in eastern Bengal (then East Pakistan) and hundreds of minority Muslims in Calcutta, the capital of West Bengal province in India. In the Kashmir Valley, however,

> leaders of the action committee, notably Masoodi and Karra, warned against violence . . . Both did wonderful work in pacifying excited Muslim crowds during the critical days of the holy relic restoration movement when a small mistake could have soaked the Valley in blood. But for Masoodi [Kashmir's top cleric] authentication of the restored relic would have been impossible and put the Indian authorities in tremendous difficulty. Karra's speeches, characterized by balance and caution, produced a moderating influence on the movement and kept agitated mobs under control. In a mass meeting at Zadibal [near Srinagar] he advised Kashmiris that while denouncing Hindu communalism in India they should not overlook the atrocities of Mus-

lim fanatics in East Pakistan. He incurred the wrath of extremists but did not retract.[36]

The tumult over the stolen relic brought back mass collective action to the Kashmir Valley and severely destabilized the Indian-sponsored regime in IJK. In late February Shamsuddin was replaced as head of government by New Delhi's favored candidate, G. M. Sadiq, who packed a reconstituted cabinet with his own loyalists like Mir Qasim and D. P. Dhar. Sadiq assessed the situation and quickly concluded that the only hope of preventing an uprising was to take the risk of releasing Sheikh Abdullah, who had been freed once before, in January 1958, but rearrested within three months. Abdullah was released in April 1964, along with his faithful comrade Afzal Beg. On 18 April Abdullah "entered Srinagar and was greeted by a delirious crowd of 250,000 people. Srinagar was a blaze of color and everyone seemed out on the streets to give Abdullah a hero's welcome . . . Addressing a huge gathering of 150,000 people on 20 April, Abdullah said that in 1947 he had challenged Pakistan's authority to annex Kashmir on grounds of religion, and now he was challenging the Indian contention that the question had been settled. A solution must be found agreeable to both India and Pakistan with due regard to the sentiments of the people of Kashmir." In late April Abdullah traveled to Delhi for talks with Nehru (who died soon after, on 27 May 1964), and in May he went to Pakistan for talks with Pakistan's military dictator, Ayub Khan. Beg and Masoodi accompanied him on both missions.[37]

The brief season of hope in Kashmir faded within months. The government of India was alarmed by Abdullah's tough stance on self-rule and by his insistence on the need for Pakistan's involvement in finding a serious, durable resolution to the Kashmir question, Sadiq was threatened by the overwhelming popular response, at least in the Valley heartland, to Abdullah's politics. Bakshi Ghulam Mohammed was smarting from his imposed marginalization, and still had the loyalty of a large number of deputies in the IJK Legislative Assembly elected in 1962. By the autumn a tactical alliance between Bakshi and Abdullah appeared in the offing, on the basis of their shared aim of bringing down the Sadiq government. In September 1964 pro-Bakshi deputies in the Assembly moved to organize a no-confidence motion against Sadiq, with Abdullah's tacit support. Sadiq's government reacted by arresting Bakshi (and six of his leading supporters) under a draconian law, the Defence of India Rules, inherited from the British colonial era. Bakshi was charged with endangering national security and sent to the same prison in Jammu where Abdullah had been incarcerated eleven years earlier. Although he was released within a few months on health grounds, the confrontation split the ruling group as a core of Bakshi loyalists continued to challenge Sadiq's authority.

Under attack on two fronts in Srinagar, Sadiq looked to New Delhi for salvation. As in 1953, the leaders of India's government sensed an opportunity in the internecine struggles of the Kashmiri Muslim elite. In December 1964 India's interior minister announced in parliament that the Union government had decided to bring IJK under the purview of two of the most centralist (and controversial) provisions of the Indian constitution—Articles 356 and 357, which respectively empower the center to dismiss elected governments of India's states in the event of a breakdown of law and order and to assume their legislative mandate. A constitutional order to that effect was immediately promulgated from New Delhi. In March 1965 central powers of intervention and control were further strengthened when the IJK Assembly passed a constitutional amendment that abolished the post of Sadr-e-Riyasat (titular head of state in IJK), elected by members of the IJK legislature, and replaced it with a governor (the standard term used in all Indian states) appointed by New Delhi. Other amendments passed at the same time changed the title of IJK's prime minister to "chief minister" (as in all Indian states), and provided for direct election from IJK to the popularly elected chamber of India's Parliament, the Lok Sabha (House of the People)—previously, representatives to India's Parliament had been nominated by IJK's legislature.

This slew of imposed integrative measures, operationalized through the cooperation of a clique of client IJK politicians, was preceded by the most breathtaking development of all. On 3 January 1965 the working committee of the National Conference (meaning its ruling Sadiq faction, Mir Qasim being party general secretary) announced that the NC would dissolve itself and merge into India's ruling Congress party. In other words, the name and identity of Kashmir's historic political movement would cease to exist altogether, and the NC would be absorbed into India's Congress as a provincial branch. It is difficult to conceive of a more drastic centralizing strategy than what unfolded between December 1964 and March 1965. On 10 January the Congress party's working committee unanimously accepted the merger offer.

This was effectively the end of the road for Article 370 and IJK's autonomous regime. Indeed, the Hindu nationalist agenda for IJK, articulated by the Praja Parishad in Jammu and by Hindu nationalist parties in India since the late 1940s, "had emerged victorious" in IJK by 1965. The irony is that the foundation for this victory had been systematically laid by the policies of the 1947–1964 government of Jawaharlal Nehru, the apparent personification of India's liberal secularism, and only carried to conclusion by his

successors. Perhaps Nehru was influenced by his own Kashmiri
Pandit origins, or, even more plausibly, was trying to compensate
for his role in the partition of India. But it is incontrovertible that
Nehru, "undoubtedly the greatest outside influence on Kashmir's
political history," was, in the words of Balraj Puri, "above all a nationalist. He subordinated democracy, morality and sub-national
aspirations [to autonomy] to the claims of Indian nationalism."[38]

The "people of the Valley reacted with unprecedented anger,"
and their "protests were again suppressed with brute force and
large-scale arrests." In mid-January 1965 Abdullah delivered a vitri-
olic speech in front of a huge PF gathering at the Hazratbal
shrine, calling on the people to resist imposition of Articles 356
and 357 and the absurd and insulting attempt to eradicate the identity of Kashmir's premier regionalist movement. "Violence and arson took place in some parts of Srinagar city" as massive crowds
returned from the meeting, "and by 7 March the situation became
sufficiently explosive to warrant a large-scale arrest of leaders of
the Plebiscite Front." (Abdullah himself was rearrested under Defence of India Rules after returning from a trip to foreign countries in May.) Sporadic unrest continued, however, and the disturbed situation in IJK probably encouraged Pakistan's military
regime to seize the moment to foment an uprising in IJK, which
led to war between India and Pakistan in the autumn of 1965.[39]

In fact, "it was no secret that Pakistan had been training young
men for three years [since 1962, when the defeat by China exposed India's military vulnerability] at different military camps
to fight as guerrillas in the mountainous recesses and foothills"
of Indian-controlled Jammu and Kashmir. But in contrast to 1989–
1990, when an insurrection aided from across the LOC but
spearheaded by Valley Kashmiris would erupt in IJK, the several
thousand armed men who crossed the CFL into IJK in August

1965 consisted of "either Pakistani nationals [mostly professional soldiers] or others [volunteers] who belonged to non-Kashmiri-speaking AJK territories." They "had taken for granted the fullest cooperation of the local Muslims but this was not forthcoming, at any rate not on the expected huge scale." The ambitious operation failed, although anti-government student demonstrations broke out again in Srinagar in October 1965, after the two countries had reached a truce, and Chief Minister Sadiq narrowly escaped assassination while visiting Baramulla.[40]

Shortly after the end of the 1965 war, the Kashmiri Pandit writer and activist Prem Nath Bazaz wrote that "for a clear understanding and realistic appraisal of the Kashmir situation it is necessary to recognize the fact that by and large State [IJK] Muslims are not very friendly towards India. An overwhelming majority of them are not happy under the present political set-up, and desire to be done with it. But they are reluctant to bring about change through warfare and bloodshed." It would take another quarter-century of repression and a generational turnover for the pacifist approach to yield decisively to armed struggle, qualifying Kashmiris as an exemplar of the political scientist Donald Horowitz's category of "reluctant secessionists."[41]

In 1966 Jayaprakash Narayan, an Indian opposition leader, wrote to Prime Minister Indira Gandhi, Nehru's daughter: "We profess democracy, but rule by force in Kashmir. We profess secularism, but let Hindu nationalism stampede us into establishing it by repression. Kashmir has distorted India's image in the world as nothing else has done. The problem exists not because Pakistan wants to grab Kashmir, but because there is deep and widespread discontent among the people." Bazaz argued at the time that while "India may reject the plebiscite and turn down UN resolutions as outdated and impractical, India cannot forever defraud the State [IJK] people of their constitutional right to free elections." He added that "if free elections are held, it may be taken for granted that the majority of seats will be captured by those unfriendly to India."[42]

This was precisely the scenario New Delhi was anxious to avoid at all costs. In 1967 elections to constitute a new Assembly, 39 of the 75 seats were filled without a contest. Congress candidates— meaning those sponsored by the Sadiq–Mir Qasim faction of the NC—were "returned unopposed" in 22 of the Valley's 42 constituencies. From the southern Valley town of Anantnag, the official candidate Khwaja Shamsuddin, who had served as IJK's prime minister for a few months in 1962–1963, was elected unopposed— after papers filed by five other candidates were rejected as invalid. In all, nomination papers of 118 candidates were rejected, 55 of them on the grounds that the candidates had failed to take the obligatory oath of allegiance to India. The government party won 60 of 75 seats in the legislature.

For the first time, simultaneous elections were held to fill 6 seats from IJK in India's Parliament (the Lok Sabha). For 2 of these—Ladakh and the Valley seat of Anantnag—Congress candidates were elected "unopposed." Another 3 were "won" by Congress candidates, as Jammu-based Indian opposition groups like "the Praja Socialist Party and the [Hindu nationalist] Jan Sangh severely criticized electoral irregularities." The irregularities common to both sets of polls included "large-scale rejection of nomination papers, arrests of [opposition] polling agents, advance distribution of ballot papers to Congress workers, absence of opposition agents at time of counting, and rampant use of official machinery to the advantage of the ruling party." Thus "Congress, which [previously] had no base [in IJK] . . . bagged five of the six parliamentary seats."[43]

There were only a couple of interesting footnotes to this fruit-less exercise. A young PF leader, Ali Mohammed Naik, made a tactical decision to swear allegiance to India, got his papers approved, and was returned to the Assembly as an independent from his hometown, Tral, in the southern part of the Valley. Bakshi Ghulam Mohammed, who had been prime minister from 1953 to 1963, ran against the Congress candidate for Parliament from Srinagar as a candidate of the rump National Conference. Puri recalls being told at the time in Srinagar by officials deputed from Delhi to "supervise" the election that "Bakshi had to be de-feated in the national interest." It has been plausibly argued that "Bakshi Ghulam Mohammed would probably not have won a free election at any point during his ten years in office." In 1967, hold-ing aloft the banner of Kashmiri regionalist resistance to New Delhi and Congress, he was elected to India's Parliament from Srinagar.[44]

In December 1970 the PF, in a shift of strategy, announced that it would contest elections to India's Parliament due in 1971 and to IJK's Legislative Assembly due in 1972. Syed Mir Qasim, Sadiq's successor as IJK's Congress chief minister, panicked. In his mem-oirs, published in 1992, Qasim wrote that at the popular level the PF had, since its emergence in the mid-1950s, "reduced the [of-ficial] National Conference to a non-entity in Kashmir's politics." "If the elections were free and fair," he added, "the victory of the Front was a foregone conclusion."[45]

It seems Qasim's assessment was correct. In early 1968 Sheikh Abdullah, imprisoned under Defence of India Rules since May 1965, was briefly released before being incarcerated again. The *Times of India* reported that "almost the entire population of Srinagar turned out to greet him" as he arrived back in the Valley in March 1968, adding that the crowds of hundreds of thousands were chanting "Sher-e-Kashmir Zindabad [Long Live the Lion of Kashmir], Our Demand Plebiscite." Days later, addressing a hundred thousand supporters in Anantnag, Abdullah warned that "repression will never suppress the Kashmiri people's urge to be free" and asked India to "redeem her promise to allow the people of the State to exercise their right to self-determination." Visiting the city of Jammu on 23 December 1970, Prime Minister Indira Gandhi declared that attempts to enter the IJK Assembly or the Indian Parliament with the intent of "wrecking the constitution" would not be tolerated. When asked by journalists how such subversion would be prevented, she answered: "Ways will be found."[46]

On 8 January 1971 "externment orders" were served on the top PF leaders Mirza Afzal Beg and G. M. Shah (Abdullah's son-in-law), obliging them to leave IJK territory. On the night of 8–9 January, across IJK, "at least 350 officials and members of the Front were arrested under the [IJK] Preventive Detention Act in a series of police raids." On 12 January the government of India declared the PF an unlawful organization under India's Unlawful Activities (Prevention) Act, on the grounds that the Front had "on diverse occasions by words, either spoken or written, and signs and visual representations . . . asserted a claim to determine whether or not Jammu and Kashmir will remain a part of India."[47] In subsequent elections in 1971–1972, Congress "won" five of six parliamentary districts and fifty-seven of seventy-five Assembly districts. The Jama'at-i-Islami, a pro-Pakistan conservative religious group, got five deputies in the Assembly, apparently after an understanding with the Mir Qasim regime that it would help oppose the PF's pro-independence politics. In the parliamentary election, Bakshi Ghulam Mohammed stood for reelection from Srinagar—a sprawling, congested capital city where outright rigging of an election is more difficult than in rural areas—this time as a regime-backed Congress candidate, consistent with his chameleon record. He was defeated by Shamim Ahmed Shamim, a PF sympathizer standing as an independent, by a large margin of 57,000 votes.

In 1975 Sheikh Abdullah finally abandoned his self-determination platform. In return for Abdullah's release and appointment as IJK's chief minister, his ever-faithful associate, Mirza Afzal Beg, signed another "Delhi accord" with the government of India whose terms verged on capitulation to New Delhi and Indira Gandhi. The agreement reaffirmed, virtually without modification, the terms of IJK's incorporation into India since 1953. A patently hypocritical clause stated that "Jammu and Kashmir, a constituent unit of the Union of India, shall continue to be governed under Article 370." In reality, between 1954 and the mid-1970s, 28 constitutional orders "integrating" IJK with India had been issued from Delhi, and 262 Union laws had been made applicable in IJK. The Delhi accord gave IJK's government the right to "review" only those laws from the shared center-state "concurrent list" of powers which had been extended to IJK after 1953, and to "decide" which of them might "need amendment or repeal." A committee was set up to examine the matter, but its recommendations were never made public. This aside, the Delhi accord patronizingly confirmed IJK's right to legislate on "welfare measures, cultural matters, social security, and [Muslim] personal law."[48]

This was not a settlement Abdullah would have accepted—or even considered—twenty, ten, or even five years earlier. His politics and popularity since 1953 had been based on defiance of New Delhi's authoritarianism. In 1995 I interviewed Abdul Qayyum Zargar, an NC veteran who had been Afzal Beg's personal secretary in 1975, in his hometown of Doda, a town in the Jammu region populated mainly by Kashmiri-speaking Muslims. Recalling the 1975 accord, Zargar said that its terms were deeply unpopular among NC-PF's activists and mass following, and swallowed as a bitter pill only because Abdullah had accepted the accord. Possibly Abdullah was worn down by age—he turned seventy in 1975—and two decades of incarceration. He probably also calculated that after Pakistan's defeat and dismemberment in the December 1971 Bangladesh war, the regional balance of power had swung decisively in India's favor, leaving him with little alternative to accepting terms dictated by New Delhi. Not everyone agreed or acquiesced—a young Valley-based activist, Shabbir Ahmad Shah, formed an organization called the People's League in the mid-1970s to keep the quest for self-determination alive, and paid for it by spending most of the next twenty years in Indian jails. Nonetheless, in an amusing contrast to 1965, Mir Qasim stepped aside as chief minister to make way for Abdullah, who was then elected leader of the house by the Congress group that was overwhelmingly dominant in the IJK legislature constituted in 1972.

The Delhi-determined circumstances of an emasculated Abdullah's return to office amounted to a clever evasion of the Kashmir conflict rather than a substantive solution to it. However, his return, and the revival of the Plebiscite Front as the National Conference under his leadership, helped foster a semblance of competitive politics in IJK for the first time since 1947. In 1977 Congress withdrew its support for Abdullah and elections were held to constitute a new Legislative Assembly. Abdullah's NC captured a clear majority—47 of 76 seats—in the legislature. Significantly, it swept the Kashmir Valley, winning 40 of 42 seats from the region (Congress was wiped out in the Valley, where the other two seats went to the Janata Party, an anti-Congress coalition which had ousted Indira Gandhi's party from power at the center earlier in 1977). The Congress and the Janata Party won 11 seats each in the Jammu region, where the NC came in a respectable third with 7 seats. Thanks to the participation of the pro-Abdullah bloc—clearly the most popular force in IJK's politics, with overwhelming dominance in the Valley—the 1977 election was a great improvement on the farcical elections between 1951 and 1972. The relative opening up of political space and election of a reasonably representative government contributed to a degree of stability.

But by the late 1970s the Lion of Kashmir was in the twilight of his life, and fundamentally he was a defeated man. He died in 1982, a year after he anointed his elder son, Farooq Abdullah, a political novice, as his successor—in keeping with the subcontinent's destructive tradition of combining democratic and dynastic politics.[49] Farooq took over as chief minister, and in mid-1983 led the NC into another Assembly election. This election was fiercely contested with Indira Gandhi's Congress, which had returned to power in Delhi in 1980 after the Janata coalition elected to govern the country in 1977 disintegrated into feuding factions. By mid-1983 India's next parliamentary elections, due by late 1984, were on the horizon and Indira Gandhi was rehearsing a strategy of majoritarian mobilization—based on thinly veiled appeals to India's Hindu majority to unite for the country's "national unity and integrity" against alleged secessionist threats from Muslim and Sikh minorities—to ensure her return to power.[50] Gandhi decided to use the IJK elections as a laboratory for her strategy, and evoked a significant response among Hindus in the Jammu region, where Congress won 23 of 32 seats at stake. But Congress won only 2 seats in the Valley, where NC again triumphed, winning 38 of 42 seats. NC also picked up 8 seats from the Jammu region and 1 in Ladakh, returning, as in 1977, a total of 47 members to the 76-seat legislature. Congress emerged as a large opposition with 26 legislators (23 from Jammu, 2 from Kashmir Valley, and 1 from Ladakh).

But Indira Gandhi, an instinctive autocrat, would not accept the verdict gracefully, and IJK's Congress would not play the role of a constructive opposition. Gandhi was especially angry because Farooq Abdullah had, shortly before the Assembly elections, aligned the NC with Indian opposition parties trying to re-create a united anti-Congress front on India's national political scene in preparation for parliamentary elections in late 1984. From the viewpoint of integrating IJK's political life with the Indian Union, Farooq's developing relationship with opposition parties in India was unequivocally a welcome development, because "the emergence of Farooq as more than a regional [IJK] figure, even if anti-Congress, automatically implied deeper political integration of Kashmir with the Union."[51] But in building this relationship Farooq was breaking a tacit understanding in the 1975 Delhi accord that had enabled his father's release and return to office, whereby the NC would support Congress rule at the center in exchange for Congress governments' toleration of NC's primacy in IJK.

In all-India parliamentary elections in 1977 and 1980, NC and Congress had contested as de facto allies in IJK, sharing out its 6 seats in Parliament between themselves. In June 1984, as Farooq's government approached the end of its first year in office, a sordid scheme, apparently engineered by the Congress government in New Delhi, saw twelve of NC's forty-seven legislators quit their party, form a new group, and form a new government with the support of the sizeable Congress caucus in the Assembly. The leader of the defectors was G. M. Shah, Sheikh Abdullah's son-in-law and a one-time general secretary of the PF, who had nursed ambitions that he, rather than the political amateur Farooq, would inherit the sheikh's mantle. All twelve turncoats, mainly NC back-benchers, were rewarded with ministerships in the new government.

According to Farooq Abdullah, the entire plan was "hatched in 1 Safdarjang Road, New Delhi" (then the prime minister's official residence), and "directed by Mrs Gandhi."[52] Its chief executor in Srinagar was a man called Jagmohan, IJK's New Delhi–appointed governor, who had assumed the post three months earlier after the previous governor apparently refused to collude in conspiracies. It was a tragic replay of the 1953 putsch, with Farooq, G. M. Shah, Jagmohan, and Indira Gandhi playing the roles of Sheikh Abdullah, Bakshi Ghulam Mohammed, Karan Singh, and Jawaharlal Nehru. Jagmohan dismissed Farooq, denied him an opportunity to try to prove his majority on the floor of the house, and rejected his appeal for fresh elections. As in 1953, protests erupted in Srinagar and throughout the Valley. These were suppressed with the aid of detachments of the Central Reserve Police Force (CRPF), paramilitary police under the Union interior ministry's control, which were flown to Srinagar from Delhi the night before the coup.

The tentative opening to political pluralism and representative government in IJK that had begun in 1977 was closed off in 1984 and never restored. G. M. Shah's main distinction in office was to earn the sobriquet "curfew chief minister"—for seventy-two of the first ninety days of his administration the Valley was under curfew orders to prevent protest demonstrations. His reign, which lasted until March 1986, brought political vacuum and institutional paralysis. The public mood was sullen. In December 1984 India's parliamentary election was held. Congress, led by Indira Gandhi's fresh-faced son Rajiv, won a massive victory throughout the country, riding on a "sympathy wave" after Indira Gandhi was assassinated by two Sikh members of her own bodyguard on 31 October 1984. But all three Lok Sabha constituencies in the Kashmir Valley returned NC candidates with huge majorities. Congreoo won the two seats from the Jammu region and one from Ladakh, but overall the deposed NC polled 46 percent of the IJK-wide vote, as opposed to only 30 percent for Congress.[53] In March 1986 violence against minority Pandits broke out in one area in the southern part of the Valley, around a town called Bijbehara, the home of Mufti Mohammad Sayeed, IJK's top Congress leader. G. M. Shah's lame-duck government was then dismissed by the center's Congress government on the basis of Article 356 (citing a breakdown of law and order), and Governor Jagmohan became the effective ruler of IJK. The political and institutional void was complete.

In late 1986 Farooq Abdullah concluded a *rapprochement* with the Congress regime at the center. Under its terms, he was re-installed as chief minister pending fresh Assembly elections in March 1987, which he undertook to contest in alliance with the Congress party (under the arrangement, NC contested 45 of 76 seats, mainly in the Valley, and Congress the other 31, mainly in the Jammu region). Farooq said that he had "come to accept" a hard political reality: "If I want to implement programmes to fight poverty, and run a government, I will have to stay on the right side of the center."[54] Farooq had decided to accept that IJK's right to a modicum of representative government (and economic development) was conditional on the whims and agenda of all-powerful New Delhi authorities, but the NC's mass following did not agree. In fact, they had had enough. A decade earlier, in 1975, they had only reluctantly accepted the imposition of the Delhi accord, and only because their supreme leader, the legendary Sheikh Abdullah, had signed on to it. His son did not have the stature and clout to achieve a repetition of 1975. To the contrary, Farooq's decision, seen as cowardly capitulation, evoked hostility and contempt. A new generation of young men, born in the 1960s, took the lead in the election campaign of the Muslim United Front (MUF) coalition, formed as an independent, pro-people organization to fight NC's opportunistic alliance with the detested Congress at the polls.

What happened in the elections of March 1987 was recounted at the beginning of this chapter. The process and its outcome irrevocably tainted Farooq Abdullah and his supporters in the eyes of their former voters as just another clique, serving as tools of the Indian state in return for the spoils of political office. This was the moment when the Valley and some of its contiguous areas lost all residual confidence in India's political system. Media and officials in India rejoiced in the victory of "forces of democracy and secularism" and vilified the MUF as Pakistan-inspired "fundamentalists arguing for a theocratic state."[55] Qazi Nissar, a prominent religious preacher in the Valley and a top MUF leader, had this to say in the aftermath of the election: "I believe in the Indian Constitution. How long can people like us keep getting votes by exploiting Islam? We wanted to prove we can do something concrete. But this kind of thing makes people lose all faith in India." (Nissar was assassinated in his Anantnag home by pro-Pakistan militants in June 1994.) Abdul Ghani Lone, another MUF leader who saw his resounding victory in Handwara turn to dust amid large-scale arrests of his supporters, queried in despair: "If people are not allowed to vote, where will their venom go but into expressions of anti-national sentiment?" (Lone, who started his political career in the Congress party in the 1960s and 1970s, was assassinated in Srinagar, also by suspected pro-Pakistan militants, in May 2002.) A shocked Srinagar lawyer who had voted for the MUF had only this to say: "I don't even pray regularly. But if you take my vote away, I lose all faith in Indian democracy."[56] The sense of disenfranchisement was absolute, but what happened in 1987 was also absolutely consistent with IJK's fate since 1947 in democratic India.

Farooq Abdullah's second term in office—until January 1990, when his government was dismissed (he says he resigned first) and IJK brought under Delhi's direct rule after the eruption of an anti-India uprising—was a disaster. His behavior during his curtailed first term, in 1983–1984, has been described as that of "a little boy with a toy" (he was given to joyriding motorcycles around Srinagar); and during the second as "a virtual abdication of governance."[57] He acquired the sobriquet "disco chief minister" because he was frequently sighted in discotheques in Indian cities, and he spent much of the rest of his time playing golf or vacationing abroad. His colleagues in government earned a reputation for corrupt practice remarkable even by IJK standards.

Meanwhile, the situation beyond the portals of officialdom turned steadily grim. In 1988 a new phenomenon emerged in IJK: increasing numbers of young men went mysteriously "missing" from their homes in towns and villages across the Kashmir Valley. They had gone "across" (the LOC), in search of weapons and combat training. In June 1988 public demonstrations in Srinagar against a steep hike in electricity rates were suppressed by police, who opened fire and killed several unarmed protesters. Then, on 31 July, bombs exploded outside Srinagar's central telegraph office and at the Srinagar Club, a gathering place for the political establishment. The attacks were carried out by Srinagar youth freshly returned from across the LOC, but were planned by Mohammad Rauf Kashmiri, a JKLF militant from Pakistani Poonch who had infiltrated into IJK.[58] In September 1988 the JKLF had its first *shaheed* (martyr): Aijaz Dar, a young Srinagar man, was shot dead during a botched attempt to assassinate a senior police officer. Strikes and "black days" were observed throughout the Valley on 15 August 1988 (India's independence day in 1947), 26 January 1989 (India's republic day in 1950), and 11 February 1989 (the day in 1984 the JKLF co-founder Mohammad Maqbool Butt was hanged by Indira Gandhi's regime for killing a policeman during a bank robbery in 1976), and in April 1989, when the elderly father of the self-determination activist Shabbir Shah died in police custody. The rhetoric of IJK's "democratic and secular" chief minister turned increasingly bellicose. Sheikh Abdullah's son declared that his regime had "the backing of the Indian government" and that he was prepared to raze particularly rebellious districts of his capital, break strikes by forcing shops to open, and break the legs of protesters before burying them alive.[59]

In August 1989 Mohammad Yusuf Halwai, a senior NC official who had been prominent in rigging the elections in March 1987 and in the subsequent repression, was shot dead by masked men in broad daylight in the heart of a congested Srinagar neighborhood. The assassination sent a wave of fear through the local hierarchy. In November, in another ominous signal, a retired Pandit judge who had sentenced Maqbool Butt to death a decade earlier was killed in the northern Valley town of Sopore. In the last few months of 1989, in a typical pre-insurrectionary pattern, a spate of targeted killings occurred in the Valley, directed especially against known or suspected agents and informers of the extensive Indian intelligence-gathering apparatus. In late November 1989 another Indian parliamentary election was held in IJK, with the underground JKLF and other pro-self-determination groups like Shabbir Shah's Pakistan-oriented People's League calling on voters to boycott the polls. The NC won "unopposed" in Srinagar, while in the other two Valley constituencies, Baramulla and Anantnag, its candidates were elected with 94 and 98 percent, respectively, of votes cast. The turnout of voters in the Valley was only 4 percent, according to official sources, and even this was apparently achieved by security forces stuffing ballot boxes at pre-selected sites (turnout was also low, 38 percent, in Udhampur, one of the Jammu region's two parliamentary districts, which has a substantial Kashmiri-speaking Muslim electorate). At no time since 1947, not even at the height of the Plebiscite Front's popularity in the 1960s, had the estrangement of a large proportion of IJK's population from India been so apparent. The Kashmir conflict was about to enter a new phase.

In *The Federalist Papers* (no. 10), James Madison wrote: "Liberty is to faction what air is to fire, an aliment without which it instantly expires. But it could not be less folly to abolish liberty, which is essential to political life, because it nourishes faction, than it would be to wish the annihilation of air, which is essential to animal life, because it imparts to fire its destructive agency." According to contemporary democratic theory: "What distinguishes democratic rulers from non-democratic ones are the norms that condition how the former came to power and the practices that hold them accountable for their actions. Democracy may give rise to a considerable variety of institutions and subtypes. For democracy to thrive, however, specific procedural norms must be followed and civic rights respected. Any polity that fails to follow the rule of law with regard to its own procedures should not be considered democratic. These procedures alone do not define democracy, but their presence is indispensable to its persistence."[60]

The political history of IJK clearly does not fulfill even the procedural minima of democratic governance. With the partial exception of 1947–1953 and 1977–1984, New Delhi elites have ruled the territory through a combination of direct control and intrusive intervention, and through sponsorship of intermediary IJK governments unrepresentative of and hence unaccountable to the population. This policy appears to have been motivated by fear of

Pakistani designs, and by suspicion and mistrust of the loyalties and preferences of most of IJK's population. The strategy has had the effect of severely retarding democratic institutional development and rights of franchise, participation, and representation in IJK. This, aggravated by systematic elimination of IJK's autonomous regime—coercive "integration" effected via compliance of client IJK governments—has in time turned Indian elites' fear of separatism into a tragically self-fulfilling prophecy.

Two points that emerge from my argument need emphasis. First, the intolerance, indeed criminalization, of political opposition in IJK has been especially destructive to the relationship between Kashmir and India. It is indisputable that "a functioning political opposition is essential to any democracy . . . Democratic systems rely on institutionalized oppositions, and it is doubtful any regime can long survive as minimally democratic without them." This is because peaceful turnover of power following elections is a *"sine qua non* of democratic politics," which in turn requires "both the permissive freedoms of speech and association, and the presence of institutions and practices that make it possible for counter-elites to organize, so as to be able to contest for power." The existence of "outlets for dissent within the regime's institutions" is thus critical to the stability of a democratic polity, for otherwise frustrated dissent may become radicalized and assume an anti-systemic form.[61]

The political scientist Juan Linz has advanced a threefold typology of political oppositions to regimes: loyal, semi-loyal, and disloyal.[62] Given the international dispute concerning rightful sovereignty over J&K, and the existence of a powerful urge to self-rule (plus pro-Pakistan factions) within IJK, perhaps the best India could have hoped for in IJK would have been oppositions "semi-loyal" to India's polity. For example, the MUF of 1987 included

pro independence and pro-Pakistan groups but was committed
to participation in Indian-sponsored institutions and political processes. Similarly, IJK's Jama'at-i-Islami, which is ideologically pro-
Pakistan, nonetheless contested Legislative Assembly elections in
1972, 1977, and 1983, as well as under the MUF umbrella in 1987.
But the cynical authoritarianism of Indian policy fostered progressive radicalization and emergence of "disloyal" opposition that rejected the entire political framework as hopelessly corrupt, denounced Indian authority over IJK as illegitimate, and launched
a campaign to overthrow it. That was how the Jama'at-i-Islami
political worker and would-be legislator Yusuf Shah metamorphosed into the Hizb-ul Mujahideen commander Syed Salahuddin
and the MUF campaign volunteer Yasin Malik was transformed
into a leader of JKLF's armed struggle for independence. But they
should not have been entirely surprised by their experience. The
hiatus between the Indian state's democratic, federal principles
and its authoritarian, centralist practices in IJK has been evident
since the inception of the Kashmir question.

That brings me to the second point I wish to clarify. Why did
uprising and insurrection erupt only in, and remain confined to,
the Indian side of the Line of Control in Kashmir? After all, the
political history of Pakistan's "Azad" Jammu and Kashmir is not
exactly a celebration of freedom and democratic rights either. The
senior pro-independence leader in AJK, Amanullah Khan, has conceded that "the area has prospered in the last twenty years . . . due
to the fact that over a million [AJK] people are working in the
Middle East, Europe and the USA." However, he has pointed out
that although "the people of AJK have regular elections, have their
own elected president, prime minister, supreme court, high court,
election commission, legislative assembly and public service commission," there are continuing restrictions on political rights and

participation. Specifically: "You have to declare in writing that you favor accession to Pakistan. If you don't you are not allowed to contest elections. In 2001, JKLF fielded its candidates for 31 of 36 seats in the "Azad" Kashmir assembly but all its nominations were rejected because its candidates stood for complete independence. About 300 JKLF activists were arrested and released only after the elections." Indeed, AJK's constitution stipulates that "no person or political party in Azad Jammu and Kashmir shall be permitted to propagate against, or take part in activities prejudicial or detrimental to, the ideology of the State's [J&K's] accession to Pakistan." Moreover, the institutional development Khan refers to is relatively recent—"from 1948 until the early 1970s, Pakistan's Ministry of Kashmir Affairs probably had the best claim to being head of the Azad Kashmir government."[63]

Several explanations are possible for why discontent translated into uprising and insurrection only in Indian Kashmir, not in Pakistani Kashmir. They include the smaller size and population of AJK, the relative historic strength of pro-Pakistan allegiances among AJK's population, and the possibility that Muslims would be reluctant to take up arms against a Muslim state (but recall Bangladesh's revolt against west Pakistan's oppressive military regime in 1971). In my view, however, the bitter radicalization of opposition to India among a large proportion of IJK's population is better explained by a different factor. Pakistan has been for most of its history, and remains, a military-bureaucratic state which has oscillated between "ruler" and "moderator" versions of praetorianism, and proven unable to stabilize basic democratic institutions and procedures.[64] India, by comparison, is a moderately successful democracy which has built and sustained such institutions and procedures, despite the challenges posed by poverty and enormous social diversity. The people of IJK had high expectations of such a system. It was thus particularly galling for them to be denied the civil liberties, democratic rights of participation and representation, and federal autonomy that by and large were respected, with imperfections, in the Indian Union. In other words, Indian policy reduced IJK to an anomalous enclave of authoritarian politics and repressive central control within an institutional framework based on robust multi-party politics and federalism. IJK's Hindus, Sikhs, and Buddhists may have been unhappy with this situation, but they would not take up armed struggle (with Pakistani support) because their ultimate allegiance, and identity, lies firmly with India. But for most of the Muslim population—especially in the long-suffering Valley—India's democracy had been exposed as a cruel hoax by the end of 1989. Their rage spilled over in early 1990.

3

THE WAR IN KASHMIR

If I did not write, my heart would explode like a bomb.

—SHAKEEL SHAN,
poet from the Kashmir Valley

ASHFAQ MAJID WANI and Nadeem Khatib grew up as best friends in Srinagar during the 1970s and early 1980s. Both boys were born in 1967 into prosperous, professionally successful upper-middle-class families and attended the city's best grammar school. Both were bright students and fine athletes. Ashfaq's ambition was to be a doctor, while Nadeem aimed to become an airline pilot.

During his teens, Ashfaq began to develop political convictions. In early 1987 he volunteered, like thousands of youngsters across the Valley, in the Muslim United Front's election campaign. On 23 March 1987 he was one of the hundreds, if not thousands, of opposition activists arrested in police crackdowns across Indian-controlled Jammu and Kashmir (IJK) to prevent organized protests as Farooq Abdullah's National Conference (NC) returned to power in Srinagar with Congress and New Delhi's support. He was released nine months later. He had been kept in solitary confinement for part of that time, charged with a minor offense allegedly committed on 4 April, on which date he had been in police custody. When released he had cigarette burns all over his body, sustained during interrogation.

Ashfaq left home and "disappeared" shortly after being released. He never came home again. But during 1989 he emerged as a household name across his homeland as one of the HAJY group—so-known after the first names of its four members, Hamid Sheikh, Ashfaq Wani, Javed Mir, and Yasin Malik—the nucleus of young Jammu & Kashmir Liberation Front (JKLF) militants freshly returned to Srinagar with weapons and training from across the Line of Control (LOC). By early 1990, as government authority collapsed in the Kashmir Valley and insurrection took hold, Ashfaq Wani was one of the most wanted men for India's beleaguered security forces. On 30 March 1990 they finally tracked him down in one of the many congested residential neighborhoods that make up the old city of Srinagar. In the first major blow suffered by the JKLF in the war for *azaadi* (freedom), Ashfaq Majid Wani was killed, at the age of twenty-three, in a fierce exchange of fire.

"I disagreed with my son and turned him out of the house," Ashfaq's father told an Indian newspaper a month later. "But he found a much larger family."[1] In early April 1990 the largest gathering ever seen in Kashmir, easily surpassing even Sheikh Abdullah's funeral in 1982, took place in Srinagar. It was for Ashfaq's funeral, attended by some five hundred thousand mourners who defied Indian curfew orders. Ashfaq's is still an honored name in Kashmir. He is buried in Srinagar's central "martyrs' cemetery," situated in the old city's Eidgah district, alongside two thousand other *shaheed* (martyrs) who have fallen as *mujahideen* (holy warriors) in the struggle for *azaadi*. Ashfaq's grave is flanked by those of two other JKLF pioneers—Hamid Sheikh, who was gunned down in Srinagar by the Indian army in November 1992, and Maqbool Butt, who was hanged in Delhi's Tihar Jail in February 1984 for killing a policeman during a bank robbery in 1976. Butt was one of very few Valley youths of the previous generation who embraced the gun—he went across the LOC in the mid-1960s from his village in IJK's Kupwara district, close to the LOC, and joined the JKLF, then newly established in Pakistani-controlled "Azad" Jammu and Kashmir (AJK). Butt's grave in the Eidgah cemetery is actually empty, since Indian authorities, fearing unrest, did not return his body to his homeland. The green Urdu inscription on his tombstone says that the people of Kashmir are in *intezaar* (eternal waiting) for his return.

Ashfaq Wani's fighting death inspired thousands of other young Kashmiri men to take up arms to continue the struggle. But his friend Nadeem Khatib was not among them. "He never even talked of joining the militants," says his father, Inayatullah Khatib. Instead, Nadeem pursued his career goal of becoming a pilot. He left Srinagar to first join a flying school near Delhi in March 1992, then went to the United States and obtained his commercial pilot's license after training at a flying school in the southern state of Georgia. In January 1994 he joined the same school as an instructor. He returned to battle-scarred Srinagar in November 1994 and stayed for almost two years. He even got engaged to a cousin, although his parents discerned that he was not keen on marriage. In October 1996 he left, telling his parents he was going back to the United States to find employment as a pilot with an

American airline. During the next two years his parents received regular telephone calls from their son—from the United States, they assumed.

Nadeem Khatib died in 1999, at the age of thirty-two, during a fierce "encounter" (firefight) between his guerrilla unit and Indian forces in a remote mountainous area of IJK's Jammu region. Apparently, he had soon left the United States for Pakistan. A close friend says: "He used to brood a lot on America's exploitation of Muslim countries. He would say that after being in the US for years, his eyes had opened." He had then traveled to AJK and enrolled as a member of Al-Badr, an Islamist group waging insurgency in IJK. After combat training, this son of Srinagar's social elite infiltrated across the LOC to fight as an ordinary foot soldier in the *jehad* against Indian forces in his homeland. After his death, two undated letters he had written during his time as a guerrilla fighter reached his parents and brother. "I am going at the call of Allah and doing what Allah has made our *farz* [duty]," Nadeem had written. "I am aware this might hurt, but duty to Allah comes first . . . Dearest Mom and Dad, it is because of the way you raised me that my *Iman* [faith] is so strong . . . It is important to remember that life on this earth is nothing more than a test and sowing ground, and that the life to come is the eternal life." In retrospect, his family reflected that during Nadeem's time in Srinagar in the mid-1990s, as a weakened but still potent war for *azaadi* raged around them, exacting a daily toll of lives and suffering, they had sensed "something brewing inside him . . . perhaps some sort of dilemma. He finally sought his answer in faith. And when he did, he left everything." Nadeem's parents are as proud as Ashfaq's of the choice their son eventually made. "I have no regrets," says his mother, Mahjabeen. "I have absolute faith my son died a martyr's

death and is therefore alive. Whenever I am alone, I feel his presence. When I stand up on the prayer mat, I feel him next to me.
He was always his mother's boy."[2]

The deaths of Ashfaq Wani and Nadeem Khatib, a decade apart,
provide key insights into the evolution of the struggle for *azaadi*
in Kashmir. Ashfaq died as a soldier of the JKLF, which launched
the armed campaign and dominated the *azaadi* movement for
its first three years, 1990–1992. The JKLF found spiritual inspiration in the Kashmir Valley's specific Islamic traditions, rooted in
the mystical piety of its Sufi saints. Its revolt was essentially the
expression of a repressed regional patriotism. Its declared ideology was (and is) an independent Jammu and Kashmir separate
from both India and Pakistan, encompassing the 1947 princely
state's borders, and it insists that its outlook towards non-Muslims
is nonsectarian. But the JKLF's armed struggle withered a decade
ago. The group Khatib joined, Al-Badr, is one of several Islamist
insurgent groups, organizationally centered in Pakistan, which
have kept the fight going in IJK since the mid-1990s alongside
the only surviving guerrilla organization composed primarily of
locals, the pro-Pakistan Hizb-ul Mujahideen (HM). The groups
dominated by non-locals, who are frequently alumni of fundamentalist *madrasas* (religious seminaries) in Pakistan, are led by
Pakistani religious zealots such as Hafiz Muhammad Sayeed of
Lashkar-e-Taiba (LeT) and Maulana Masood Azhar of Jaish-e-
Mohammad (JeM), and their motivation is of a radical Islamic
character. Ashfaq Wani died in 1990, during the heady euphoria of
the first months of the uprising, and in Srinagar, unquestionably
then the epicenter of the revolt. By the time Khatib joined the insurgency in the late 1990s, Srinagar, although far from normal,

had ceased to be a city dominated by huge pro-*azaadi* processions and hundreds if not thousands of "boys" openly flaunting weapons on the streets. The locus of insurgency had moved out to rural, often remote forested areas of the Valley, and had spread to new theaters, principally Muslim-dominated mountainous tracts of the Jammu region such as the twin districts of Rajouri and Poonch on the LOC. It was in one such zone—a remote mountainous area called Mahore in Jammu's Udhampur district—that Nadeem Khatib fell while playing his part in a protracted war of attrition with the Indian state. Unlike Wani's, his was a largely unsung death. By 1999 hundreds of martyrs' graveyards dotted towns and villages across the Valley and some parts of the Jammu region, and Khatib's is just another among thousands of *shaheed* tombstones.

The Intifada Phase (1990–1995)

In keeping with the history of most protracted struggles between state power and popular insurrection, the *azaadi* movement has had a tortuous trajectory and traversed several distinct phases. In this account of the war in Kashmir, I distinguish three such phases: the *intifada* or uprising phase, which lasted from 1990 until 1995; a period of demoralization and atrophy (1996–1998); and the *fidayeen* phase (1999–2002), marked by the renewal of insurgency with a radical Islamist ideological color and the ascendancy of Pakistan-based militant groups using *fidayeen* (suicide-squad) tactics against Indian forces.

In January 1990 the simmering rebellion of 1988–1989 (described in Chapter 2) came to a boil in mass resistance to Indian rule in the Kashmir Valley. The JKLF's campaign of selective assassinations of alleged Indian spies and political "collaborators" in the Valley escalated sharply in the final months of 1989, starting with the shooting of a prominent NC functionary, a Muslim, on a Srinagar street in August 1989. Over the next six months more than one hundred such killings occurred, effectively paralyzing the government's administrative machinery and severely damaging its surveillance and intelligence apparatus. Approximately three-fourths of the victims—a mix of officials of the local political hierarchy, alleged spies and intelligence agents, and prominent citizens accused of pro-India leanings—were Muslims, and the rest were Pandits, members of the Valley's small but high-profile Hindu minority.[3] By December 1989 a total boycott of India's late-November parliamentary elections had taken place in the Valley, and the decisive moment had arrived. In early December, the daughter of the Kashmiri Muslim interior affairs minister in India's federal cabinet, a medical student in Srinagar, was kidnapped by JKLF activists. Her captors demanded the release of six top JKLF activists then in jail. When the militants were freed, they were greeted by thousands of Srinagar residents amid scenes of jubilant celebration (the JKLF released the young woman, unharmed). In January 1990 the incapacitated IJK government of Farooq Abdullah was dismissed by the federal government, citing Article 356 of the Indian constitution—a breakdown of civil order—and IJK was brought under New Delhi's direct rule. Jagmohan, who as New Delhi–appointed IJK governor had played a murky if not nefarious role in IJK between 1984 and 1986 (see Chapter 2), was sent back to Srinagar—this time by an anti-Congress coalition government which had ousted Rajiv Gandhi's Congress from power in New Delhi—to confront an explosive situation.

In the second half of January, massive demonstrations calling for Kashmir's *azaadi* from India erupted in Srinagar and other towns in the Valley. Even the JKLF's still relatively few underground militants were initially stunned by the spectacular scale and emotional intensity of the protests. Hundreds of thousands marched in the streets of Srinagar; even in smaller towns like Sopore, Baramulla, and Anantnag tens of thousands participated. Squads of stone-throwing youths confronted heavily armed personnel of the federal government's Central Reserve Police Force (CRPF) and Border Security Force (BSF) in every Srinagar neighborhood, prompting comparisons to the first Palestinian *intifada,* which began in the Israeli-occupied West Bank and Gaza in December 1987. The local Jammu and Kashmir police seemed to have disappeared from the Valley practically overnight. The CRPF and BSF units—known as "paramilitary forces" because their structure, organization, weaponry, and role place them in the gray area between ordinary police and the professional military—consisted almost entirely of non-Muslim Indians from outside IJK. By 1990 some of their personnel had acquired combat experience against long-running guerrilla insurgencies in India's volatile northeastern borderlands (adjoining Myanmar, Bangladesh, Bhutan, and China) as well as in Punjab province, the site of a secessionist revolt by some Sikhs in the 1980s and early 1990s. But the challenge they encountered in the Valley—an entire society in the throes of uprising—simultaneously unnerved and enraged them.

During just three days of mass protests, 21–23 January 1990, some three hundred excited but unarmed demonstrators were shot dead in Srinagar by these paramilitary troopers. A Srinagar resident, Farooq Wani, employed as an engineer in a department of the IJK government, narrated his experience of one such demonstration, which took place on 21 January 1990:

> I fell down on the road [after being hit by gunfire]. I saw
> small boys being shot. I remained lying. Then I saw a

paramilitary officer coming. I saw him pumping bullets into the bodies of injured people lying on the road. A young boy trying to hide under the bridge [over the Jhelum River] was killed . . . As I lifted my head, a CRPF man shouted: "He's still alive!" I pleaded: "I'm a government employee, please don't shoot." The officer shouted abuses at me and said *Islam mangta hai?* [you want Islam?], and fired at me. My back and hands were hit. Another paramilitary moved up to me and shouted—*tum sala zinda hai, mara nahin hai?* [you bastard, you haven't died yet?] He left after kicking my back . . . Then a truck was brought, and all of us, dead and injured, were piled into it—they loaded about 30–35 dead bodies. As there was no space for more, the officer ordered the driver: *Baaki ko naale mein phenk do* [throw the rest into the stream]. A tarpaulin was thrown over us. After driving for some time we stopped, and I heard voices speaking Kashmiri. One of the injured among us cried out. The tarpaulin was lifted and we saw a local policeman, who said: "My God, there are living bodies here." Three other people were still alive.

Wani survived with six bullet wounds to various parts of his body. He later heard that the policeman who saved his life had suffered a heart attack.[4]

Mirajuddin Munshi, a well-known Srinagar physician, had been an intellectual mentor to the JKLF's youthful leaders from 1988 on. I first met him in the United States in 1994, after he left Kashmir fearing assassination by pro-Pakistan radicals, following a rash of murders of pro-independence members of the Valley intelligentsia during 1992–1993. In our conversation, Dr. Munshi recalled

the horror he had felt as an eyewitness to the indiscriminate killing of hundreds of unarmed Srinagar protesters in the first weeks
of the uprising. Dr. Munshi had no illusions about the nature of
India's relationship with Kashmir—he would otherwise not have
become a JKLF ideologue—but the brutality of the Indian state
still came as a profound, bitter shock. In 1990 it reinforced his belief that the time had come to part ways with India.

International events played a significant role in steeling insur-
rectionist resolve in late 1989 and early 1990. The first Palestinian *intifada* against Israeli occupation was an important reference
point, as was the collapse of repressive one-party regimes in central and eastern Europe after mass demonstrations in the autumn
of 1989. In the words of a Srinagar academic, "We felt that if the
Berlin wall could be dismantled, so could the Line of Control."[5]
The young Kashmiri guerrillas, for their part, were inspired by the
1989 Soviet withdrawal from Afghanistan in the face of Afghan
mujahideen resistance, and by the success of Tamil Tiger guerrillas
in Sri Lanka in stalemating a vastly superior Indian military force
sent to suppress them between 1987 and 1990.

In retrospect, it is clear that these were dangerously naïve analo-
gies. Soviet forces would withdraw from Afghanistan, as Indian
forces would from Sri Lanka, once it became clear that these foreign expeditions were fundamentally misguided and increasingly
costly in terms of resources and combat casualties. The Indian
state would not contemplate any such course in Kashmir, the cornerstone of its identity as an inclusive, secular state and the focal
point of its bitter enmity with Pakistan. The Indian state's response to the uprising was instead to institute a policy of ruthless
mailed-fist repression, a policy supported by virtually the entire
spectrum of Indian political opinion. On 24 January 1990 JKLF
gunmen responded to the Srinagar massacres by killing four un-

armed Indian air force officers on the outskirts of the city. Thereafter, the Valley was caught up in an escalating spiral of violence and reprisal.

As shown in Chapter 2, state-sponsored violations of civil liberties and fundamental democratic rights of citizens had been normal, indeed institutionalized practice in Indian Jammu and Kashmir for four decades prior to 1990. But what unfolded in IJK from 1990 on was of a different order and magnitude—a massive human rights crisis. From the perspective of Indian counterinsurgency strategy, a "surgical" response was not feasible given the manifestly popular nature of the uprising. Indeed, an Indian journalist reported in April 1990 that the *azaadi* movement had united "workers, engineers, schoolteachers, shopkeepers, doctors, lawyers, even former MLAs [members of the IJK legislative assembly] and Jammu and Kashmir police."[6] The nonsurgical response rapidly turned the relationship between the Indian state and the Valley's population into an occupier-occupied relationship, sealing a bitter divide. Between July and September 1990 the Valley was brought under the purview of martial law, as the Indian government enacted an Armed Forces Special Powers Act and a Disturbed Areas Act to back up existing IJK emergency regulations and its own draconian law, the Terrorism and Disruptive Activities (Prevention) Act.

But most Indian counterinsurgency operations in the Valley made no reference to *any* framework of law. The BSF, the CRPF, and other specialized paramilitary formations such as the Indo-Tibetan Border Police took over policing of the Valley's cities, including Srinagar, while in the countryside and border areas close to the LOC absolute power passed into the hands of the regular Indian army. In the eyes of the several hundred thousand soldiers and paramilitary troops flooding the Valley, the whole population was suspect not just disloyal to India but, much worse, in league with the enemy state across the LOC. A correspondent of an Indian newspaper reported from Srinagar in April 1990 that for the average Indian soldier fighting insurrection in the Valley, "the face of the Kashmiri has dissolved into a blurred, featureless mask. He has become a secessionist-terrorist-fundamentalist traitor." Even "affluence and influence are no longer safeguards," the correspondent wrote, against the policy of blanket repression.[7]

In August 1990 an article in an Indian magazine described a trade union activist in the Valley's northwestern Kupwara district, who had participated in numerous labor agitations in India. When he tried to tell those torturing him in a local army camp about his Indian friends, they retorted: *"Humme sab kuch pata hai. Tum sab pakistani ho"* (We know everything. You are all Pakistanis).[8] In the summer of 1995 I spoke with Afzal Hussain, a schoolteacher in the village of Drugmulla, just off the road running from the town of Baramulla to Uri, a town on the LOC in the northwestern part of the Valley. Hussain said he had been arrested by the army in a "general crackdown" in May 1990, in which all able-bodied men in the area were indiscriminately picked up. He said he had been tortured with electric shocks and red-hot iron rods in three different army camps in Baramulla district over the next forty days. "You know," he told me with a wry smile, "I did my master's degree in philosophy from an Indian university. As a realist and a secularist, I was quite comfortable with Kashmir being part of the Indian Union."

"Crackdowns" were—and indeed still are—the main instrument used by Indian forces in the war against insurgency. The term denotes operations in which large detachments of gun-toting troops arrive in convoys of jeeps and trucks, cordon off an urban neighborhood or a village, and require all men to come out of their homes and gather in an open space, such as a schoolyard. Masked *mukhbirs* (informers)—often suspects captured in earlier operations and softened up through interrogation—would then be set to work identifying "militants" (the term for guerrillas) and those civilians especially active in helping and harboring them. In the meantime, soldiers would conduct house-to-house searches looking for weapons, explosives, and hidden insurgents. Allegations of theft of money and valuables, vandalism, and molestation of women and girls during these intrusive searches rapidly became commonplace. In response to such accusations, the authorities sometimes also required women and girls to gather outside, in a group separate from the men. Some crackdowns would last a whole day or longer, even in harsh winter conditions.

Those identified as suspects would then be driven away to army or paramilitary camps, or to special "interrogation centers" which sprouted in Srinagar and across the Valley. Torture, often in gruesome forms, became routine and widespread. According to an American journalist who covered the Valley in 1990–1991, "in interviews officers of the security forces stated that the use of torture was absolutely vital to obtain information on weapons caches, hideouts and insurgent groups' memberships, and the whereabouts of the leaders." Numerous people returned from interrogation either physically crippled or mentally disturbed, or both; others never returned at all. In August 2002 a major IJK newspaper estimated that since 1990, 3,500 persons had disappeared after being taken into custody; in early 1999 Amnesty International estimated the figure at over 800.[9]

Srinagar and other towns were frequently placed under curfew orders, sometimes lasting weeks, to prevent the recurrence of mass demonstrations. Even so, huge *azaadi* rallies took place, for example in March 1990 when over three hundred thousand peo-

ple gathered in the town of Charar-e-Sharief, thirty kilometers
from Srinagar, at the shrine and mausoleum of the Valley's patron saint, the fourteenth-century Sufi mystic Sheikh Nooruddin
Noorani, and took a collective oath, in the presence of JKLF
leaders, to struggle for "self-determination." Another massacre of
about sixty pro-*azaadi* marchers took place in Srinagar in May
1990. Such incidents continued to occur as late as October 1993,
when thirty-seven participants in a pro-independence demonstration in Bijbehara, in the southern part of the Valley, were killed
by BSF personnel. Between 1990 and 1993 the central market
squares of one town after another—Srinagar, Sopore, Bijbehara,
and Handwara in the Valley, Doda in the Jammu region—were either gutted or severely damaged by security forces running amok
after guerrilla raids targeting their personnel. Numerous civilians
were killed during these rampages. In April 1993, for example,
Srinagar's famous Lal Chowk (Red Square, so-named in 1947 in
honor of the Moscow original by NC leftists) was partially gutted
by BSF soldiers. Sixteen civilians were killed during the incident.
In February 1991 members of an army unit are alleged to have
raped dozens of women in a mountain village, Kunan Poshpora,
in the Valley's Kupwara district. One woman, who was in late
pregnancy at the time, was also kicked in the stomach and subsequently gave birth to an infant with a fractured arm. A decade
later, in 2002, incidents of egregious sexual violence by Indian soldiers against Kashmiri women continued to be reported.[10]

When I toured the Valley and the Doda-Kishtwar district of
Jammu in 1995, the entire region resembled an armed garrison,
teeming with soldiers, and a vast prison camp for the population.
Roadblocks were ubiquitous in both towns and rural areas, and
verbal abuse as well as beatings of citizens was common at these
checkpoints. Srinagar had become a "bunker city," adorned with

hundreds if not thousands of bunkers manned by paramilitary soldiers crouching behind sandbags and wire netting (the latter as protection against grenade attacks), their guns peering out through firing slits. Soldiers fingering their triggers were stationed ten yards apart on all major roads, and groups of soldiers constantly patrolled neighborhoods on foot or in special patrol vehicles. The same regime was in place in other towns. Srinagar turned into a ghost city, its streets monopolized by heavily armed soldiers, as soon as dusk fell. On roads connecting the Valley's towns, military convoys traveled at all hours, the lead vehicle sporting a mounted machine gun. Even remote villages existed cheek-by-jowl with Indian military encampments.[11]

This regime of repression had the effects of further radicalizing public opinion and of convincing thousands of Kashmiri youths to take up arms to fight the Indian state. The years 1990–1993 were the boom period of armed struggle in the Valley, a time of immense turmoil and suffering but also of great enthusiasm and optimism about the mass movement. During my field research in IJK in the mid-1990s, I repeatedly heard how during 1990–1992 droves of young men, determined to avenge humiliations, abuse, and brutality endured at the hands of the Indian state, would leave their homes in cities and villages and either undertake the hazardous LOC crossing or seek training and arms in militant camps established in the Valley. In January 1990 Indian security officials were already speaking of "a defiant new breed of Kashmiri." In early May 1991, at the start of the summer infiltration season, seventy-two young men from the Valley were killed by Indian troops on the LOC on a single day while attempting to return from AJK to join the fight. Visiting the Valley in 1992, an Indian journalist found that "children no longer dream of becoming doctors or engineers; their ambition is to become *mujahids*," and that repression had succeeded in "eliminating militants in arithmetical progression and generating militants in geometrical progression." The Valley was rife with Indian troops, but they were unable to gain the upper hand over exponentially multiplying guerrillas fervently supported by almost the entire population.[12]

Two features of the *azaadi* movement during this ascendant phase merit emphasis. First, the insurgent groups fighting Indian forces consisted overwhelmingly of local Kashmiri recruits, in sharp contrast to 1947 and 1965, when principally non-IJK elements—Pakistani nationals and volunteers from AJK—had taken on the Indians. For example, of 844 guerrillas killed in fighting during 1991, only two were *not* residents of IJK, according to official figures of the Indian counterinsurgency command in Srinagar.[13] India's Kashmir problem had finally come home to roost. The "internal" conflict was now at least as critical as the international dimension. The independentist JKLF had been formed in Pakistani Kashmir in the mid-1960s, and for more than twenty years had had a negligible presence on the Indian side of the LOC, since the pro-independence political space was solidly occupied by the National Conference/Plebiscite Front of Sheikh Abdullah vintage. In the transformed political context of 1989–1990, however, a new, radicalized generation in the Kashmir Valley, flying the JKLF's banner of independent Kashmir, emerged as the vanguard of a mass uprising.

Second, the insurgency was initially very largely specific to the Valley—a geographically and culturally compact region with a powerful tradition of autonomist politics developed over fifty years, expressed first by the historic National Conference movement and then by the Plebiscite Front. In 1990 it was essentially the old NC-PF brand of politics that, radicalized under the leadership of a militant younger generation, rebelled against India. The impact of the uprising was at first minor in the Jammu region (and in thinly populated Ladakh, where it has remained so). In the early 1990s the guerrilla movement made its first inroads into Jammu in the Doda district, a huge, mountainous expanse covering the northeastern part of the Jammu region. The vast area and rugged, forbidding terrain, through which the Chenab river runs a meandering course, make it an ideal base for guerrilla fighters, and the district is contiguous to the southern Valley district of Anantnag. But demographic and political factors, rather than merely topography and geography, made Doda district into one of the toughest zones of the guerrilla war by 1992. The district's population is at least 57 percent Muslim (1981 census) and most of these are Kashmiri speakers, ethnolinguistically identical to the dominant Valley population, making Doda's Muslim society substantially a sociocultural and political extension of the Valley. Significantly, Indian-controlled Jammu's two other Muslim-majority districts, Rajouri and Poonch, whose Muslims belong predominantly to non-Kashmiri ethnolinguistic communities such as Gujjars and Rajputs, remained quiet in the *intifada* phase of the war, even though both districts adjoin the volatile LOC—their turn would come several years later, in the *fidayeen* phase.

Ethnolinguistic community with a religious base, rather than an overarching pan-Muslim identity, was clearly the decisive factor in the 1990–1995 phase of the *azaadi* movement. Doda's Kashmiri-speaking Muslim enclaves embraced the Valley's cry of self-determination with enthusiasm. In July 1992 the bustling market of Doda town (which is 80 percent Kashmiri Muslim) was razed by the CRPF in retaliation for a militant raid. As in the Valley, experience of repression drove the resistance. In the summer of 1995 I interviewed Maulana Farooq Hussain Kitchloo, the middle-aged *imam* (head preacher) of the mosque in Kishtwar, a picturesque mountain town (52 percent Kashmiri-speaking Muslim, 48 percent Hindu and Sikh) located in the most disturbed part of Doda district. He told me of a defining moment in the town's history: in March 1995, when his nephew Marouf Ahmed Hub, a twenty-two-year old shopkeeper, was arrested by the town's BSF commandant and tortured to death in custody. Twenty thousand people from the town and surrounding villages demonstrated for *azaadi* the next day, and guerrilla recruitment and activity picked up significantly in Kishtwar *tehsil* of Doda district.

Years later, at the time of writing in the autumn of 2002, Doda-Kishtwar remains one of the most difficult areas of operation for Indian counterinsurgency forces (the locally recruited guerrillas of Hizb-ul Mujahideen, HM, have proven especially resilient) and a simmering cauldron of communal tension because of the mix of religious groups in its population. In November 2001, for example, thirteen soldiers were killed when their convoy was ambushed at Ramban, a Doda township on the highway connecting Jammu city to Srinagar through the Banihal pass. In August 2002 an army colonel commanding counterinsurgency operations died in a mine blast in the interior of Doda district (after which security forces burned four nearby Muslim villages). Both attacks were attributed to HM units active in the area, and Shakeel Ansari, HM's commander for Doda and adjoining mountainous parts of Udhampur district, is one of most wanted guerrilla leaders in IJK.[14]

The spread of insurrection throughout Kashmiri-speaking areas of IJK obscured emerging problems in the *azaadi* campaign. The first of these was the exodus from the Valley of the bulk of the region's main religious minority, the Kashmiri Pandits, shortly after the uprising began. According to the government of India's 1981 census, Hindus made up only 4 percent—124,078 of 3,135,000 people—of the Valley's population. The vast majority of these were Kashmiri Pandits, so the Valley's Pandit population was probably 130,000–140,000 in 1989–1990 (numerous Kashmiri Pandits already lived permanently outside Kashmir, in various Indian cities, where many achieved prominence in various professions, the civil service, and the military). As the uprising broke out across the Valley in early 1990, approximately one hundred thousand Pandits left their Valley homes for Jammu city and Delhi in a few weeks in February and March, in one of the most controversial episodes of the war in Kashmir. Organized groups representing Pandit migrants have since claimed that they were forced out of the Valley by a systematic terror campaign of "ethnic cleansing" and even "genocide." Pro-*azaadi* Muslim opinion in the Valley tends to argue that the migration was encouraged and even actively facilitated by Indian officials, particularly Governor Jagmohan, in a deliberate attempt to stigmatize the *azaadi* movement as sectarian and "fundamentalist."

While it is not possible to resolve such conflicting versions conclusively, the facts of the matter appear to lie somewhere between the two poles. The JKLF's campaign of selective assassinations claimed some Pandit lives between September 1989 and February 1990, although Muslim victims numbered three times as many. High-profile Pandit victims included the president of the Kashmir Valley unit of India's Hindu nationalist Bharatiya Janata Party (BJP) in September 1989, the retired judge who a decade previously had sentenced the JKLF cofounder Maqbool Butt to death in November 1989, and the director of the Srinagar station of India's government-run television network in February 1990. These highly publicized killings may well have contributed to the spread of fear in the Pandit community. Some of the agents of Indian intelligence agencies targeted by JKLF assassins were also Pandits, who, to the resentment of some local Muslims, have a history of being overrepresented relative to their proportion of the population in government employment in IJK. The sight of huge pro-*azaadi* demonstrations chanting Islamic religious slogans across the Valley in January–February 1990 may have further intimidated local Pandits and contributed to their exodus. On 15 March 1990, by which date the Pandit exodus was substantially complete, the All-India Kashmiri Pandit Conference, a community organization, asserted that a total of thirty-two Pandits had been killed by Muslim militants since the previous autumn—a plausible claim.[15] The displacement of Pandits from the Valley has been the prime tool of Indian officials, politicians, and media in the propaganda war over Kashmir since 1990.

But the Pandit issue is more complex and ambiguous than that propaganda suggests. In 1995 I visited squalid camps housing poorer Pandit refugees in Purkho and Misriwala, settlements near the city of Jammu in IJK's Hindu-majority south, and was touched by their condition. These were rural folk uprooted from their farms and orchards in the Valley; lacking the professional qualifications and connections of the urbanized majority among the Valley's Pandits, they were having a difficult time. They uniformly narrated horror stories of intimidation and violence that had forced their departure, and portrayed the Valley's Muslim majority as crazed fanatics. However, when I continued my journey to the Valley, I met a number of Pandits, in some cases entire families, living in the Valley's towns and villages. Their narratives were markedly different. These were representatives of the sizeable minority among the Pandits who had not joined the 1990 exodus, and there were also a few who had left in 1990 but returned in the intervening years. They spoke, in private interviews, of being well-treated and in some instances protected by Muslim neighbors and friends. Several expressed sympathy and solidarity with the Valley's majority population living under Indian repression, although all were unequivocal in their opposition to armed militancy against the Indian state and to the politics of *azaadi*.[16]

Indeed, a young Pandit visiting his parents in Srinagar in the summer of 1992, for the first time since the insurrection began, wrote: "Our *mohalla* [neighborhood] had not changed except for two CRPF bunkers on the street. I was amazed at the friendliness and warmth with which I was greeted. Muslim neighbors turned up with *mithai* [sweets] and blessed me as soon as word got out that I was in town and invited me to their houses to celebrate with *sevion-ki-kheer* [vermicelli pudding, a traditional delicacy]. There was not a single Muslim friend or acquaintance who did not greet me as he would have before the troubles began."[17] When a pre-dawn crackdown took place in their *mohalla* during his stay, "Hindu, Muslim and Sikh neighbors were united in their resentment against the security forces" conducting the operation.

Even more dramatic testimony is available from a prominent Pandit couple kidnapped in Srinagar in November 1991 by members of an armed group calling itself Hizbullah, who were released after forty-five days in captivity:

> During this time we lived for varying periods in 57 [Muslim] homes. All those people showered love and hospitality on us. We owe them all a debt of gratitude. With their sympathy we were better able to cope . . . We met a cross-section of people in the villages and a sizeable number of youth belonging to militant organizations. We talked with them about education, religion, social life, politics, *Kashmiriyat* [the meaning and values of Kashmiri identity], human emotions, and above all,

ways of building bridges and winning hearts. These
interactions reinforced our faith in the values of love
and goodness which are still deeply ingrained in the
Kashmiri ethos.[18]

In response to persistent allegations by Indian media and right-
wing Hindu politicians about desecration and destruction of
scores of Hindu temples and shrines in the Kashmir Valley, a leading Indian magazine undertook an investigation in February
1993.[19] Its journalists were armed with a list of twenty-three such
sites supplied by the Delhi office of the BJP—whose top leader
L. K. Advani (India's interior minister post-1998 and deputy prime
minister since 2002) said after Hindu extremists demolished the
disputed Babri mosque in the north Indian town of Ayodhya in
December 1992: "Nobody raised a voice when over forty temples
were desecrated in Kashmir. Why these double-standards?" The
investigators, who inspected and photographed each site, found
that twenty-one of the twenty-three shrines were completely in-
tact (the other two had sustained minor damage in unrest after
the razing of the Babri mosque). They reported that "even in villages in which only one or two Pandit families are left" since the
exodus of 1990, "the temples are safe . . . even in villages full of
[armed] militants. The Pandit families have become custodians of
the temples. They are encouraged by their Muslim neighbors to
regularly offer prayers."[20] This is consistent with a syncretistic feature of Valley society, in which shrines and saints are often revered
by people cutting across formal religious boundaries.

In the recent, *fidayeen* phase of the insurgency, Pandits living in
the Valley have been occasionally targeted, including one massacre near Srinagar in which twenty-three villagers were killed. At
the same time, some Pandits have steadily trickled back to live in

Srinagar since the mid-1990s, and many more have resumed visits to the Valley from Delhi or Jammu. In mid-2002, for example, fifteen thousand Pandits, mostly migrants, participated in an annual festival held at one of the most famous Hindu shrines, Khir Bhawani in the village of Tulmulla, near Srinagar, where "local Muslims welcomed them with open arms." In April 2002, twenty-five hundred Pandits living in the Valley, including a large number of women and children, organized a major Hindu religious ceremony in the heart of Srinagar.[21] Nonetheless, the *azaadi* movement has never been able to live down the taint of the Pandit exodus in the first months of the uprising. The embarrassment has been especially acute for JKLF, the organization that pioneered the insurrection and dominated its first three years, since its struggle was (and is) supposedly motivated by a vision of an independent Jammu and Kashmir in which all religious faiths, ethnicities, and regions can coexist with dignity and equality. However, most of Kashmir's Pandit minority became the first collateral casualties of the independence war, and the movement's leaders cannot avoid a measure of moral if not actual culpability for their fate. The Pandit flight also exposed a critical flaw embedded in the "independent Kashmir" concept—its complete inability to accommodate the multiple political allegiances regarding sovereignty and citizenship that exist even in the Kashmir Valley (the stronghold of pro-independence sentiment) and even more extensively in IJK as a whole (see Chapter 4). The Pandits, whose history, culture, ethnicity, and language are the same as the Valley's Muslims, suffered because as a community ultimately loyal to India they could not identify with the "patriotic" anti-India uprising sweeping their home region.

The second problem that emerged in the *azaadi* campaign, paradoxically because of the movement's meteoric growth, was an alarming proliferation of armed groups in the Valley. In the first heady years, with revolution in the air and the Valley awash in weapons procured from across the LOC—from shadowy sources in AJK or Pakistan proper or in the booming arms bazaars of the North-West Frontier Province bordering Afghanistan—it was distinctly fashionable to become a "freedom fighter." It was almost equally easy for newly minted "commanders" to gather a band of gunmen from their locality or extended family and float a *tanzeem,* a guerrilla group. The Valley's history of endemic political factionalism also played a role in this. For example, two factions of the People's League, a pro-Pakistan political party formed in the 1970s, spawned two separate *tanzeems:* Muslim Jaanbaaz Force and Jehad Force, which were only uneasily amalgamated as Al-Jehad. Young adherents of the People's Conference party in the Valley's northern Kupwara district formed their own guerrilla outfit, Al-Barq. In Srinagar, elements of the Islamic Students' League, an organization active in the 1980s, emerged in 1990 as a group called the Allah Tigers, whose main activities appeared to be making statements to the press emphasizing the *mujahideen* ban on alcohol, cinema, and beauty salons and issuing puritanical strictures on the dress and behavior of women. The group disappeared after 1990.

But the fragmentation of the armed struggle was only partly a spontaneous process generated by factionalism and the heat of the moment. The Pakistani military's Inter-Services Intelligence (ISI) had, during the 1980s military regime of General Zia-ul Haq, acquired vast resources and autonomy as the nodal agency coordinating the Central Intelligence Agency (CIA)–sponsored war against the Soviet occupation of Afghanistan. By 1989 Soviet forces were on their way out of Afghanistan and the ISI was in a position to focus on the new war in Kashmir, Pakistan's sacred national cause since 1947. In an unexpected windfall for the ISI, sizeable numbers of youth from Indian Kashmir were, for the first time since 1947, prepared to take up arms against Indian rule. Between 1988 and 1990 ISI operatives assisted the JKLF, which saw Pakistan as a vital strategic ally, in launching the insurrection. Like the JKLF vanguard, they were initially taken aback by the explosion of anti-India feeling in the Valley. As the armed revolt rapidly acquired a popular character owing to the severe and indiscriminate nature of Indian repression during 1990, thousands of Valley youths started to cross the LOC in search of weapons and training. The Kashmir *jehad* was on.

The ISI sensed that a long-awaited window of opportunity for Pakistan had finally opened in Kashmir. However, the JKLF, the agent and vehicle of the uprising, was dogmatically committed to the ideology of an independent, reunited Jammu and Kashmir state, separate from both India and Pakistan—an ideology elaborated as early as 1970 by the movement's veteran ideologue Amanullah Khan.[22] From 1991 the ISI cut off aid to the JKLF and adopted a twin-track strategy to mold the Valley uprising to Pakistan's conception and interests.

The first strategy aimed to divide and weaken the JKLF by encouraging its pliable elements to break away and form pro-Pakistan guerrilla groups. By 1991 at least two such factions had emerged—Al-Umar Mujahideen and Ikhwan-ul Muslimeen (literally, Muslim Brothers). Al-Umar was led by Mushtaq Ahmed Zargar, alias Latram, a Srinagar JKLF militant who had become notorious for executing suspected collaborators by exploding grenades tied to their bodies.[23] In late 1993 I interviewed an Ikhwan-ul Muslimeen commander, a Srinagar resident who said that after basic training in Pakistan the ISI had sent him to acquire practical training in war by participating in the 1991 Afghan *mujahideen* siege of Khost, a city in eastern Afghanistan whose fall heralded the countdown to the end of the pro-communist Najibullah regime in Kabul in 1992.

The second strategy was to build up a pro-Pakistan guerrilla organization operating in the Valley, the Hizb-ul Mujahideen (HM), as a force that could rival and then displace the JKLF. HM, a guerrilla group with close links to the IJK branch of a conservative Islamic party, the Jama'at-i-Islami (JI), which also has organizations in Pakistan and Bangladesh, was chosen to be the Pakistani state's surrogate in IJK. In 1991 the leader of HM in the Valley, Ahsan Dar, a native of the town of Pattan in Baramulla district, was purged as insufficiently reliable and replaced by the veteran JI activist Yusuf Shah, alias Salahuddin (whose antecedents are described in Chapter 2). Abdul Majid Dar, a native of the town of Sopore in the northern Valley, an area where JI has influence, became the key HM operational commander in the Valley.[24] By 1993 the ISI had further diversified its Kashmir portfolio by encouraging zealot Islamic groups based in Pakistan, such as Harkat-ul Ansar, to enter the Kashmir war. In 1994 Maulana Masood Azhar, a top Harkat-ul Ansar activist from Bahawalpur, in the southern region of Pakistan's Punjab province, was captured by Indian forces in the southern Valley district of Anantnag.[25]

By 1994, in addition to "crackdown," "blast," and "firing," a new term had entered the vocabulary of war in Kashmir: "gun culture." It carried a pejorative meaning. The *mujahideen*'s halo of heroism was gradually giving way to a painful realization among the public that because of the phenomenal expansion of the armed struggle from 1990–1993, the ranks of freedom fighters contained politically shallow people, opportunists, and even criminals.

By mid-1994 it was being reported from the Valley that "Kashmiris are sick of growing criminal tendencies among proliferating armed groups."[26] But public disenchantment with the climate of insecurity created by roaming groups of gunmen was outweighed by an even bigger problem facing the *azaadi* movement.

As the dominant guerrilla organization, the JKLF bore the brunt of repression imposed by the Indian counterinsurgency machine between 1990 and 1992. Of 2,213 guerrillas killed in that three-year period, the majority were JKLF fighters, including the cream of its fighting cadres, and hundreds more were captured. In 1993 another 1,310 guerrilla fighters were killed; in 1994 the guerrilla death toll was 1,596. In 1992–1993 reports emerged that Indian counterinsurgency authorities were operating a "catch-and-kill" policy in the Valley, under which guerrilla suspects were being summarily executed.[27] One civilian official responded to the allegations by saying, "Yes, they're killing them. Perhaps because the jails are full—or they want to frighten the people," while a paramilitary commander asserted in April 1993: "We don't have custodial deaths here, we have alley deaths. If we have word of a militant, we will pick him up, take him to the next lane, and kill him."[28] In 1992 members of the local Jammu and Kashmir police staged a revolt in Srinagar after one of their members was tortured to death. Of the JKLF's original four-man HAJY group, Ashfaq Wani died on 30 March 1990, and Yasin Malik was captured in a wounded condition on 6 August 1990 and not released until May 1994. Hamid Sheikh was also captured; released in the autumn of 1992 by BSF intelligence to counteract the rising influence of pro-Pakistan elements in the guerrilla struggle, he was killed along with several associates by Indian army intelligence, which apparently did not agree with the BSF's decision, in Srinagar in November 1992.[29] By 1992 the JKLF's dominance of the armed struggle was under siege on three fronts: relentless pressure from the Indian security forces, the formation of splinter groups with Pakistani support, and the rapidly rising strength, again with Pakistani support, of HM as a military force.

The first known armed clash between JKLF and HM guerrillas occurred in Srinagar in April 1991, and a JKLF area commander was killed. Further clashes, and casualties on both sides, occurred during 1991 and 1992, more the result of local turf wars than of ideological disagreement. Attempts to patch up differences in the broader interest of the movement were not successful. In February 1992 the JKLF temporarily retrieved its position when the JKLF organization in AJK attempted a highly publicized march on the LOC to stress the unity in struggle of the two Kashmirs. Pakistani and AJK authorities dismissed the independentists' move as a political stunt and reckless provocation to Indian armed forces positioned at the LOC. Some thirty thousand people joined the JKLF's march, which was broken up by Pakistani border troops who opened fire just short of the LOC, killing twenty-one marchers. When news of the killing of Kashmir independentists by Pakistani forces reached Srinagar, "60,000 people gathered" at the Hazratbal shrine, taken over by JKLF militants since 1990, "defying [Indian] curfew," to condemn the Pakistani action and express solidarity with the independence movement. The episode was described as "a major [political] victory for JKLF groups operating in the Valley over Pakistan-sponsored factions like HM."[30]

But besieged on three fronts, its best cadres dead or jailed, the JKLF was fighting a losing battle. The year 1993 marked the decisive ascendancy of HM as the dominant guerrilla group in the armed struggle. In May 1993 Javed Mir, the sole member of the HAJY group still active in the field, admitted as much when he said, "Gun-power is not the only thing that matters. The public are the most powerful weapon and they are on our side."[31] In mid-1994 Yasin Malik, freed after four years in prison, declared an indefinite JKLF ceasefire, partly to preserve what remained of the JKLF's cadre. He was not particularly successful in that goal. In January 1995 Malik told me that since mid-1994 he had lost almost a hundred activists to continuing Indian operations against the group. A veteran IJK journalist has told me that in his estimation a total of three hundred surviving JKLF members were killed by Indian counterinsurgency forces after the group's unilateral ceasefire in mid-1994, often after HM members provided information regarding their identity and whereabouts, thus completing the decimation of JKLF's field presence.[32] The JKLF's ceasefire decision did not discernibly reduce violence in IJK, since the group was already a marginal player in insurgency by that time. The middle of 1994 was nonetheless a political turning point in the *azaadi* movement, as the pioneer militant organization effectively laid down its arms.

Javed Mir's brave claim was both right and wrong. Bereft of "gun power" in a heavily militarized environment, the spokesmen of the independence movement would struggle to retain political relevance from 1994 on. However, he was right about the limitations of gun power. In 1993–1994 HM emerged as the leading guerrilla organization in the field, but its ideology of *Kashmir banega Pakistan* (Kashmir will become Pakistan) remained a minority orientation, at odds with the continuing popular appeal of independentist ideology in the pro-*azaadi* areas of IJK. HM's sacrifices in the cause of *azaadi* were (and are) widely admired, but its political affiliate JI's brand of orthodox Islam—preached in a network of religious schools run by the party—is regarded with distaste by most Muslims in the Valley and other Kashmiri-speaking areas like Jammu's Doda-Kishtwar, who prefer their more liberal, eclectic Sufi-influenced version.

In 1995 a senior JI activist in Kupwara's Nowgam sector, dominated by HM militants, told me that despite his best efforts at indoctrination, "80 percent of the *awaam* [people] here support the idea of independence." In Pampore, a town twenty kilometers south of Srinagar that is the birthplace of Sheikh Abdul Aziz, then jailed commander of Al-Jehad and now a senior figure in the All-Parties Hurriyat Conference (APHC), the umbrella coalition of IJK parties favoring self-determination, most people did not agree with Aziz's pro-Pakistan views. "We don't want to exchange one *gulami* [slavery] for another," I was told. In war-torn Doda's Kishtwar town, Maulana Farooq Hussain Kitchloo, the Muslim community's spiritual leader, made it clear to me that his heart lay with the marginalized JKLF's crusade for independence. There are sizeable pockets of hard-core support for Pakistan in the Valley and in the Jammu region's Muslim-populated areas, but consistent with the historical pattern, those who consider their national identity Pakistani constitute a minority opinion in IJK. They are vastly outnumbered by adherents of the radicalized variant of the old brand of regional patriotism.

By 1994 the *azaadi* movement had reached a crossroads. The underlying division in the movement—the existence of two competing definitions of "freedom" or "self-determination," the rallying cry of 1990—had been laid bare by the rise of pro-Pakistan militants as the fighting force of a population that was still largely independentist. HM hardliners aggravated the dilemma by attempting to impose their understanding of the *azaadi* concept. Between 1992 and 1994 several prominent members of the Srinagar intelligentsia known for independentist convictions and

JKLF leanings were mysteriously murdered. Some of these killings—including that of Hriday Nath Wanchoo, a Pandit human
rights advocate—were probably the work of elements within the
Indian security apparatus. But others, such as the murder of Dr.
Abdul Ahad Guru, a cardiologist and JKLF ideologue, were probably carried out by pro-Pakistan militants.[33] The problem extended
well beyond the elite. In 1995 I spoke with an elderly working-
class man, Mohammed Shafi Bhat, in Ganderbal, a town north of
Srinagar. Bhat was consumed with hatred for HM, whose members he described as "fundamentalists." He said that in 1993 both
his brothers had been called out of their home and shot dead by
HM men simply because they had collected donations to repair
the shrine and mausoleum of a Sufi saint which had been damaged by HM cadres.

In June 1994 Qazi Nissar, a respected cleric who held the position of *mirwaiz* (high priest) of the southern half of the Kashmir
Valley, was murdered in his home near the town of Anantnag by
gunmen said by locals to be from HM. The *mirwaiz* of the northern Kashmir Valley, Maulvi Farooq, had already been killed by
gunmen said to be from HM in his Srinagar home in May 1990;
now it was the turn of Qazi Nissar, who had been prominent in
the Muslim United Front in 1987 and had lately "accused HM of
holding Kashmir to ransom, to hand over to Pakistan on a plate."
Nissar's assassination was a turning point in the Kashmir uprising.
An "unprecedented outburst of fury at pro-Pakistan insurgents
erupted at his funeral" as "more than 100,000" mourners chanted
slogans such as *Hizb-ul Mujahideen murdabad* (Death to HM), *Jo
mangega Pakistan, usko milega kabristan* (Those who want Pakistan
will be sent to the graveyard), and *Hum kya chahtey? Azaadi!* (What
do we want? Freedom!). A *hartal* (general strike) called to protest
the murder was successful, and "houses all over the Valley turned

off their lights between 7pm and 10pm in a show of solidarity." It was argued that "the slogans in no way indicate that Kashmiris want to live within the Indian Union. Rather, they send a clear signal that Kashmir wants independence from both its neighbors."[34]

One account of the war in Kashmir that appeared in the mid-1990s observed: "In the Valley, Pakistan's heavy influence on the movement is deeply resented, especially among JKLF supporters. India clearly hopes to exploit the sentiment, once the Kashmiris find the fight is futile. In the long run, Pakistan's powerful intervention may prove to have undermined the very uprising it sought to fortify." Another account, also published in the mid-1990s, predicted that "in the end, Pakistan's policies may push Kashmir, however reluctantly, deeper into India's fold."[35] These prognoses were substantially fulfilled by 1995–1996, when a new term, "renegades," was added to the lexicon of the Kashmir war.

The "renegades" were guerrillas who gave up the struggle against India and enlisted as auxiliaries in the Indian war on insurgency. Some were criminal elements, while others were men of weak political commitment who had joined the guerrilla war at the peak of *azaadi* fervor in the early 1990s, discovered that they had no stomach for a protracted fight against huge Indian forces, and opportunistically switched sides. But others were genuinely disillusioned by what they perceived as Pakistan's corrupting influence on the struggle and the willingness of the pro-Pakistan hard core to perpetrate violence against those among their own people who did not agree with them. Those disillusioned in this manner included front-ranking militants who had been active in pro-Pakistan guerrilla groups in the first half of the decade. For example, in May 1996 two former commanders of the Muslim Jaanbaaz Force and Al-Jehad, and one former commander of HM, publicly gave up the struggle and resumed civilian lives. By 1995

HM had acquired a bad reputation for attacking and killing not just JKLF's pro-independence supporters but also members of smaller guerrilla groups. Many of these ex-guerrillas, and their relatives and friends, sought protection, or vengeance, or money—or all three—through collaboration with the Indian counterinsurgency campaign.

Two large concentrations of such counterinsurgents—also known as "pro-India militants" and "Ikhwanis"—emerged around the town of Pattan (Baramulla district) in the northern Valley and around the town of Anantnag in the southern Valley. Smaller groups sprang up elsewhere. Their emergence was a great help to India's security forces.[36] For the first time since the eruption of insurgency, Indian authorities had the benefit of local collaboration. Some of the former guerrillas were absorbed into a special counterterrorism force of the Jammu and Kashmir police, known first as the Special Task Force and later as the Special Operations Group (SOG), which has become notorious since its formation in the mid-1990s for corruption and brutality. Others were given the status of special police officers and attached to paramilitary and army units operating in their localities, especially to four specialized and notoriously brutal counterinsurgency army formations collectively called the Rashtriya Rifles (RR; National Rifles), created to fight guerrillas in the Kashmir Valley and the war zones of the Jammu region.[37] With their assistance, Indian forces were able to reassert a significant degree of control over Srinagar and other Valley towns and some rural areas in the Valley.

The military tide had turned in the Kashmir war. The last mass protests characteristic of the *intifada* phase came in May 1995, when the shrine and mausoleum of Sheikh Nooruddin Noorani, in the town of Charar-e-Sharief, was gutted by fire after a battle between the Indian army and guerrilla fighters. (Prior to that, hundreds of thousands flooded Srinagar's streets in May 1994 and again in October 1994, to welcome the independentist activist Yasin Malik and the veteran "self-determination" advocate Shabbir Shah back to their homeland from extended captivity in Indian jails, in scenes reminiscent of the mass outpourings of emotion whenever Sheikh Abdullah was released from Indian jails between the late 1950s and the mid-1970s.) Valley residents generally blamed the Indian army for the shrine's destruction. But in a telling illustration of the infiltration of the local struggle for self-determination by "foreign" or "guest" militants, the leader of the guerrillas holed up in Charar-e-Sharief turned out to be Manzoor Ahmad, alias Mast Gul, a Pakistani veteran of the 1980s war in Afghanistan. In August 1995 five Western tourists trekking in the southern Valley were kidnapped by a shadowy group calling itself Al-Faran, suspected of being a front for the Harkat-ul Ansar group consisting of religious zealots from Pakistan. One of the tourists, a Norwegian, was found beheaded; another, an American, managed to escape; and the other three remain missing to this day. The grim incident, severely condemned by the APHC and attributed by many locals at the time to a sinister Indian plot to defame "the movement," was an early warning that the *fidayeen* phase of insurgency in Kashmir was on the horizon.

Demoralization and Atrophy (1996–1998)

One of my friends and informants in Srinagar throughout the 1990s was a resident of Khanyar, a lower-middle-class neighborhood in the old city of Srinagar. Khanyar, a maze of lanes and alleys packed with wooden houses built in traditional Kashmiri style, has had a powerful reputation as a militant stronghold since 1989. During the first half of the 1990s my informant, a trader of Kashmiri shawls and carpets then in his thirties, would relate the exploits of Khanyar militants with great pride and enthusiasm, as well as stories of "Akbar Bhai," an Afghan "guest" who had helped local boys take on the BSF before being killed in 1993. I met several local members of militant groups—the JKLF, Ikhwan-ul Muslimeen, and Al-Jehad—through him. They were all his relatives, friends, or neighbors.

In July 1995 I was, for the first time, advised not to visit the neighborhood because a few "foreign militants" had taken shelter there, and locals could not guarantee my safety. In March 1996 my friend was in a disconsolate mood, reflecting the state of the *azaadi* movement. "People still deeply desire *azaadi*," he said, "and almost nobody accepts the legitimacy of the *hindustani hukumat* [Indian rule] from their hearts . . . But there is a loss of hope, because the struggle, after so much violence, suffering, and *qurbani* [sacrifice], has not led to the realization of our *huq* [rights]." This was a snapshot of the exhaustion and loss of morale that gripped the Valley in 1996–1997. The JKLF was crushed, most of the other local guerrilla groups formed in the early 1990s had disbanded or become defunct, and the sole survivor, HM, was facing a determined offensive from the counterinsurgency forces and their new allies, the "renegades." Staring defeat in the face, my friend was now hoping that activists of *jehadi* groups from Pakistan, who had been steadily infiltrating into IJK since 1993, would keep the struggle alive.

It was not that violence ceased in IJK during this period. According to official Indian figures, 1,209 guerrillas were killed in 1996, 1,075 in 1997, and 999 in 1998 (after 1998 the figure started climbing again, to 1,082 in 1999 and 1,612 in 2000; during the first eleven months of 2002 as many as 1,581 guerrillas were killed). The human rights situation continued to be grave—it was in 1996 that Jaleel Andrabi, a human rights lawyer associated with JKLF, was picked up in the streets of Srinagar by RR soldiers and "rene-gades" and tortured to death. But by and large the armed conflict was now less visible—centered in rural, often remote areas in the Valley and Jammu's Doda district and in newly emerging theaters of war, such as the twin LOC districts of Rajouri and Poonch in the Jammu region.

The beginnings of superficial normalcy became visible in the urban landscape of Srinagar, a city that had been under virtual siege from 1990 to 1995. The unsightly bunkers were reduced in number, the checkpoints were fewer and less aggressive during daylight hours, and there was even some pedestrian and automo-bile traffic in the city center after dusk. During the summer of 1997, thousands of middle-class Srinagar families made the excur-sion to Gulmarg, a popular resort forty-five kilometers from the city, for the first time in almost a decade. In 2002 a Srinagar news-paper noted the change since the end of the *intifada* phase: "The streets are silent. The crowds of boys dispersed. Many resting in graves and others struggling to survive as ordinary citizens."[38] Indeed, the spontaneous crowds never returned to the streets on a mass scale, although localized protests, usually in response to mistreatment and alleged atrocities at the hands of Indian secu-rity forces, remained a frequent feature of community life in IJK. When the struggle was renewed after the period of relative lull, it took a deadlier form than the popular upsurge of the early 1990s.

The government of India saw the relative quiet of 1996–1998 as an opportunity to complete its pacification campaign. Its strat-egy was to supplement continuing repression with reinstallation of a civilian IJK government. In May 1996 India's parliamentary elections were held in IJK (IJK had been excluded from the previ-ous parliamentary election, in 1991). Then in September 1996 elec-tions were held, after a gap of almost a decade (since March 1987), to constitute a new IJK legislative assembly. Farooq Abdullah and a gaggle of his NC retainers were resurrected from political oblivion and won a two-thirds' majority in the eighty-seven-member legislature (forty-six deputies elected from Valley, thirty-seven from Jammu, and four from Ladakh). Abdullah was duly reinstalled as IJK chief minister at the head of a new government. The Hurriyat Conference, formed during the *intifada* phase of the uprising as a coordinating body of IJK's spectrum of parties favoring "self-determination," mounted a boycott against the Indian-sponsored electoral process—in the face of harassment by security forces and pro-India militants—demanding instead tripartite talks on the Kashmir question between India, Pakistan, and representatives of the *azaadi* movement. Both sets of elections, particularly the first, were severely marred by low turnout in most Valley constituencies and pro-*azaadi* areas of Jammu, widespread allegations of people being coerced to vote by security forces and "renegades," especially in rural communities, and other forms of fraud.[39]

Just prior to the autumn 1996 elections, I traveled around Badgam, a district in the center of the Kashmir Valley. Some areas of Badgam, and contiguous pockets in the neighboring Baramulla district, are dominated by Shia Muslims, the minority sect in Islam and in the Valley. After leaving Srinagar, I stopped first in the main market in the district town of Badgam. There a middle-aged shopkeeper told me that he was going to vote in the forthcoming elections, in the faint hope that reestablishment of some sort of civilian administration in Srinagar would bring relief from "the gun culture of the security forces, the militants, and the renegades." But, he said, "if you ask me what I really want from my heart and you want me to give a truthful reply, I can only say: *azaadi* and *khudmukhtari* [self-rule]." I then drove to Soibugh, known throughout the Valley and beyond as the home village of a number of leading militants, including HM's leader Yusuf Shah, alias Syed Salahuddin; Ashraf Dar, a senior HM commander killed by Indian forces in 1993; and Shabbir Siddiqui, a senior JKLF leader killed by Indian forces in March 1996. During the elections to the Indian parliament in May 1996, the village had registered an apparently impressive voter participation, including Salahuddin's own brother.

As a Kashmiri companion (a Srinagar lawyer) and I passed a fortified army camp and entered the village, we encountered the older brother of the recently slain JKLF leader Shabbir Siddiqui. He politely declined to be seen engaging in an extended conversation with me. He said that the village and its environs were classified as a super-sensitive "red zone" by the security forces, the army was patrolling constantly, and he feared there were informers in the village. He did not want to risk a nocturnal visit from soldiers and renegades inquiring about his conversation with a visitor. (Six years later, Soibugh was still a war zone. In September 2002 three policemen and a HM fighter were killed in an hour-long battle on the village's outskirts.)[40] At the tea shop on Soibugh's dusty main street, my companion and I were met with suspicious stares from the assembled group of villagers. On being informed that I was an Indian researcher, they assured me with alacrity that "there will be a huge turnout of voters here in the assembly elections." My companion then spoke to them in Kashmiri, trying to convince them, he later told me, that I was not an Indian army officer in plain clothes or an intelligence agent. The tune changed. "We want *azaadi*," the villagers chorused in unison, with a conviction that had been markedly absent in the earlier response.

On the way back to Srinagar, I stopped at a martyrs' cemetery—one of hundreds that dot the war zones of IJK—in another

Badgam village, Warapora. As I walked around the cemetery, followed by a friendly crowd of curious children, I noticed from the inscriptions on the tombstones that while almost all the graves from 1990–1994 were of locals who had fallen in the guerrilla struggle, the more recent 1995–1996 graves were a mix of locals and volunteer fighters from towns and districts in Pakistan (mainly Pakistani Punjab). Around the time I visited that village cemetery, Nadeem Khatib was making the decision of his life in an affluent Srinagar home. The war in Kashmir was far from over; it was merely simmering.

The Fidayeen Phase (1999–2002)

The onset of the *fidayeen* phase of insurgency was presaged by a brief thaw in India-Pakistan relations. The year 1998 was South Asia's nuclear summer, when India tested five nuclear devices and Pakistan responded with six tests a few weeks later. Initially it seemed that overt nuclearization of the subcontinent might produce some benign side effects. In February 1999 India's prime minister Atal Behari Vajpayee traveled to Pakistan on the first run of a bus service connecting Delhi with Lahore, a major Pakistani Punjab city close to the border with Indian Punjab. Vajpayee and his Pakistani counterpart, Nawaz Sharif, "sharing a vision of peace and stability" and "recognizing that the nuclear dimension of the security environment of the two countries adds to their responsibility for avoidance of conflict," signed a "Lahore Declaration" during the visit. The declaration pledged a "composite and integrated dialogue process" on the basis of an "agreed bilateral agenda," and resolved to "intensify efforts to resolve all issues, including the issue of Jammu and Kashmir."[41]

Vajpayee's decision to extend an olive branch to Pakistan was possibly encouraged by the Indian security establishment's upper hand over guerrilla militancy in IJK. But the promise of Lahore evaporated on the barren peaks and ranges of Kargil, in IJK's Ladakh, in the summer of 1999, as Pakistani regular units supported by *jehadi* volunteers infiltrated the Indian side of the LOC and the Indian military launched a massive land and air campaign to evict the infiltrators. Indian officials and commentators have claimed that the Pakistani operation was masterminded by General Pervez Musharraf, then Pakistan's chief of army staff. Six weeks into the fighting, Nawaz Sharif agreed to withdraw Pakistani forces after a tense meeting with U.S. President Bill Clinton on 4 July 1999 in Washington. The humiliating climbdown sealed the fate of Sharif's civilian regime, already unpopular in Pakistan because of rampant corruption and persecution of critics and political opponents. In October 1999 Sharif moved to dismiss Musharraf in a failed preemptive strike, and the armed forces deposed Sharif. The border conflict in Kargil aroused jingoistic nationalism throughout India, with the notable exception of Indian Jammu and Kashmir, where public opinion in most areas ranged from sullenly indifferent to bitterly hostile.[42]

The first *fidayeen* (literally, life-daring) raid occurred in July 1999, shortly after the end of the Kargil hostilities, when two guerrillas simply barged into a BSF camp in Bandipore, a northern Valley town, firing indiscriminately from automatic rifles and lobbing grenades. The Indian army's cantonment area in Srinagar's Badami Bagh locality was penetrated with the same simple but deadly tactic later in 1999. Between mid-1999 and the end of 2002, at least 55 *fidayeen* attacks, usually executed by two-man teams, were targeted against police, paramilitary and army camps, and government installations in IJK, mostly in the Kashmir Valley. Of these, 29 took place in 2001, making that year the high point of the *fidayeen* campaign. According to Indian counterinsurgency authorities, 161 military, paramilitary, and police personnel died in these attacks (the Indian army alone lost 82 men), and 90 militants perished while executing them.[43]

The bulk of the raids have been attributed by Indian security sources to one militant group, Lashkar-e-Taiba (LeT), which consists of religious radicals from Pakistan and was headquartered until early 2002 at Muridke, near Lahore in Pakistan's Punjab province. Most of the rest have been attributed to Jaish-e-Mohammad (JeM), another zealot group that is led by Pakistanis, has a predominantly Pakistani membership, and is the direct descendant of Harkat-ul Ansar, which was active in IJK in the mid-1990s.[44] LeT denies that its raids are suicide missions—preferring to call them "daredevil" actions—since the group follows an ultra-orthodox version of Sunni Islam that strictly prohibits suicide, but the raids nonetheless have an undeniably suicidal character. The attackers almost never return from these penetrate-and-kill missions—their aim is not to save their own lives but to maximize the frightening psychological impact on the enemy by inflicting death and destruction on their targets. The LeT's mouthpiece *Jihad Times* (published until 2001 from Islamabad, Pakistan's capital) and JeM's fortnightly Urdu journal (also published in Pakistan) have both discussed suicidal warfare in Kashmir. LeT refers to members who execute such operations as *fidayeen* (those who dare their lives), while JeM refers to its *khudkush shaheed dasta* (self-sacrificing martyrs' unit).[45]

In December 2001 a heavily armed five-man squad managed to enter the compound of India's Parliament building in New Delhi and then attempted to enter the building itself, where hundreds of parliamentarians and government ministers were present at the time. The attackers were killed by security officers after a forty-five-minute battle with guns and grenades. Nine other people, including security staff, parliament stewards, and a gardener tending the grounds, also died. Indian authorities said the raiders were Pakistanis and had been helped and harbored by three men from the Kashmir Valley residing in Delhi. India began a massive military buildup on Pakistan's borders. Primarily in response to U.S. pressure, in January 2002 General Musharraf announced a crackdown on *jehadi* groups operating across the LOC from Pakistani territory. LeT and JeM were banned along with several other violent sectarian groups active within Pakistan.

But after a four-month lull, three gunmen struck again in *fidayeen* style in May 2002, targeting a camp near Jammu city housing families of Indian soldiers. They killed more than thirty people, mostly civilians, and war tensions escalated sharply in the subcontinent. In July 2002 gunmen suspected by Indian authorities to be LeT members struck on the outskirts of Jammu city, massacring twenty-nine Hindus in a slum district before fleeing. Whether by design or accident, the date of the massacre was the seventy-first anniversary of the 13 July 1931 Srinagar massacre of twenty-one Muslim protesters by police, the incident that catalyzed mass political awareness in Kashmir. The Hurriyat Conference coalition and other groups favoring "self-determination" organized protests in Srinagar against the massacre. In an interview given to an Indian news agency by satellite phone from his mountain base, the top Hizb-ul Mujahideen commander for the Jammu region condemned the carnage as "inhuman and un-Islamic" and said he "suspect[ed] that the massacre was carried out by foreign militants."[46] In early August 2002 an annual Hindu pilgrimage in the southern part of the Kashmir Valley was attacked, and nine pilgrims and a gunman were killed. In November 2002 two gunmen struck in the heart of the old bazaar in Jammu city, and one of them entered a popular Hindu shrine in the neighborhood, firing indiscriminately. A dozen people, mostly civilians, were killed in the incident, along with the two attackers. Indian authorities once again suspected the LeT of being behind the raid. By the end of 2002, however, it was clear that the frequency of *fidayeen* raids had decreased significantly in IJK compared to 2001 or even 2000. At the same time, the selection of targets had widened beyond the security forces, and targets appeared to be chosen, and attacks timed, to increase communal antagonisms in IJK and, most important, to keep India-Pakistan relations in a precarious limbo. The highly publicized attacks, especially those against "soft" targets, provided the Indian government's Hindu nationalist leadership with the main justification for its hard-line stance rejecting resumption of a dialogue on Kashmir with the Musharraf regime—branded in India as the "sponsor" of "cross-border terrorism"—overruling mild pressure on New Delhi by the United States and other Western countries.

Peace efforts faltered in this atmosphere of violence. In July 2000 HM, the only insurgent force composed predominantly of IJK residents (augmented by some from AJK), declared a temporary ceasefire, but withdrew it after two weeks amid a sharp escalation of guerrilla violence, including a car-bomb explosion in the center of Srinagar claimed by HM and a series of massacres of Hindus in the Kashmir Valley and the Jammu region for which *jehadi* groups of Pakistani origin were generally considered responsible. The episode exposed a rift between moderate and hardline HM members, and pro-truce commanders were purged from the organization in 2001. In November 2000 Prime Minister Vajpayee announced a one-month halt to offensive operations by Indian security forces in IJK to coincide with the Muslim holy month of Ramzan/Ramadan. This too petered out within months amid intensified guerrilla and state violence. In July 2001

Musharraf visited India at Vajpayee's invitation for talks with the top members of India's government, which proved inconclusive. The Indians emphasized the destabilizing effect of "cross-border terrorism" originating in Pakistan, while the Pakistanis emphasized the need for Indian commitment to a serious political dialogue on the Kashmir question.

Three points can be made about the *fidayeen* phase of insurgency in Kashmir. First, the use of suicidal tactics as a weapon of war is neither novel nor the monopoly of militant Muslims. The Japanese *kamikaze* of World War II used the tactic extensively. Among contemporary political movements, Palestinian militants—especially but not exclusively their Islamist wing—have resorted to the tactic with increasing frequency and decreasing discrimination since the second *intifada* began in the autumn of 2000. But the most effective and most deadly practitioners of suicidal warfare in the South Asian subcontinent—and possibly in the world—since the 1980s have been the Tamil Tigers of Sri Lanka, whose fighters are Hindu, Christian, agnostic, or atheist.[47]

Second, it is true that the main ideologues and practitioners of suicidal warfare in the Kashmir war are radical Islamist groups of Pakistani provenance. JeM, for example, claimed responsibility for an October 2001 raid by a *fidayeen* squad on the Indian legislative assembly complex in Srinagar in which thirty-eight people were killed—mostly local Muslim policemen on guard duty and Muslim civilian employees of the legislature secretariat—and even identified a member from Peshawar, Pakistan, by name as the driver of the jeep bomb that exploded at the heavily guarded entrance and enabled the other members of the suicide squad to enter the complex (the group retracted the claim two days later).

However, suicidal warfare in Kashmir is *not* exclusively a "cross-border" phenomenon, but rather is the product of the incendiary infusion of the ideology and tactics of trans-national Islamist militancy into a brutalized, desperate local environment—that is, of a conjunction of internal and external factors. In May 2000 JeM carried out its first suicide attack in the Kashmir Valley when a JeM militant exploded a car bomb at the entrance to the Srinagar headquarters of the Indian army's 15th Corps, which is deployed in the Valley. The militant was Afaq Ahmed Shah, aged seventeen, a high school student from Srinagar's Khanyar neighborhood. Born in 1983 into a religious family, Afaq had endured a childhood consumed by rebellion, oppression, and despair. Like Nadeem Khatib, he was internally tormented by what he saw around him and eventually decided that he could no longer be a passive witness.

If Ashfaq Wani and Yasin Malik personify the *intifada* generation of the *azaadi* movement, Afaq Shah and Nadeem Khatib represent its *fidayeen* generation. In December 2000 another JeM car bomber attempted to breach the perimeter of the 15th Corps headquarters—this time it was twenty-four-year-old Mohammed Bilal from Manchester, England, a British citizen of Pakistani descent. In September 2000, on a day I happened to be in the Kashmir Valley, a RR camp in the town of Beerwah in Badgam district—not far from the village of Soibugh—was attacked by two *fidayeen*. They killed an Indian major and thirteen soldiers before they were finally cornered and killed. One of them was a *jehadi* militant from Pakistan, the other a Kashmiri-speaking Muslim from a mountain village in the Jammu region's Udhampur district. Two years later, in November 2002, a *fidayeen* duo armed with assault rifles and hand grenades penetrated a CRPF camp in the heart of Srinagar, killing six troopers and losing their own lives. A LeT spokesman named the attackers as Abu Younis, a Pakistani militant, and Reyaz Ahmad Khan, a local fighter from the southern Valley town of Qazigund.[48]

The third point about the *fidayeen* phase is that its most spectacular and most publicized attacks have been directed against such high-profile targets as the Indian army's cantonment and operational headquarters in Srinagar, the headquarters of the SOG in Srinagar, Srinagar's airport, and the legislature's premises in Srinagar, in addition to multiple attacks at various locations in Jammu city, including its railway station, its old bazaar, and at least one shantytown district. However, the crucial theaters of war in this phase lie away from urban centers, in the rural areas, dotted with small towns, of IJK's sprawling interior. These remote locales and frontiers of conflict in Rajouri-Poonch (Jammu region) and Kupwara (Kashmir Valley)—scenes of a deadly, daily war of attrition—are key to an understanding of the complexity of the contemporary Kashmir problem.

As fighting in the Kashmir Valley diminished in 1996–1997, the twin Jammu districts of Rajouri and Poonch were becoming the most active theater of the Kashmir war. Their relative tranquillity during the *intifada* phase is something of a puzzle, since both are Muslim-dominated districts (Rajouri 65 percent, Poonch 90 percent) and lie alongside 250 kilometers of hilly border on the LOC. There are three explanations for the puzzle. First, unlike Doda district in the Jammu interior, which was gripped by insurgency from the early 1990s on, the Muslim majorities of Rajouri-Poonch are not ethnolinguistically identical to the Valley's population. Except in a Kashmiri-speaking Muslim belt in the northeastern corner of Poonch district, abutting the Valley, Rajouri-Poonch's Muslims belong largely to non-Kashmiri ethnic communities—

Gujjars, Bakerwals, Rajputs, even a sprinkling of Pathans. The single largest ethnic group in the two districts is the Gujjars, a traditionally nomadic people who rear livestock and cultivate farmland in highland areas. Gujjars make up 48 percent of the population in Poonch and 50 percent in Rajouri.[49] The dominant language in the hill tracts of Rajouri-Poonch is neither Kashmiri nor Dogri, which is spoken in Jammu's Hindu-dominated south, but Pahadi, a dialect of Punjabi. Because of ethnolinguistic distance from the core area of the *azaadi* campaign, the Kashmir Valley, Rajouri-Poonch Muslims, unlike the Kashmiri speakers of Doda-Kishtwar, were not swept up in the movement.

Second, because of their location on or near the border, Rajouri-Poonch Muslims suffered greatly in the India-Pakistan conflicts of 1947–1948, 1965, and 1971. The area was fiercely contested during the hostilities of 1947–1948. During the 1965 war, older residents recalled to me thirty-five years later, truckloads of Muslim men were arrested by the Indian army for suspect loyalties and taken away to Jammu city for interrogation, where many were brutally treated and some killed. Indeed, in 1965 "100,000 Hindus and Sikhs were forced to flee from Chhamb-Jaurian area in [southwestern] Jammu when the Pakistan army overran it, and 70,000 Muslims had to leave their ancestral homes in Poonch-Rajouri and cross into Azad Kashmir partly . . . because they were harassed" by the Indian army and local Hindus and Sikhs.[50] Displaced people of all religious communities were largely able to return after the war, but this precarious history made local Muslims wary of retribution at the hands of the Indian military if they joined the 1990 uprising. Third, the 250 kilometers of the LOC running on a north-south axis in Poonch and Rajouri have been a major route for guerrillas infiltrating the LOC into IJK since 1990. The entire stretch is full of infiltration corridors known locally as *galis* (alleys); Indian army brigades stationed on the LOC are named after *galis* in their areas of responsibility—BG Brigade (Bhimbar Gali Brigade), JWG Brigade (Jharan Wali Gali Brigade), and so on. However, from 1990 to 1995 guerrillas infiltrating through the Rajouri-Poonch sector (often with the assistance of Gujjar guides) preferred to simply pass through the two districts to the high-priority areas of insurgency—the Valley and Doda district.

As insurgency faltered in the Valley, the post-1995 generation of infiltrating militants began to pay greater attention to Rajouri and Poonch. By 1998 the twin districts were in the grip of guerrilla war. As violence and repression engulfed the area, *jehadi* infiltrators from Pakistan and AJK began to acquire some support among local Muslims. As Majid Khan, a popular trade union leader in the worst-affected zone, Poonch district's Surankote *tehsil*, told me in the autumn of 2000: "There is a socioeconomic basis for militancy here. Most people are quite poor, and often lack drinking water, educational opportunities, and health care. The local administration and India-backed politicians are usually callous to their needs. In some parts of India, similar problems of poverty and marginalization have spawned ultra-leftist movements. Here, in a border area of a disputed territory, grievance finds a different outlet. Humiliating experiences at the hands of the army can turn people into guerrilla sympathizers and even active militants in some cases."

According to the commander of Romeo Force, the specialized counterinsurgency wing of the Indian military in Rajouri-Poonch, his soldiers killed 166 guerrillas during the six-month period between 15 March and 15 September 2000, of whom 89 (54 percent) were "foreigners"—that is, Pakistani nationals and AJK residents. By 2001 the fighting had got worse. In the ten-month period between 1 January and 31 October 2001, the Romeo Force killed as many as 572 insurgents, almost half of all guerrilla casualties in IJK during the period. During 2002 the fighting continued unabated. On a typical day, 28 April 2002, twelve guerrillas were killed in the twin districts, six while trying to infiltrate through Bhimbar Gali and another six inside Indian territory.[51]

All the major *jehadi* groups dominated by Pakistanis—LeT, JeM, Al-Badr, Tehreek-ul Mujahideen, Harkat-ul-Mujahideen, and Harkat-ul-Jehad-i-Islami—are active in the area. In addition, HM has a significant presence, especially in the Pir Panjal mountains, a range that traverses a massive east-west arc across the northern Kashmiri-speaking part of Poonch district, the southern part of the Valley, the mountainous Gujjar and Kashmiri Muslim-dominated upper reaches of Jammu's Udhampur district, and finally Doda district. The HM's fighting units in this area are called the Hizb-ul Mujahideen Pir Panjal Regiment and, as in the Valley and Doda, are mostly recruited from the local population, augmented by a sizeable AJK element. In April 2002 it was reported that leaders of the main guerrilla outfits had met in Surankote's hills and established a mechanism, headed by a commander of local origin, to coordinate operations in ten sectors across the Jammu region.[52]

The 250-kilometer, eight-hour journey by road from Jammu city to the town of Poonch, which I undertook in the autumn of 2000, is a lesson in the complex dynamics of the Kashmir conflict. The road snakes in a northwesterly direction parallel to one of the most disturbed and militarized borders in the world, where small-arms exchanges as well as mortar, machine-gun, and artillery duels between the Indian and Pakistani armies are routine. For the first fifty kilometers the road runs alongside the "working boundary" between Indian Jammu and Pakistani Punjab (Jammu city and Sialkot, a large Pakistani Punjab town, are just thirty kilometers apart). Near the Indian town of Akhnur, the working boundary becomes the Line of Control as Pakistani Punjab gives way to AJK on the other side. Beyond Akhnur the Jammu plains gradually give way to Rajouri district's hills, and the road begins to climb in sharp twists and turns. It is dotted from there on with milestones put up by the Indian army's border roads organization, entreating drivers to "be gentle on my curves." There are also numerous army billboards, written in Hindi-speaking north India's Devanagari script, which proclaim *Kashmir se Kanyakumari tak, mera Bharat mahaan!* (From Kashmir to Kanyakumari, my India is great; Kanyakumari, previously known as Cape Comorin, is the southernmost tip of the Indian subcontinent.)

The reality is far less sanguine. These are classic borderlands, where no magnitude of manpower or firepower can ensure secure control, and where the allegiances of much of the population are at least somewhat suspect. Indeed, religion, ethnicity, and intense inter-state rivalry over territory and the allegiance of people—the defining features of the Kashmir conflict—come together in an incendiary mix in the borderlands of Rajouri and Poonch. Until partition and war in 1947–1948, Rajouri and Poonch had close economic and ethnolinguistic ties not only with the AJK districts of Mirpur and Muzaffarabad but also with the western (Pakistani) Punjab districts of Rawalpindi, Jhelum, Campbellpur, and Mianwali and even the districts of Abbotabad and Mansehra in Pakistan's Frontier Province. Many families in border villages of Poonch and Rajouri still have relatives on the Pakistani side of the LOC. In fact, the historic, pre-1948 Poonch district, which played such a central role in the events of 1947 (see Chapter 1) is bifurcated by the LOC, and the Pakistani-controlled part of Poonch is still a prime source of recruits to the Pakistani army. In an interesting twist, although both (Indian) Poonch and Rajouri are

Muslim-majority districts, the *towns* of Rajouri and Poonch—
which are the districts' centers of administration, commerce, and
education—have predominantly Hindu (and Sikh) populations
(the countryside is largely Muslim, overwhelmingly so in the case
of Poonch). Many of these Hindus and Sikhs are 1947 refugees,
and descendants of those refugees, from Pakistani Kashmir. For
example, many Hindus and Sikhs in Rajouri town trace their origins to Kotli, an AJK town and district directly to the west across
the LOC, and those in the town of Poonch to Rawalakot, an AJK
town and district to its west.

The first sign of the war zone, apart from Indian military convoys, appeared in Rajouri's southern foothills, on the way from
Akhnur to a town called Nowshera, in the form of a Village Defence Committee (VDC) foot patrol. The VDCs are a network
of "self-defense" militia set up by Indian authorities across the
Jammu region, and draw mainly on Hindu and Sikh villagers living in or on the periphery of insurgency-affected areas. The patrol
we encountered consisted of some twenty villagers, all Hindu,
dressed in tattered clothes and scuffed shoes and clutching anti-
quated .303 rifles. They had a litany of complaints: they are paid a
pittance, given bolt-action rifles and a rationed supply of bullets to
confront the guerrillas' AK-47s and grenade launchers, and denied
wireless sets needed to communicate news of guerrilla movements and attacks to the nearest army base. However, they were
determined to defend their village to the best of their ability.
Leaving this clutch of ragged but gallant warriors behind, we
reached the district town of Rajouri after a five-hour, 150-kilome-
ter drive from Jammu city. Although the market was bustling and
Muslim, Hindu, and Sikh shops were trading side by side, there
was a discernible air of tension in the town.

The surrounding countryside is convulsed with guerrilla warfare and counterinsurgency, and there is deep distrust between the town's Muslim and non-Muslim citizens. In November 2001 the headmaster of a village school near the town, a Kashmiri-speaking Muslim, was executed by guerrillas in front of his students "because one of his daughters, a doctor, is married to an army major, while another daughter is a police sub-inspector." In December 2001 a district judge, a Hindu, was shot dead along with two bodyguards and a friend by guerrillas who ambushed their car on the Rajouri-Poonch road. In January 2002 nine Muslims from a nearby village were killed when they were allegedly used by RR troops as human shields during an operation against guerrillas. The town of Rajouri is a tinderbox, and violence spills over regularly from the hinterland. In February 2002 guerrillas fired 170mm. Chinese rockets from a hill overlooking the town at the Indian army's divisional headquarters in the town. In July 2002 four LeT guerrillas infiltrated the town's high-security enclave housing the residences of senior police officers and civil administrators. All four were killed, along with an Indian army captain, in the ensuing overnight encounter.[53]

Our destination, the town of Poonch, is another hundred kilometers north of Rajouri town, a three-hour drive on mountain roads. We covered the distance as fast as possible; dusk was approaching and much of the route passed through Poonch district's Surankote *tehsil*, the hotbed of armed conflict. In November 2001 eleven army personnel, including a major and a junior commissioned officer, died in a guerrilla ambush near a village twenty kilometers from the town of Surankote. In July 2002 seven guerrillas and three army personnel, again including a major, were killed in a single day in two separate battles in Surankote *tehsil*. In late July an army officer and two local policemen, both Muslim, were killed in another guerrilla ambush, and in August two brothers in a Surankote village were killed by the army because they allegedly aided guerrillas. Also in August, seven infiltrating JeM militants were intercepted and killed by the army in the neighboring *tehsil* of Mendhar.[54]

The war intrudes periodically into the grimy town of Surankote, which is permanently on edge. In late April 2002 "militants lobbed a grenade on an Army vehicle at Hadi Mohalla Bazaar [Surankote's market] . . . The grenade exploded injuring five soldiers and some pedestrians. An encounter broke out and in the crossfire, two civilians were killed and fourteen injured including three women. Two militants were also killed and a shop destroyed in the exchange." In late August 2002 two guerrillas entered the house of Azad Ahmed Khan, an SOG officer, shot dead his father, brother, sister-in-law, and nephew, and critically wounded two other family members. In September 2002 guerrillas exploded bombs and opened fire at the main bus stand in the town, killing eight paramilitary BSF personnel, three local police officers, and two civilians. Two of the attackers also died; at least ten civilians and several BSF men were wounded.[55] For most of the thirty kilometers between the towns of Surankote and Poonch, the paved road degenerates into a barely passable dirt track. As we drove along this road as dusk fell, crossing decrepit bridges over mountain streams and passing ghostly hamlets seemingly inhabited only by watchful Indian soldiers, my driver joked: "Sir, whenever I travel along this stretch of road I never know whether I'm going straight to Poonch or straight to heaven." This was among other things a reference to the condition of the road, which is pitted with craters of varying sizes caused by land mines and IED (improvised explosive device) blasts, requiring an uncommon mastery of the steering wheel.

We found the town of Poonch, which has a mixed population

of Hindus, Sikhs, and Muslims, in a state of virtual siege. As armed police patrolled the darkened streets, Yashpal Sharma, a political leader in the town and a Hindu, told us that the surrounding villages were "teeming with militants" and anything could happen at any time. Indeed, guerrillas attacked the town's police station with rocket-propelled grenades shortly after my visit. In the *dak bungalow* (rest house) where we spent the night, my next-door neighbor turned out to be a young police commander, a leader in the local fight against insurgency. A Kashmiri-speaking Muslim from the Jammu region's Doda district, he spoke with frustration of the Indian state's unsympathetic attitude toward IJK's aggrieved people, and recounted how the army frequently mistreats locals and mishandles situations. But, his Sikh deputy commander at his side, he also described with pride how his unit had "eliminated" eight infiltrated JeM militants in a fierce encounter near the town a month earlier.

He showed me an inventory of equipment seized from slain guerrillas and mountain hideouts since the beginning of 2000. The arsenal included assault rifles, sniper rifles, machine guns, grenade launchers, mortar bombs, hand grenades, antitank rockets, antitank and antipersonnel mines, IEDs of various types, remote controls for detonating mines and IEDs, large quantities of plastic explosive, flame-throwers, night-vision devices, binoculars, state-of-the-art radio sets, and decoding sheets for coded communications. As I perused this arsenal and the officer tuned his own radio set to two guerrilla units in nearby mountains bantering in rustic Punjabi, one reason for the spread and tenacity of insurgency in Rajouri-Poonch became clear to me: this *jehad* was a highly sophisticated operation supported by a professional military establishment across the LOC.

The "proxy war" being waged against Indian rule from across

the LOC was not, however, the whole story. The police commander adroitly avoided answering my question of whether it was possible for a relatively small number of infiltrated *jehadi* militants from Pakistan to generate this level of disturbance across a large area without support from at least part of the local population (Rajouri and Poonch districts together have almost nine hundred thousand people).

The following morning my companions and I drove back from Poonch toward Surankote. Our plan was to have a late breakfast with Chaudhary Mohammad Aslam, the top leader of the Gujjar community of Rajouri-Poonch, at his home in a village called Lassana, just off the Poonch-Surankote road. A few kilometers before Lassana, we were stopped by a "road-opening party" of the Romeo Force, whose thankless job is to check the road every morning for mines and IEDs planted by guerrillas during the night.

The soldiers, from homes in diverse parts of India, were equipped with mine-proof armored patrol vehicles manufactured in South Africa, and were very tense. They had reason to be nervous. In late August 2001, "militants beheaded two priests of a Kali [Hindu] temple near the Dhundak bridge" spanning the Suran river, from which the town and *tehsil* take their name. (On the same day, in nearby villages, guerrillas massacred a Muslim family of five who had refused to give them food, and killed two Muslim village officials.) "An indefinite curfew was imposed in Surankote and Poonch towns" following the beheading of the priests to prevent communal violence between Hindus and Muslims, and "police forces were deployed in the sensitive areas of Rajouri town." By "the bodies of the two priests, left along the Surankote-Poonch road near Lassana village, the security forces found a box of fruit containing an IED with a 10-kilogram RDX

[plastic explosive] charge. Army vehicles frequently use this particular road." In May 2002 "three ultras of Jaish-e-Mohammad outfit
were killed in an encounter during a joint operation by the police
and army in Lassana village in Poonch district." In November 2002
"four persons were killed when unidentified gunmen ambushed a
private vehicle near Lassana on the Rajouri-Poonch road."[56]

Chaudhary Aslam, a courtly man in his sixties, greeted us
warmly in his heavily fortified and guarded hilltop farmhouse.
Currently senior vice president of the Congress party in IJK, he
has had a long, distinguished career in IJK's political establishment. At various times over three decades he has been education
minister, agriculture minister, speaker of the IJK legislative assembly, and president of the Congress party in IJK. "Nobody wants
Pakistan here," he assured me with an air of confidence. If any
Gujjars provide food, shelter, or intelligence to insurgents, or act
as their guides and couriers, he said, the reason was *majboori se*
(they are threatened or coerced into doing so) or else *garibi se* (because of poverty, they give some assistance for money). But, I
asked, was it not a fact that some Gujjar youth had actually joined
the insurgents? "Yes," he replied with a pained look, "the rhetoric
of *jehad* has had some effect, unfortunately."

It was only after our meeting over a delicious breakfast of meat,
bread, and cheese that I discovered that Chaudhary Aslam's own
antecedents are more fluid than he might like to acknowledge.
During the 1947–1948 fighting in Rajouri and Poonch, Aslam's father, a Gujjar notable called Chaudhary Ghulam Hussein, sided
with Pakistan and migrated to the Pakistani side of the ceasefire
line in early 1949. He returned in 1954, under an amnesty law
passed by Sheikh Abdullah's government, after which his son em-
barked on his career as an Indian politician. But the allegiances of
the next generation of Gujjars had once again, apparently, be-

come indeterminate. Aslam did not disclose to me that one of his nephews was a guerrilla in the area. In September 2002 Aslam was sharing a dais with senior Congress leaders at a party rally in Surankote town when guerrillas attacked the town's bus stand a stone's throw away, killing sixteen people, mostly Indian security personnel.

About two hundred kilometers north of Poonch, guerrilla war continues in Kupwara, the Kashmir Valley's most infiltration-prone district. In late April 2002 I visited Kupwara's remote and picturesque Lolaab valley, a militant redoubt close to the LOC. A Lolaab village, Trehgam, is the birthplace of Maqbool Butt, co-founder of JKLF in the 1960s. The atmosphere was tense. The previous day nine HM guerrillas had died in a battle with the army in the neighboring Nowgam sector of Kupwara district's Handwara *tehsil*. Eight of the slain militants were natives of Kupwara villages, the ninth a guest fighter from Pakistan.[57] We drove out of Kupwara town and through the checkpoint at the army's Zangli garrison, the entry point to the sprawling Lolaab valley. As we entered the Pothushahi forest area of Lolaab, we saw SOG and army personnel engaged in a major crackdown in a village called Wavoora. The next day we discovered that we had witnessed mopping-up operations after a "LeT battalion commander, Farmanullah of Pakistan, was killed in an encounter with Army and Special Operations Group of local police at Pothushahi forest in Lolaab area of Kupwara district."[58] We continued toward Sogam, the only town in Lolaab, through an idyllic landscape of farming villages and orchards watered by mountain streams. We drove along rural back roads saturated with military vehicle traffic and Nepalese Gurkha soldiers on foot patrol alongside peasants driving *tongas* (horse carts), and through peaceful-looking villages guarded by Ikhwanis, onetime guerrillas turned pro-India gunmen.

Sogam has a political history. A bastion of the historic National Conference, it was a major center of the Quit Kashmir movement of 1946 (see Chapter 1) and the site of mass arrests. An atmosphere of repression and fear still prevailed in Sogam fifty-six years later. In late June 2002 insurgents fired rifle grenades at the house of Sogam's representative in the IJK legislature, Mushtaq Ahmed Lone, a minister in the NC government. Lone was in Srinagar, but his elderly parents were in the house. The attack injured five CRPF paramilitary police posted on guard duty, two seriously. In September 2002 Lone was assassinated along with five bodyguards in a Lolaab village while campaigning for reelection to the assembly. One civilian also died in the attack, and twelve others were injured, four critically.[59] The minister's funeral in Sogam, attended by various Indian dignitaries who flew into the remote area, was marred by guerrillas firing heavy machine guns and rocket-propelled grenades from the surrounding hills. Indeed, "when personnel of the J&K police stood for the guard of honor" before the minister's coffin, "their bugles and gunshots were drowned in the noise of militant fire," and two soldiers were killed and five wounded while fighting guerrillas who attempted to storm the funeral site.[60]

On the way back from Sogam to Kupwara town, we stopped for tea at the residence of Lolaab's chief forest officer. It turned out that the officer, in his fifties, had served four years in jail, from 1989 to 1993, for being a member of the pro-Pakistan People's League. In mid-July 2002 five fighters of Jamiat-ul Mujahideen, a guerrilla group, were killed in another bout of fighting in the Nowgam sector's forests. In late July the Indian army shot dead four HM militants, including two AJK residents, who were trying to infiltrate the LOC in Kupwara. In mid-August three LeT guerrillas were killed in an encounter in the Lolaab valley, during which a SOG operative named Farid Khan was injured.[61] Further violence took place in the town of Sogam in the final months of 2002, including a bomb blast that killed six paramilitary troopers in October and the assassination of murdered minister Mushtaq Lone's brother, a surrendered former guerrilla leader, in December.

On India's independence day, 15 August 2002, Indian counterinsurgency authorities in Srinagar announced that 1,052 "terrorists" had been eliminated between 1 January and 15 August 2002, compared with 1,059 during the corresponding period in 2001 (by 30 November 2002 the number of "terrorists" eliminated during the year had climbed to 1,581). It was also disclosed that 1,012 AK rifles, 1,179 kilograms of RDX and other explosive material, and 317 wireless sets had been recovered from January–August 2002, compared with 880 AK rifles, 651 kilograms of bomb-making material, and 291 radios captured during January–August 2001.[62]

The human tragedy of a dehumanized conflict continues. The Bakshi family live in Srinagar's central Batamaloo district, a "separatist" stronghold. Of the family's three sons, one, Showkat, a pioneer JKLF militant, was in prison continuously from 1990 until late 2002; another, Shakeel, a junior APHC leader, is also incarcerated; and the third, Shariq, lost his life fighting Indian forces. The Bhat family are from Tral, an HM-influenced town in the Valley's south. The father, Mohammad Subhan Bhat, once a NC legislator, was killed by guerrillas in 1991. One of his two sons, Showkat, was also killed by guerrillas in 1994, and the other, Fayaz, a local government officer, was assassinated in late July 2002. Fayaz Bhat had been shortlisted by the NC as a possible party candidate from Tral in IJK elections scheduled for the autumn of 2002. After his death, Ghulam Hassan Jan, Tral zonal president of NC, became the party's top prospective candidate. Jan had been living in Srinagar for years because Tral was too unsafe. In early August 2002 he was shot dead in central Srinagar. Tral's previous NC zonal president had also been assassinated. And Ghulam Hassan Jan's younger brother, Ghulam Nabi Jan, who in the mid-1990s "began helping security forces in anti-militancy operations" in the Tral area, in the late 1990s was "killed along with twelve others [pro-India guerrillas] when militants blew up his vehicle in a IED blast."[63]

Lessons of Conflict

The history of thirteen years of war in Kashmir suggests three conclusions.

First, the policies of the Indian state have been crucial to the eruption, spread, decline, and renewal of insurgency. The Pakistani state's manipulative and malign interventions have also had an important effect on the trajectory of conflict, but the Indian state's role has been crucial to both the shaping of the "internal" conflict and its radicalization and trans-nationalization. According to the figures of India's own counterinsurgency command, in the first eight months of 1999 its forces killed 617 guerrillas, of whom 167 were "foreigners" (27 percent) from outside IJK (the "foreigner" count includes residents of AJK). During the first eight months of 2000, 941 guerrillas were slain, of whom 261 (28 percent) were such foreigners.[64] This implies a local-to-"foreigner" ratio of approximately 70 percent to 30 percent in guerrilla ranks. The war in Kashmir, even in its *fidayeen* phase, is not reducible to simply a problem of "cross-border" terrorism and infiltration fomented from and/or by Pakistan. The onus of any process to develop a peaceful approach to the Kashmir conflict thus falls primarily on India, and secondarily on Pakistan.

Second, the society and politics of IJK, the principal arena of the conflict, are remarkably complex. This is a richly diverse, multi-textured society with *matryoshka*-doll layers of political complexity. A cacophony of intersecting and competing tunes, rather than a single melody, is the result of this social and political plurality. The unitary-sounding categories of "self-determination" and "the Kashmiri people" are overly simplistic when the "self" is in fact differentiated, if not fractured, into multiple social groups and contending political segments with very different aspirations. The sources of the Kashmir conflict are multiple, and require a sophisticated approach.

Third, the "internal" and "international" dimensions of the Kashmir conflict are inextricably entangled. This was the case in 1947, and remains the case in a different political context more than half a century later. In November 2001 Professor Mohammad Ibrahim, head of the conservative Jama'at-i-Islami party in Pakistan's North-West Frontier Province, sat in the Hadiqat-ul-Uloom *madrasa* (seminary) in Peshawar and ruminated on the struggle in Kashmir after the defeat of the Taliban in neighboring Afghanistan: "We consider Kashmir part of Pakistan. Afghanistan was another country. I expect the Government of Pakistan to help the Kashmiri people against Indian tyranny." Meanwhile, outside the *madrasa*, "Karamat Ullah, general secretary of Hizb-ul Mujahideen, was talking to young men sitting around the grounds or playing cricket. Many were recruits heading for training in Kashmir— courses of one month and three months are standard—or were coming or going from the war-zone. Karamat Ullah said that 500 to 600 members of his organization crossed the frontier dividing

Indian and Pakistani forces in Kashmir every month, many rotating in or out in advance of winter closure of passes."[65]

In late July 2002 militant spokesmen in Pakistani Kashmir's capital, Muzaffarabad, were admitting that in response to Indian threats of war and American pressure, General Pervez Musharraf's government had "sharply curtailed" their activities in AJK. But, a HM source pointed out, "we have many mobile training camps in the hills and forests of [Indian] Kashmir where youths are trained . . . [and] we have munitions stockpiled over the years. The recent series of attacks on Indian forces [inside IJK] is proof that we are capable of continuing our struggle."[66] In late August 2002 Sheikh Jameel-ur Rehman, general secretary of the United Jihad Council, an alliance of over a dozen *tanzeems* active in IJK, asserted that "during the past thirteen years we have never sought permission from Indian soldiers to cross the ceasefire line and we do not need permission from Pakistani soldiers either," pointing out that the region's topography facilitates infiltration and exfiltration at many points of almost a thousand kilometers of frontier—740 kilometers of LOC and another 200 kilometers of "working boundary" on Indian Jammu's southwestern border with Pakistan.[67] The "cross-border" character of the Kashmir conflict is therefore an inescapable reality. In the long run, the only solution to cross-border violence lies in institutionalized ties of cross-border cooperation.

4

SOVEREIGNTY IN DISPUTE

Kashmir is neither an integral part of India nor the jugular
vein of Pakistan, but a disputed territory which requires a
solution through talks. Kashmir belongs to all the residents
of the [pre-1948] undivided state [of Jammu and Kashmir].

—GHULAM MOHAMMED SHAH,
former chief minister of IJK, July 2002

AT ITS CORE, the Kashmir conflict is a dispute
over sovereignty. It is a sovereignty dispute defined by the mutually reinforcing intersection of "domestic" and "international"
sources of conflict. At the international level, sovereignty over the
territory and people of Jammu and Kashmir is disputed between
the states of India and Pakistan. The international dimension of
conflict is complemented, and compounded, by sharply different
preferences on the sovereignty question *within* the contested territory. Inside Kashmir, the two state-centered claims to sovereignty
have a rival in a third conception of sovereignty, a construct of in-

dependentist ideology, which argues that sovereignty resides in neither New Delhi nor Islamabad but with the citizens of Jammu and Kashmir. The crux of the contemporary Kashmir problem is this three-way disagreement over the legitimate locus and unit of sovereignty. For purposes of sovereignty, citizenship, and governance, are the legitimate borders India including its "integral part," Pakistan including its "jugular vein," or an independent Jammu and Kashmir separate from both countries? In their maximalist versions, these claims are mutually exclusive. They permit no space or scope for meaningful dialogue, let alone any actual prospect of crafting a solution to the basic conflict.

What ways exist of establishing the legitimate borders of political community? Suggested approaches seem many and varied on superficial inspection, but practically all fall into one of two broad categories: plebiscitary or partitionist. Both approaches—and the different variants of each—are hobbled by political tunnel vision and underlying motivations of imposing the agenda of one of the contending parties as a definitive "solution" to the dispute. Neither type of approach provides a viable basis for transcending the internal and international antagonisms that cumulatively define the Kashmir stalemate. Both suffer from one or both of two salient flaws: a fixation on territory; and an unbending belief in the absolute legitimacy of one of the three nationalist (in the case of the Kashmir independentists, perhaps more accurately described as quasi-nationalist) perspectives and the rejection of competing perspectives as utterly illegitimate.

The Plebiscitary Approach

During the first decade of the Kashmir dispute, the sovereignty question was proposed to be settled "in accordance with the will of the people, expressed through the democratic method of a free and impartial plebiscite conducted under the auspices of the United Nations." Between 1948 and 1957 the U.N.'s Security Council repeatedly passed resolutions calling for such a process. A United Nations Commission for India and Pakistan (UNCIP) was established primarily to work with the two governments in organizing and administering a popular referendum to decide the key question of rightful sovereignty over the contested territory, and pending that exercise, a United Nations Military Observer Group (UNMOGIP) was set up to monitor the truce along the ceasefire line dividing Jammu and Kashmir into Indian- and Pakistani-controlled zones. A half-century later, a skeletal UNMOGIP of forty-five officers still operates on the Line of Control, but its white four-wheel-drive vehicles flying the blue standard of U.N. peacekeeping are a forlorn, less than token presence alongside hundreds of thousands of heavily armed troops massed on either side of the LOC. The promised plebiscite has long receded into distant memory.

Of the parties to the Kashmir dispute, India alone dismisses the plebiscite as irrelevant, obsolete, and unnecessary. Its foreign ministry's standard line is that "the question of plebiscite in any part of India, including Jammu and Kashmir, simply does not arise. The people of Jammu and Kashmir have exercised their democratic rights repeatedly, as have people in other parts of India."[1] This is a dubious stance. It appears to suggest that the people of Indian Jammu and Kashmir (IJK) have freely and voluntarily consented to be part of the Indian Union through participation in Indian-sponsored political processes and representation in Indian-sponsored institutions. The Security Council resolutions—notably those of March 1951 and January 1957—are unequivocal that such participation and representation could not be regarded as a substitute for an internationally supervised plebiscite. More important, the myth of freely and voluntarily given consent to Indian sovereignty is exploded by the appalling record of New Delhi–instigated subversion of democratic procedures and institutions and abuse of democratic rights in IJK over more than fifty years (recounted in Chapter 2). India's leaders exploited Pakistan's decision to join U.S.-sponsored Cold War security pacts as a pretext to openly renege on the plebiscite commitment as early as the mid-1950s, despite Prime Minister Nehru's flowery "pledge . . . not only to the people of Kashmir but to the world" to hold such a plebiscite.

That India's dismissal of the plebiscite is fundamentally opportunistic does not, however, detract from the reality that after more than fifty years of conflict, the plebiscite *is* indeed an obsolete idea. U.N. Secretary-General Kofi Annan admitted as much on a visit to the subcontinent in 2000, when he described the decades-old Security Council resolutions on Kashmir as unenforceable and essentially defunct. The United Nations does not deny that Kashmir is an unresolved international dispute, but its position is that it can consider playing a role in either mediating or facilitating a settlement only if both India and Pakistan agree to its participation. India is squarely opposed to such a role for the United Nations. Since India is one of the parties to the conflict, its absolute rejection of a plebiscite does render that option infeasible—effectively a non-option.

In contrast to India, both Pakistan and supporters of independent Kashmir continue to consider the plebiscite a relevant reference point. They do so motivated by subtly different considerations and agendas, however. For the state of Pakistan, the revisionist power in the territorial dispute over Kashmir, the existence of unfulfilled U.N. resolutions on Kashmir—unfulfilled, according to the Pakistani version, because of India's prevarications and duplicity—still constitutes the main, if tenuous, basis in international law for Pakistan's *locus standi* on Kashmir. Pakistani leaders and diplomats thus routinely invoke Security Council resolutions in ritual sparring with their Indian counterparts over Kashmir, just as Indian officials tend to emphasize the legality and finality of the maharaja's October 1947 accession of J&K to India—the linchpin of the Indian state's legal claim to Kashmir— at every opportunity. (In practice, Pakistani leaders, including General Musharraf, have indicated a willingness to pursue an intergovernmental peace process with India on Kashmir which is not straitjacketed by formal pronouncements such as the declaratory commitment to the principle of plebiscite.) This is partly a reflexive instinct conditioned by lengthy habituation, and partly a deliberate ploy intended to irritate the other country as much as possible. The established positions of the two countries are also somewhat ironic in light of history since it was originally India, and not Pakistan, that internationalized the Kashmir question before the United Nations by complaining to the world body about Pakistani-backed armed aggression to forcibly seize a territory that had legally acceded to India.

The Pakistani state's formal commitment to ascertaining the "will" or "aspirations" of the people of Jammu and Kashmir, through the implementation of U.N. Security Council resolutions, tacitly restricts that choice to the two practical options of 1947— India or Pakistan. This state-centered, legalistic interpretation of the "right to self-determination" is significantly different from the highly populist version articulated by proponents of an independent Kashmir. These proponents—a fractured and fractious collection of factions and personalities in both IJK and Pakistani-controlled "Azad" Jammu and Kashmir (AJK)—seek to give voice to a popularly based, largely inchoate but nonetheless resilient sentiment that feels it has been systematically stifled and denied by India and cruelly used and manipulated by Pakistan.

In historical terms, this ideology is descended from the Jacobin conception of popular sovereignty coined by the National Conference in the 1940s (see Chapter 1), and it has a powerful resonance among a very large segment of J&K's population, especially in the Kashmir Valley. In its pristine form, this alternative conception of sovereignty is expressed in the text of a declaration adopted by the independentist Jammu and Kashmir Liberation Front (JKLF) at a public meeting held in the AJK town of Mirpur on 5 January 1995: "Jammu & Kashmir State as it existed on 14 August 1947—including Indian-occupied areas, Azad Kashmir, and Gilgit and Baltistan—is an indivisible political entity. No solution not approved by a majority of the people of the entire State as a single unit will be accepted."[2] For adherents of this view, the preferred mechanism for resolving the sovereignty question is a referendum with three options on the ballot—India, Pakistan, and an independent, reunified state of Jammu and Kashmir—the outcome to be decided by a simple majority of the electorate.[3]

This view on the sovereignty conundrum and how it ought to be resolved is more democratic than the two state-sponsored versions, for it at least vests the right to decide squarely in the people of Kashmir. It is, however, infeasible as a political agenda because India is against a plebiscite in principle, while Pakistan's advocacy of U.N. resolutions appears to be a tactical device deployed in wrangling with India, rather than indicative of a genuine commitment. In any case, Pakistan is at least as hostile as India to the concept of an independent Kashmir, as manifested in its treatment of independentist groups in AJK and the Northern Areas and in the concerted attempts by the Pakistani military and its intelligence agencies to turn the independentist uprising in IJK into a movement dominated by pro-Pakistan elements (see Chapter 3). Although a referendum on sovereignty is a historically legitimate idea, the reality is that India would never agree to any kind of plebiscite, while Pakistan would like any such exercise to be conducted on its original terms—that is, excluding the "third option" of independence. In the mid-1990s in Srinagar, Syed Ali Shah Geelani, a prominent conservative Islamist in the Valley and the Hurriyat Conference's senior pro-Pakistan member, told me that a choice between independence and Pakistan would confuse and severely divide the Muslims of J&K, and he was probably correct.

The dogged advocates of the plebiscitary vision of independent Kashmir are generally aware of the hopelessness of their cause. But they persist in asserting their case at a declaratory level, for two reasons. First, this vision, however hopeless in practical terms, has immense romantic appeal and hence a certain political currency among a large segment of Jammu and Kashmir's population, not just in IJK but in AJK as well. In 1989 members of the Kashmir Liberation Cell, a research body supported by the Pakistan and AJK governments, presented an American scholar visiting Pakistani Kashmir with maps depicting the entire pre-1948 princely state and "asserted with some fervor that this is what Jammu and Kashmir was before and will be again when we are independent." The scholar rightly concluded that "it is not only India that has cause for concern about the future of its relationship with Kashmir."[4]

The urge to *azaadi* (freedom) and *khudmukhtari* (self-rule) has a long and distinguished historical lineage, associated with the politics of the National Conference in the 1940s, the Plebiscite Front between the mid-1950s and the mid-1970s, the People's League in the 1980s, and the JKLF in the 1990s. The forms of struggle have varied over time, but in one form or another this tenacious urge has defined politics in Kashmir for the past six decades. The evidence suggests that it can be suppressed but not extinguished. Even if the demand for a plebiscite and the goal of an independent, reunified Kashmir are politically unrealizable aims, an honorable accommodation of the urge to *azaadi* and *khudmukhtari* is essential to any framework for democratically resolving the Kashmir question. That is the second reason why die-hard independentists such as the young JKLF leader Yasin Malik persist in articulating the maximalist argument for "self-determination." They feel they owe it to their political forebears, their people, and their "martyrs" not to allow this important element in Kashmir's political life to be marginalized and destroyed by state-led authoritarianism.

The independentist vision is, however, potentially as intolerant as the repressive state-led nationalisms it opposes. In an uncanny replication of Indian and Pakistani official nationalisms—which in their maximalist versions claim Kashmir to be *atoot ang* (integral part) and *shah rag* (jugular vein) of their respective states—independentists also subscribe to an idealized sacred geography, the territory of the pre-1948 princely state of Jammu and Kashmir. That "state" existed under British imperial power for barely a century (1846–1947) and cobbled together diverse regions and ethnic and religious communities under a despotic, semi-feudal monarchy (see Chapter 1). It is not at all clear why a territory with a relatively brief and distinctly undistinguished genealogy of "statehood" should be elevated to a sacrosanct status. Such an ideological doctrine smacks of the same syndrome—fetishization of "territorial integrity" and a rigid, monolithic conception of sovereignty—characteristic of state-led nationalist stances on the Kashmir question.

The flaw inherent in the independentist perspective—and in

the mechanism proposed for its actualization, the plebiscite decided by majority vote—is all the more acute because Jammu and Kashmir is a territory fractured along the most fundamental and intractable of fault lines: national identity and state allegiance. The Indian and Pakistani states and the independentist tendency each have the allegiance of segments of the population. On the smaller, less populous Pakistani side of the LOC, the population is divided among those strongly loyal to Pakistani nationalism and the Pakistani state and those who support independentist or at least autonomist politics. In IJK, two national identities (Indian and Pakistani) and one quasi-national identity (Kashmiri independentist), and the three accompanying political orientations, exist with mutually incompatible notions of the meaning of "self-determination."

The plebiscitary formula is blind to the *matryoshka*-doll complexity of political allegiances in IJK. In a hypothetical referendum, the Kashmir Valley would probably return a strong pro-independence majority, but even in this region, a significant minority consisting of Hindu (the Pandits) as well as Muslim citizens (especially the Gujjar and Shia minorities) would vote for India, while another sizeable minority of Muslim citizens would vote for Pakistan. The Jammu region, whose population is almost two-thirds Hindu, would probably produce a strong pro-India majority overall, but Muslim-dominated districts within the region (Doda, Rajouri, Poonch) might well vote differently or at least return a more mixed verdict, while predominantly non-Muslim enclaves within these Muslim-majority districts (such as the towns of Rajouri and Poonch and the town of Bhaderwah in Doda district, all of which are dominated by Hindus plus Sikhs) would probably vote differently from the rest of their areas. "Self-determination" for "the Kashmiri people" sounds distinctly unitary, while the reality is an extremely plural society where the "self" is fractured on the most basic questions of identity and allegiance.

In such a complex situation, a plebiscitary approach is not just deeply simplistic and inadequate but, potentially, deeply destabilizing. In IJK, the crucial arena of the Kashmir problem, any attempt to impose one of the three perspectives on sovereignty on the other two segments of the population is a recipe for conflict, repression, and violence, as the past and present of authoritarian Indian policy in IJK clearly reveals. A majoritarian plebiscite, the most direct method of settling a sovereignty question, is by its very nature a winner-take-all mechanism. It has been pointed out that such referenda "cannot measure intensities of belief" and preclude "working things out through discussion."[5] In a deeply volatile context such as Kashmir's, where different segments of the population hold intense, sharply conflicting beliefs about the legitimate borders of sovereign authority, a plebiscitary approach is bound to have inflammatory, polarizing consequences. In fact, it is more than likely to herald a short countdown to all-out civil war.

The sovereignty dispute that led to bitter civil war in Bosnia and Herzegovina (BiH) from 1992 to 1995 had a configuration similar to that of the problem in Kashmir. When the federal state of Yugoslavia, of which BiH was one of six units, disintegrated in 1991 as Croatia and Slovenia seceded, the political future of Bosnia became an open and explosive question. Among Yugoslavia's units, BiH had by far the most mixed, multinational population— its 4.4 million people approximately 45 percent "Bosniac" (Bosnian Muslim), 35 percent Bosnian Serb, and 18 percent Bosnian Croat. Broadly speaking, most Bosnian Serbs wanted BiH to remain within a shrunken, Serbia-dominated Yugoslav union, while most Bosnian Muslims increasingly favored a sovereign Bosnian state.

The third community, the Bosnian Croats, were also by and large against Bosnia remaining within a rump Yugoslavia dominated by Serbia, and were increasingly influenced by the virulent nationalist politics of newly independent Croatia, whose secession from Yugoslavia in mid-1991 sparked an armed revolt by Croatia's own Serb minority. At the urging of an arbitration commission established by the European Union (EU) to deal with the conflicting claims to "self-determination" that arose with the unraveling of Yugoslavia, a referendum on sovereignty was organized in BiH on 29 February and 1 March 1992. Sixty-three percent of the eligible electorate participated, and 98 percent of these voters supported the independence option.

There were a couple of deadly problems with this apparently straightforward outcome. First, the referendum was massively boycotted by Bosnian Serbs, who disagreed strongly with its very premise. But the referendum nonetheless provided the basis for international recognition of Bosnia's independent status in early April 1992. Within weeks the radicalized Bosnian Serbs launched a large-scale military campaign to seize control of as much of BiH as possible, with the moral and material support of the government of Serbia and the by then largely Serb-controlled army of federal Yugoslavia, the Yugoslav People's Army. In the summer of 1992 BiH descended into full-fledged civil war, as Bosnian Serb forces ruthlessly overran two-thirds of the newly independent state in a matter of months, "ethnically cleansing" hundreds of thousands of Muslims and Croats from these territories, and besieged the capital, Sarajevo.

The second problem became evident by early 1993. Most Bosnian Croats had voted for independence not because of a commitment shared with Muslims to a united state of Bosnia and Herzegovina, but as a tactical move to ensure that BiH would be separated from what remained of the Yugoslav federation after the departure of Slovenia and Croatia. The Muslim-Croat alliance which won the referendum in 1992 dissolved chaotically during the first few months of 1993. It became clear that Bosnian Croat nationalists had viewed that alliance in purely tactical terms, as a stepping-stone to their own vision of a "Greater Croatia" which would include sizeable Croat-populated regions of BiH. By April–May 1993 Bosnian Croat forces, with the full backing of the aggressively nationalist government of Croatia and its army, launched their own land-grab and expulsion campaign in certain regions of BiH, engulfing those regions in bitter warfare with Muslim forces. By the end of 1993 BiH had been effectively partitioned by war into three zones of military control and three national(ist) statelets. The sovereignty plebiscite had unleashed a series of events culminating in bloody partition. There are parallels with Kashmir here. Like Bosnia, Kashmir has three national/quasi-national identities and three rival allegiances/preferences on the sovereignty issue on the same territory. As in Kashmir, the internal Bosnian conflict was severely compounded by the external regional/international dimension, which involved two larger and aggressively nationalist neighboring states (Serbia-Montenegro and Croatia), both with territorial interests and strongly motivated groups of co-nationals in Bosnia and Herzegovina.[6]

The Bosnian case suggests that a plebiscitary approach is not just inappropriate but positively dangerous for Kashmir, which is also the site of a complex and volatile sovereignty dispute with inseparable internal and international dimensions. The complexity and sensitivity of the Kashmir problem call for tools of surgical precision, not the blunt instrument of plebiscitary majoritarianism. A plebiscitary approach guarantees a winner-take-all outcome. This has the inevitable effect of inflaming and sharpening the fundamental conflict over the legitimate unit and locus of sovereignty.

Even in societies where the potential for violence is not as pronounced as in Bosnia or Kashmir, plebiscites have a polarizing effect. In October 1995 an independence referendum in Quebec was defeated by the narrowest of margins, 50.4 percent to 49.6 percent. Almost 60 percent of Quebec's Francophone majority (who make up 80 percent of the total population) voted for secession from Canada, and they were barely thwarted by the "no" vote cast by the very large anti-independence minority among the Francophones and the 20 percent of Quebecers who are Anglophone or members of the Native American communities. Prior to the referendum, the Native American groups who inhabit vast, sparsely populated tracts of northern Quebec held parallel referenda—much like the Serb communities of Croatia and Bosnia in 1991–1992—and overwhelmingly affirmed their desire to remain in a united Canada. A very volatile situation would have ensued had the outcome of the referendum been exactly the reverse—50.4 percent in favor of independence, 49.6 percent against (a difference of fewer than fifty thousand votes). Half the citizenry would then have triumphantly celebrated the dawn of "freedom," while the other half would have felt insecure and quite possibly furious at the prospect of a change in sovereignty against their will.

In a society divided along the crucial fault line of national identity and state allegiance which is also the subject of an inter-state sovereignty dispute, the basic thrust of peace-building must be *not* to further inflame and polarize, but to devise a framework that can turn the competing, mutually antagonistic political logics of the contending parties into a positive-sum game. In Northern Ireland, a good example of such a society, the peace process based on

the Good Friday Agreement of April 1998 has sought to imple
ment precisely such a broadly based, accommodative settlement.
The Northern Ireland model involves three key elements: devolution of power from London to Belfast; a broadly inclusive, power-
sharing regime in Northern Ireland with equal representation in
government for parties representing the pro-British (Unionist) and
pro-Irish (Nationalist) communities; and cross-border institutional
arrangements linking Northern Ireland, which remains under
British sovereignty, with the Republic of Ireland. This multidimensional solution to a centuries-old intractable conflict has been enabled and is reinforced by the developing confederalization of Europe under the aegis of the EU, which both the United Kingdom
and the Republic of Ireland joined in the early 1970s.

The Good Friday agreement has retained one potentially troublesome plebiscitary provision, however. It stipulates that British
sovereignty over Northern Ireland will not yield to Irish sovereignty (that is, a unified Ireland) unless and until a majority in
Northern Ireland ratify such a change in a referendum. This effectively puts the prospect of such a change in cold storage for some
years to come, since demographic projections show that the pro-
British Protestant population will continue to be a thin majority
of Northern Ireland's population for at least another decade. If
the pro-unification Catholic population becomes the majority in
Northern Ireland, nonetheless, a sovereignty change effected via
majoritarian plebiscite will still be rife with inflammatory possibilities in a society which continues to be fractured on the basic fault
line of national identity and state allegiance.

Ultimately, a consideration of the plebiscitary approach provides a compelling lesson on how *not* to go about attempting to
untangle a complex sovereignty dispute in and over a territory
such as Jammu and Kashmir.

The Partitionist Approach

The partitionist approach to resolving the Kashmir conflict comes in a variety of forms and from diverse quarters. In a way, the partitionist approach represents the logical opposite of the plebiscitary approach. The plebiscitary approach is either in denial of or insufficiently sensitive to the complexity of political allegiances and preferences on the disputed territory. The partitionist approach seeks to respond to such complexities by drawing or redrawing the borders of political community and sovereignty in ways that are claimed to be more conducive to prospects of peace and stability. In fact, the partitionist proposals fall far short of that promise. They tend to be unviable in practical terms, and dangerous in that they threaten to aggravate rather than resolve conflict.

The simplest variant of this approach is the idea of converting the Line of Control that divides the Indian and Pakistani parts of Jammu and Kashmir into a de jure international border between the two countries. The LOC, which originated in January 1949 as a ceasefire line between the Indian and Pakistani armies at the end of their first war over Kashmir, shifted only slightly in subsequent military conflicts in 1965 and 1971, and was renamed the Line of Control—to be "respected by both sides without prejudice to the recognized position [on the Kashmir dispute] of either side"—by the Simla Agreement concluded between the leaders of the two countries in 1972. The larger and significantly more populous part of Jammu and Kashmir lies on the Indian side of the LOC, making India the status quo power in the Kashmir dispute and Pakistan the revisionist power. For decades, Indian leaders have sought to convert the border drawn in blood through Jammu and Kashmir in 1947–1948 into a legal, permanent international frontier. As discussed in Chapters 1 and 2, India's prime minister Nehru suggested such a "solution" to his Pakistani counterpart in the mid-1950s, and indeed may have first broached the subject as early as late 1948. Pakistani leaders from Liaquat Ali Khan to Mohammed Ali Bogra to Pervez Musharraf have always rejected the suggestion vehemently. In the autumn of 2002, asked whether he was amenable to dividing Jammu and Kashmir along the Line of Control, Musharraf tersely replied: *"Main bewkoof nahin hoon* [I am not an idiot]."[7]

Converting the LOC into the juridical boundary between India and Pakistan is not the official Indian stand on the Kashmir dispute. Formally, India claims the entire territory of the pre-1948 princely state of Jammu and Kashmir and refers to the portion beyond the Line of Control as "Pakistan-occupied Kashmir," which it claims rightfully belongs to India under the instrument of accession signed by the maharaja of Kashmir in late 1947. For practical purposes, however, official India harbors no illusions about the possibility of recovering these territories, and would ideally like the de facto territorial status quo to be given the stamp of permanent, juridical legitimacy.[8]

This Indian stance is at once astonishingly naïve and cynically unconstructive. No Pakistani regime or leader can or will accept turning the LOC into part of the India-Pakistan border as the starting point or defining element of a political dialogue with India on Kashmir, since such acceptance would preempt the basis of the international dispute over Kashmir on India's preferred terms. Without the agreement of Pakistan—the party on the other side of the fence, quite literally—no stabilization of or change to the LOC's status is possible. The LOC is without doubt one of the most important and difficult issues in the Kashmir conflict, but it is appropriately the subject of "final-status" talks, at an advanced stage of a comprehensive, multidimensional peace process.

I believe that either redrawing or erasing the LOC is not only practically impossible but unnecessary as well as undesirable for a democratic compromise on Kashmir—although the de facto border's meaning and character would need to be redefined, and the line itself probably renamed, as part of such a compromise. However, official India's inordinate interest in sealing the LOC as the de jure international frontier amounts to putting the cart before the horse—in the absence of any apparent willingness on India's part to meaningfully engage the multiple dimensions of the Kashmir problem at either internal or international levels—and smacks of a tactic intended to eliminate the possibility of any meaningful dialogue on the Kashmir question. As an opening gambit, the Indian perspective on the LOC is unacceptable not just to Pakistan but to several million people in IJK, supplemented by a sizeable number in AJK, who favor an independent Kashmir. Permanently partitioning Kashmir along the LOC would do nothing to address India's core problem in IJK—the existence of very large numbers of citizens who do not accept the legitimacy of Indian sovereignty over their lives and land. Official India's apparent preoccupation with the LOC reveals that its perspective on the Kashmir conflict is narrowly fixated on territorial control. This is a recipe for international stalemate and continued "internal" conflict, not peace.

If India's myopic status quo partitionism is destructive to prospects of moving toward peace in Kashmir, so is any brand of revisionist partitionism that may enjoy currency in Pakistan. It is difficult to cite hard evidence for the latter type of agenda, which is practically never expressed publicly or explicitly. However, there is a widespread perception in India, shared by some observers in Western countries, that elements of the Pakistani elite would really prefer a redrawing of the LOC in a way that is, in a Pakistani view, more balanced and fairer to Pakistan. For example, the

Kashmir Valley, with its overwhelming Muslim majority, could become part of Pakistan, in exchange for which Pakistan might withdraw any claim on the rest of IJK, including substantial Muslim-majority areas in the Jammu region and in Ladakh (the Kargil district). This variant of partitionism, driven by irredentist motives of territorial aggrandizement, is utterly bankrupt and fantastic. The Indian state cannot and will not cede *any* part of IJK, including (indeed perhaps especially) the Valley, to Pakistan. Moreover, the bulk of the Valley's population is attached to the idea of independence, not integration into Pakistan, and although pro-*azaadi* feelings are especially deep-rooted and widespread in the Valley, a minority of the Valley's Muslims (and, of course, its small Hindu minority) continue to identify with India. The *Kashmir banega Pakistan* (Kashmir will become Pakistan) ideology has resonance with only one of three segments, also a minority, of the Valley's population. Revisionist partitionism of the kind just described is thus doubly untenable. It is unacceptable to the Indian state, and it is not consistent with the first-order preferences of most people in the Valley, the most coveted real estate in Kashmir.

In 2001–2002 the leader of Pakistan's military regime on more than one occasion outlined his vision of a South Asian peace process: "The first step should be the resumption of peaceful dialogue. The second should be to accept Kashmir as a central issue. The third is to negate any solution that is not acceptable to both the countries. The fourth is to apply what remains of a solution according to the wishes of Kashmiris."[9] Although this is a somewhat simple, even glib statement, it has its positive points. The characterization of Kashmir as "a central issue," rather than "the core issue" of India-Pakistan relations (the preferred Pakistani terminology), appears to be an attempt to assuage Indian complaints about an alleged Pakistani fixation on Kashmir. The third element—a frank recognition that any "solution" will have to be a compromise between contending maximalist ambitions—is genuinely promising. Taken at face value, it effectively eliminates a number of so-called solutions from the slate, including the chimerical prospect of any negotiated repartition of Kashmir that would involve revision of borders and a transfer of some areas from de facto Indian sovereignty to de facto Pakistani sovereignty.

Alternative partitionist formulas are equally untenable. The idea of making the Valley—the region of J&K where support for "self-determination" is most developed and widespread—a fully sovereign unit has been bandied about from time to time.[10] This sort of proposal is not feasible, since it would be seen as an intolerable loss of territorial integrity and sovereignty by Indian state elites and the vast majority of the Indian public, and a fully sovereign authority in any part of the disputed territory would probably not be regarded as acceptable by Pakistani elites either. But there are other problems as well. A sovereign Kashmir Valley would include a significant minority of Muslims whose basic loyalty is to Pakistan, and another sizeable minority of Hindus, Sikhs, and Muslims (especially among the Valley's minority Shia Muslims and ethnic Gujjars) whose national identity is ultimately with India. The pro-India group would be likely to see themselves as "orphans of secession," and would probably migrate permanently from their homeland rather than put up with such a "solution."[11] The pro-Pakistan segment would perhaps see such an outcome as merely a stepping-stone to a merger with Pakistan, somewhat like the nationalist Croats of Bosnia and Herzegovina during the Bosnian war.

A sovereign Kashmir Valley would thus not only *include* groups who consider their fundamental rights violated, indeed negated, but also *exclude* people who identify or sympathize with the independentist agenda. For example, a pro-independence population exists among the Kashmiri-speaking Muslims of Doda district (as does a pro-Pakistan element), in the Jammu region, and to a lesser extent possibly also in other Muslim-dominated areas of Jammu like Rajouri, Poonch, and highland areas of Udhampur district. An independent Kashmir Valley would thus create "stranded" communities both within and without, because of the *matryoshka*-doll complexity of political allegiances, a "problem" that can only be "solved" through large-scale population transfers. That situation would carry a high potential for sectarian violence and reciprocal expulsions in numerous locales, which could lead to a much bigger conflagration involving India and Pakistan. If the Pakistani-controlled AJK districts across the LOC from IJK were not included in any sovereign entity centered on the Kashmir Valley, a sizeable pro-independence population in AJK would be left out. However, if these districts were included, a possibly even larger population in AJK whose basic allegiance is to Pakistan would have to become unwilling citizens of a sovereign entity dominated demographically and politically by Valley Kashmiris whose spoken language (Kashmiri not Punjabi) and political traditions are very different from those of AJK.

"Solutions" premised primarily on a territorial fixation are not just infeasible given the constraints of realpolitik and the entrenched interests of states, but also are unviable because of the sheer complexity and multi-layered differentiation of political allegiances in Kashmir. Another example of such a misguided "solution" is that of a U.S.-based group financed by a wealthy Kashmiri-American businessman and consisting mainly of retired American diplomats and academics. This group has published a document which "recommend[s] that a portion of the former princely state of Jammu and Kashmir be reconstituted as a sovereign entity."[12]

The document does not precisely specify the intended "portion." However, during an invitation-only conference at a university in the United States that I attended in May 2000, the group's sponsor circulated maps specifying the area in question, which encompassed the Kashmir Valley, all of Poonch district in IJK's Jammu region, most of Rajouri district, all of Doda district, parts of Udhampur district, and all of the Kargil district in Ladakh. According to the plan presented, this area would either be one of two "sovereign" Kashmir entities, the other being Pakistani-controlled AJK, or, preferably, the greater part of a single, amalgamated entity including the AJK districts.

This proposal shares the crippling problems of territorially fixated, partitionist ideas in general. In addition, the attempt to expand the boundaries of the "sovereign entity" beyond the core area of the Kashmir Valley—which is itself not as socially and politically homogeneous as the proposal presumes—to cover certain Jammu and Ladakh districts renders it even more precarious. These areas of Jammu and Ladakh are included in the territory of the putative sovereign state apparently on the grounds that they are predominantly Muslim, Kashmiri-speaking, or both. The social and political realities are infinitely more complicated. The Kargil district of Ladakh is indeed populated mainly by Shia Muslims, but its social history and political dynamics are distinct from those of the Valley. The cry for self-determination, which has a huge popular base in the Valley, does not have discernible support in Kargil. Unlike the Valley's Kashmiri-speaking population, the Muslim communities of the Jammu region's war-torn border districts of Rajouri and Poonch (see Chapter 3) belong mostly to non-Kashmiri-speaking ethnic groups like Rajputs, Gujjars and Bakerwals, and Pathans, and have ethnolinguistic, geographic, and political distance from the Valley. Their allegiances cannot

be taken for granted by Indians, Pakistanis, or Kashmir independentists. Moreover, significant non-Muslim minorities live in
Rajouri-Poonch. The towns of Rajouri and Poonch (unlike the
districts as a whole) are dominated by Hindus together with a
considerable sprinkling of Sikhs.

The Muslim majority in the Jammu region's Doda district are
principally Kashmiri speakers who share an ethnic identity and
close political affinities with the Valley. However, Muslims are
only 57 percent of Doda district's population. The other 43 percent consists of Hindus together with some Sikhs. Of the three
towns in the district, Doda has a Kashmiri-speaking Muslim majority (and a sizeable Hindu minority), Bhaderwah has a majority
of Hindus (and a large Muslim minority), and Kishtwar's population is evenly split between Muslims and non-Muslims, principally
Hindus.

The scenic and historic mountain town of Kishtwar is in a way
a microcosm of the complexity of the Kashmir problem. Its rugged hinterland, dotted with remote villages (some Hindu, some
Muslim), is a major theater of war between India's army and paramilitary forces and tenacious guerrilla formations, whose fighters
are mostly locally recruited young men intermixed with a significant "foreign" *jehadi* element. One of the first massacres of
Hindu civilians in Kashmir took place on a mountain road near
the town in August 1993, when a local bus was stopped by gunmen and sixteen Hindu passengers lined up and shot dead. Despite such provocations, the president of the Doda district unit of
the Hindu nationalist Bharatiya Janata Party (BJP), a resident of
Kishtwar town, told me in 1995 that locals belonging to different confessional communities still had a degree of tolerance and
respect for each other. He indicated that this was both a tradition and a practical compulsion, given the town's population mix.

However, a conversation with him in the garden of the local *dak bungalow* (rest house), followed by an interview with the pro-independence *imam* (chief preacher) of the town's ornate mosque and a cross-section of Muslim citizens in a house on one of the winding lanes of the Muslim residential quarter, made it amply clear to me that this town was a powder keg—deeply divided in fundamental political allegiances and preferences. As I returned to the *dak bungalow* for the night, I passed rows of Muslim and Hindu shops standing cheek by jowl on the dusty main street, already eerily deserted because the nightly curfew was about to begin.

The example of Kishtwar illustrates particularly vividly why both plebiscitary and partitionist approaches—both fixated on territory and premised on a belief in the absolute legitimacy of one view of self-determination to the exclusion of its competitors—are deeply inappropriate ways of dealing with the Kashmir problem. In February 2002 "unidentified militants appeared near the dak bungalow in Kishtwar and hurled a grenade at the security picket guarding the bungalow. However, the grenade missed its target and exploded on the main street." One person was killed—a Muslim citizen. Of the thirteen other civilians seriously injured in the blast, six were Muslim and seven Hindu.[13] The future of Kishtwar—and of Kashmir—depends on devising a framework that can accommodate, however uneasily, the various contending preferences on sovereignty and self-determination. Plebiscitary and partitionist approaches both fundamentally violate the logic of that essential goal.

Yet another variant of partitionism is articulated by sectarian Hindu groups on the extreme right wing of Indian politics. Although their perspective on the Kashmir problem has remained essentially constant over more than five decades, their views have assumed greater importance than before because of the move of right-wing Hindu sectarianism from the margins to the center stage of Indian politics since 1990.[14] During 2002 the Vishwa Hindu Parishad (VHP, World Hindu Council), a zealot organization which has a worldwide network, adopted the following stance on Kashmir:

> VHP on Sunday demanded division of [Indian] Jammu & Kashmir into four parts including a separate enclave with union territory [that is, administered directly from New Delhi] status for resettling migrant Kashmiri Pandits [in the Kashmir Valley]. Alleging neglect, discrimination, injustice and deeply rooted bias against Jammu and Ladakh by successive regimes in Srinagar, VHP's central board demanded carving out of a separate state [of the Indian Union] comprising Jammu, Kathua, Udhampur, Doda, Poonch, and Rajouri. The resolution on Kashmir passed at the meeting [also] demanded partition of the Kashmir Valley and the creation of a union territory for resettling Kashmiri Pandits in the area north-east of the Jhelum river. The VHP also demanded union territory status for Ladakh, and immediate abrogation of Article 370 of the [Indian] Constitution which provides special status [a regime autonomous of New Delhi] to the state [of IJK].[15]

Following this declaration, the Rashtriya Swayamsevak Sangh (RSS, National Volunteer Organization), which is the ideological and organizational core of India's Hindu sectarian movement, also took up the agenda of partitioning Indian-controlled Jammu and Kashmir: "Close on the heels of the VHP demand for division of Jammu & Kashmir into four parts, the RSS today sought trifurcation of the state—carving out Kashmir Valley and Jammu as separate states and Ladakh as a union territory. The resolution of the RSS national executive also demanded abrogation of Article 370."[16]

The VHP and RSS demands were rejected by India's BJP interior minister and deputy prime minister, L. K. Advani, a hardline right-wing politician with close connections to the RSS. The minister and his party's spokesman both asserted that they favored maintaining the status quo in IJK.[17] Nonetheless, a reporter for the *Indian Express* astutely observed that the Hindu sectarian movement "has now neatly put forward three faces on [Indian] Jammu & Kashmir—BJP the moderate, RSS the hard-line and VHP the extreme—tailored to the requirements and constituency of each outfit." Indeed, the RSS launched a campaign based in Jammu city on the "trifurcation" and "statehood for Jammu" platform, in partnership with the Jammu BJP, to coincide with the run-up to elections to the IJK legislature in the autumn of 2002. Advani's denial in Delhi notwithstanding, the IJK BJP unit's manifesto for these elections pledged to abrogate Article 370 and to detach Ladakh from IJK and make it a union territory.[18]

As it turned out, RSS-BJP candidates campaigning in the Jammu region on the "trifurcation" and "separation of Jammu from Kashmir" planks fared disastrously in the elections, consistent with a historical pattern in which the BJP and its predecessor parties have never been able to win more than marginal support among the Jammu region's Hindu electorate. In a debacle for the extreme right's agenda, only one such candidate was elected among the Jammu region's thirty-seven deputies to the IJK assembly. In Ladakh's Buddhist-dominated Leh district, RSS emissaries persuaded the leaders of the Buddhist community (who are of Tibetan ethnic stock) to form a Ladakh Union Territory Front, which subsequently won Leh district's two seats in the eighty-seven-member IJK assembly "unopposed."[19]

This particular partitionist agenda is premised on an absolute denial that any unresolved sovereignty issue exists in Jammu and Kashmir, at either the internal or the international level. In this view, the Kashmir problem exists because IJK's integration with Hindu-majority India has been disrupted by "pseudo-secular" New Delhi governments' misguided policy of "appeasement" of IJK's Muslim majority, particularly the overwhelmingly Muslim population of the Kashmir Valley—exemplified above all by Article 370 of the Indian constitution, the IJK autonomy statute. This argument has long had currency in sectarian Hindu politics both in IJK and in India proper. The demand for trifurcation of IJK to enable self-determination for "Hindu" Jammu and "Buddhist" Ladakh has its origins in the early 1950s, in the agitation against Sheikh Mohammad Abdullah's government by the Praja Parishad (see Chapter 2), the progenitor of Hindu reaction in urban Jammu. Abolition of Article 370, viewed as a blight on the organic unity of India, has been one of the sacred shibboleths of the BJP during its long years as a minor opposition party in Indian politics. The demand for a separate, Pandits-only enclave in the Kashmir Valley is more recent but still over a decade old. In the formulation of one Pandit organization, this enclave, "sanitized" of Muslims, would cover 55 percent of the Valley's land area (8,600 of 15,853 square kilometers) and include four of its five largest towns—Srinagar, Baramulla, Anantnag, and Sopore.[20] Pandits, including displaced persons, make up 4 percent of the Kashmir Valley's population.

The partitionist posture of India's far right is based on a host of myths, misrepresentations, and distortions. Article 370 could not possibly have engendered secessionism in Kashmir because IJK's autonomous regime was drastically eroded by central intervention from New Delhi beginning in the mid-1950s and practically ceased to exist in all but name by the mid-1960s (see Chapter 2). The argument that the grant of autonomous status served as the thin end of the secessionist wedge is therefore baseless. To the contrary, *liquidation* of IJK's autonomous regime through authoritarian central intervention led to the entrenchment of secessionist longings, particularly in the Kashmir Valley. The people of the Kashmir Valley have by and large been disenfranchised citizens of the Indian Union since the 1950s—with rare semi-democratic interludes and exceptions—ruled either through unrepresentative client governments foisted on Srinagar by New Delhi's manipulation or through overt use of police methods and military repression (or, more commonly, a variable mix of manipulation and repression).

Any grievances regarding inequitable treatment or marginalization that exist among certain segments in the Jammu and Ladakh regions cannot therefore be blamed on the people of the Kashmir Valley. The voices of extreme Hindu communalism and reaction in Jammu, while consistently vocal and encouraged by patrons in India proper, have moreover never been able to demonstrate anything resembling mass support among the overall Hindu majority in IJK's Jammu region. The demand for partition of the Valley to create a Pandits-only area is simply bizarre, and at odds with the complex picture of Pandit-Muslim coexistence and conflict in the Valley before, during, and after the watershed year of 1990.

The kind of internal partition of IJK favored by India's far right is probably illegal under international law, given J&K's status as a disputed territory, and probably also under India's own constitution, given the continuing presence of Article 370, even if only on paper, in that document. The prescription is also at variance with social and political realities on the ground in the Jammu and Ladakh regions of IJK. As noted earlier, three and a half of the Jammu region's six districts—Doda, Rajouri, Poonch, and parts of Udhampur—have majority Muslim populations. The Jammu region as a whole has a Hindu majority because the Muslim-majority areas, largely rural and mountainous, are more thinly inhabited than the plains and foothills dominated by Hindu populations. The RSS-inspired agenda of partitioning IJK to carve out a Hindu-majority Jammu is unacceptable to the Muslims of Rajouri, Poonch, Doda, and the Udhampur uplands, not just to their pro-independence and pro-Pakistan elements but also to those reconciled to Indian rule. It is a recipe for inflammation of communal divides in volatile, confessionally mixed locales like Rajouri and Kishtwar (besides, even the city of Jammu, which is solidly Hindu-dominated, has a sizeable Muslim minority population). It was pointed out as early as the 1960s by a seasoned observer of Kashmir politics, a Kashmiri Pandit from the Valley, that "the proposed separation of Jammu cannot be effected in the manner its sponsors fondly hope. The Muslims living in the districts of Doda and Poonch, where they are the majority, will almost certainly refuse to be bracketed with the Dogra Hindus and prefer to stay with the Valley's Muslims."[21] The same situation persists today. Faced with such a prospect, Jammu's Muslim communities are likely to forge a common front overriding internal ethnolinguistic and political differences, and to insist on remaining connected to their fellow Muslims in the Valley.

Like Jammu, Ladakh is a heterogeneous region and does not have a unitary regional personality. For several decades, Buddhists, concentrated in the Leh district, made up a very slight majority of the sparsely populated high-altitude region's mixed Buddhist-Muslim population. Census results from 2001 reveal that the demographic balance has shifted slightly but significantly, so that Ladakh's population of 250,000 now has a thin Muslim majority of 52 percent. Ladakh's Kargil district is almost 85 percent Muslim, principally adherents of the Shia version of the faith. The Leh district is over 80 percent Buddhist, the main minority being a Muslim community called Arghuns, descendants of Sunni Muslims who migrated to Leh from the Kashmir Valley in the seventeenth century and intermarried with local ethnic Tibetans.

In August 2002 it was reported that while "the trifurcation demand of the RSS may have sent a wave of optimism through the Ladakh Buddhist Association (LBA) which is spearheading the campaign for a union territory in Leh, opposition is gaining ground in Kargil." In response to the trifurcation campaign, an all-party meeting was held in Kargil, and those attending the meeting "unanimously opposed any division of the state [of IJK]." Asghar Karbalai, vice president of the Imam Khomeini Trust, Kargil's premier religious body, asserted: "We strongly condemn the RSS and VHP move and whatever be the solution to the Kashmir dispute, we will always go with the [Muslim] majority in the state. In fact, we want unification of Gilgit, Baltistan and the other part of Kashmir [the Pakistani-controlled Northern Areas and "Azad" Kashmir] with the state as those are also parts of our state." Sheikh Ahmad Mohammadi, secretary of Kargil's Islamia school, commented: "We have never supported LBA in their demand and we will not allow trifurcation. Anything claimed by LBA should not be attributed to us." Another speaker, Kargil's NC representative in the IJK assembly, who was also a junior minister in the IJK government, deplored the myth that Ladakh has a solely or predominantly "Buddhist" character. The meeting also complained that Buddhist groups based in Leh were receiving an unfair share of development funds granted to Ladakh, at Kargil's expense.[22] The partition plan advocated by the Indian far right is likely to open a Pandora's box of contending claims, identities, and preferences in IJK, and add yet another incendiary element to a volatile "internal" conflict.

The range of partitionist possibilities surveyed here reveals how tenuous, and counter-productive, the partitionist approach is as a "solution" to the Kashmir conflict. This is consistent with rigorous comparative research that has found the claims of academic advocates of partition as a conflict-resolution strategy to be empirically unsustainable, and with my own critique elsewhere of partition both as a general prescription for divided societies and for the post-Yugoslav Balkans in particular.[23]

Lessons for Peace

The primary insight that emerges from this survey of plebiscitary and partitionist approaches to the Kashmir conflict can be stated with brevity. None of the three "nation-state" perspectives on Kashmir—the authoritarian, integrationist Indian version; the irredentist, revisionist Pakistani version; and the simplistic view of self-determination often promoted by Kashmir independentists—can hope to impose its will as a solution to the contemporary Kashmir problem.[24] Attempts to impose any one of these perspectives are bound to degenerate into repression, and ultimately guarantee prolongation of both internal and international conflict. The three ideologically based and territorially fixated nation-state perspectives, in their maximalist forms, lead to nothing but an impasse. The only possibility of moving from conflict toward peace is by a different approach, which is sensitive to the constraints of realpolitik and the basic interests and aspirations of *all* the contending parties, but is nonetheless able to transcend the trap of contending nation-state perspectives. Such an approach and framework is developed in Chapter 5.

Contested sovereignty—disagreement over the legitimate borders of political community—remains the core of the Kashmir crisis. In the autumn of 2002 the government of India held elections to constitute a new IJK legislature and government. The elections were condemned by Pakistan as a farcical diversion and boycotted by the Hurriyat Conference, the coalition of groups in IJK favoring self-determination, some of whose leaders were wooed with the lure of office and other inducements to participate by Indian officials but eventually declined to take the bait. In mid-September 2002 the first phase of these elections was held, covering constituencies in the northern Valley districts of Baramulla and Kupwara, the Jammu districts of Rajouri and Poonch, and the Kargil district in Ladakh. The public response, and the rates of polling recorded, presented a mixed picture, underlining the extreme complexity of politics in Kashmir. In the districts of Baramulla and Kupwara, major towns such as Baramulla, Sopore, and Bandipore, as well as extensive tracts in rural areas, witnessed negligible polling verging on a total boycott in some cases. Small demonstrations against Indian-sponsored elections and for *azaadi* took place at several locations, including the towns of Baramulla and Pattan. "Elections are irrelevant and an attempt by the government of India to mislead the international community," said a citizen in Sopore. "Even if the [Indian] security forces cut us into pieces we will not vote. This is no alternative to the right of self-determination."[25] This is the opinion and stance of a large segment of IJK's population, especially in the Kashmir Valley.

There were also reports of Indian military and paramilitary soldiers intimidating and terrorizing citizens to force them to vote,

especially in rural areas. In Kulangam, a large Kupwara village off
the Sopore-Handwara road, "one 25-year-old man, who was too
afraid to give his name, said he went to vote after being beaten by
soldiers who came to his house. 'When I refused to go, they hit
me. Then they took us to the main road and told local policemen
to escort us to the polling station. They told us they would come
back later to check whether we had an ink mark on our finger'"
(polling officials put indelible ink on the fingernail of every person
who votes to prevent multiple voting). A shopkeeper in the same
village "said three or four soldiers knocked on his door soon after
polling began. They said to me go to the polling station and cast
your vote. Why are you inside? We're worried they will come
back and beat us. I don't want to vote, I'm on a poll boycott. The
people want freedom from India, they don't want elections [that
seek to legitimize Indian rule]."

At the polling station, "a long queue of voters waited . . . Many
said they were voting because the army gave them no choice. 'I
was on the road going to my house when 10–12 soldiers told me I
have to vote. So I have come here. I am in favour of independence. I didn't want to vote,'" one voter said. Another Kulangam
citizen claimed that "the army came to my house at 6.30 AM, I
hadn't even taken my tea," while in Dangapora, a village in neighboring Baramulla district, yet another said, "The army threatened
us, telling us that if we did not vote they would say we had been
found with a gun and arrest us." In Loland, another village in
Baramulla district, "soldiers were seen moving through the streets
speaking to shopkeepers and people on the streets. After they had
passed, people said they were being told to go to the polling stations. Virtually noone from the village had voted so far as they
were boycotting the elections. The soldiers denied they were coercing voters and said they were searching for terrorists."[26]

When a group of journalists "reached Karihama, Dedikote,

Pazipora and adjacent villages [in Baramulla], people were seen being herded by security forces to polling booths. 'They have asked us to vote and we will have to abide by their directions. They will conduct a nail-parade in the evening to check if we have voted, whether our nails are marked with ink or not,' said a Karihama villager." In another village in Kupwara, "local youth sitting on the road said they were trying to procure a bottle of indelible ink" to mark their own fingers.[27]

In Chogal village, near the town of Handwara in the Kupwara district, a young man who had worked as a polling agent for a candidate said, "The boycott here is so absolute that even my own family did not turn up [to vote]. I am now worried what to do when I return home." Earlier that day the following sequence of events unfolded in Chogal: "Around 9.30 AM a group of Army personnel appeared, and started knocking on doors asking villagers to vote. They barged in and asked everybody to come out. We tried to resist but they pushed us with their rifle butts. They took us at least a kilometer, then we saw a crowd gathered in the *chowk* [market square]. The crowd started shouting slogans for *azaadi* and the army men then left us alone.'" Another citizen said, "They called me and asked me why I had not gone to vote. I was so scared I said I don't have a vote and they started hitting me. I was slapped and hit with rifle butts."[28]

There were many other reports of threats and beatings, including of women in villages near Handwara and Bandipore. In a village near the Baramulla town of Sangrama, a crowd of twenty-five hundred enraged locals burned the jeep of the NC candidate after security forces arrested a village woman because one of her sons was a guerrilla.[29] Indian authorities claimed that 40 percent of eligible citizens had exercised their franchise in Baramulla district and 55 percent in the much smaller Kupwara district. These figures include numerous involuntary voters, in addition, up to a million and a half eligible citizens in the Kashmir Valley have simply not registered to vote and are thus not counted when calculating these percentages. Participation by women was also extremely low in most areas.[30]

Not all of the voting was fraudulent or coerced, however. In at least half of fourteen constituencies in the two districts (ten in Baramulla, four in Kupwara), there was substantial genuine polling. In some remote constituencies dominated by ethnic Gujjar electorates (Uri and Gurez in Baramulla, Karnah in Kupwara), anti-India sentiment is less strong than in Kashmiri-speaking areas and opposition to Indian-sponsored processes and institutions is less pronounced. In other constituencies some people voted out of loyalty to a particular local candidate, or to ensure the defeat of a detested candidate. Both motivations were at work in the Baramulla constituency of Sonawari, in the hinterland of the town of Pattan. Parts of this constituency are the base of the Valley's best-known guerrilla-turned-pro-India-gunman, Kuka Parray, a hero to some and a criminal to many others.

The major factor motivating people to vote, however, was the presence of a number of credible candidates opposing the ruling NC party in the two districts. In Kupwara, these candidates, standing as independents, mostly belonged to the locally influential People's Conference (PC) party, a moderate party favoring self-determination whose veteran leader, Abdul Ghani Lone, had been assassinated in Srinagar by suspected pro-Pakistan extremists in May 2002. In Kupwara's Handwara constituency, a PC bastion, the decision of Ghulam Mohiuddin Sofi, a Lone lieutenant, to run as an independent candidate (the PC being a constituent of the Hurriyat Conference coalition boycotting the polls) against the sitting legislator, a minister in the NC government, evoked a great deal of local enthusiasm.[31] Sofi eventually won the Handwara seat by a narrow margin over his NC rival, but other PC men standing as independents in the Kupwara district surprisingly lost to the unpopular NC, highlighting the difficulties of a ballot-oriented strategy for advocates of self-determination in the absence of a real Kashmir peace process at the internal and international levels.

In several constituencies of the sprawling Baramulla district, people inclined to vote saw an attractive option in the People's Democratic Party (PDP), a basically pro-India party in the Valley which nonetheless adopted a "pro-people" posture against abuses of human rights and brutalities committed by Indian security forces. The PDP was formed in 1999 under the leadership of the political veteran Mufti Mohammad Sayeed, formerly the Valley's top Congress leader, who quit Congress and formed his own IJK-based party. Its best-known face is Sayeed's elder daughter Mehbooba Mufti, a fiery and popular campaigner for citizens' human and civil rights. The PDP campaigned on a platform of defense and restoration of those rights and on a vision of a comprehensive Kashmir peace process involving India, Pakistan, and all sections of political opinion in IJK. This progressive program appealed to a section of the Valley's electorate, where the PDP won sixteen of forty-six electoral districts and subsequently formed a government, headed by Mufti Mohammad Sayeed, in coalition with the Congress (which did very well in Hindu-dominated parts of the Jammu region) and with the support of several smaller parties and independents.[32]

I argued in Chapter 2 that the prime reason for the radicalization of political dissent in IJK, culminating in insurrection in 1989–1990, was the purposeful stifling of opposition *within institutional politics* by the Indian state, operating in collusion with local client elites, since the 1950s. In the autumn 2002 elections, it appeared that some citizens even in areas supporting self-determination were trying to make the most of limited opportunities to find an institutional outlet for opposition voices to the deeply unpopular NC government, installed in office since 1996. The NC, led by Sheikh Mohammad Abdullah's elder son Farooq and grandson Omar, was widely viewed not just as hopelessly corrupt and incompetent and an unapologetic sponsor of brutal counterinsurgency policies, but also as a major obstacle to a wider peace process involving the Hurriyat Conference groups and Pakistan.

Thus in the Kupwara village of Trehgam, the birthplace of the JKLF pioneer Maqbool Butt, 83 percent of the electorate voted—without duress. Butt's aged mother denounced the voting as "betrayal of the blood of martyrs"; the villagers listened respectfully but voted anyway. An elderly woman explained: "Our vote isn't against freedom. It is against the National Conference." Indeed, "a group of villagers started shouting pro-independence slogans after casting their votes at 8.30 AM. India shouldn't think our vote is to legitimize its rule in Kashmir," several village men cautioned. It is for "dislodging the NC." In Lone-Harie, Abdul Ghani Lone's ancestral village, a young man asserted: "We will continue to work for the cause of Lone. This vote is not against the Hurriyat and the freedom struggle, just against the NC."[33]

In the Baramulla constituency of Gulmarg, which includes the famous holiday resort of the same name, "early-morning voters talked of 'defeating people who create obstacles to peace.'" "Standing in the long queue of voters at 8.15 AM outside the polling booth," a man in his sixties said, "Today I am voting for a new party that has promised to work with all people to bring peace." The PDP, then in opposition, was an especially strong contender in this area, and its candidate, the senior party leader Ghulam Hassan Mir, subsequently won the seat by a huge margin over his

NC rival, Sheikh Mohammad Abdullah's younger son Mustafa Kamal. In a nearby village in the same constituency,

> mist blanketed the village and Farooq Ahmad Bhat shivered in the early-morning chill, walking to the nearest polling center to cast his vote. Bhat, 22, was the first voter in Gulmarg's Batapora village . . . Bhat reached the polling center at 7.20 AM. [After voting he spoke of his hopes]: "The candidate I have voted for would strive for peace between India and Pakistan. He would fight for removal of [Indian] Army installations from residential areas, and the removal also of the SOG [counter-terrorism Special Operations Group] of the J&K police, which is even worse than the Rashtriya Rifles [the army's counterinsurgency wing] . . . This violence cannot go on endlessly."[34]

The overwhelming majority of the people of Jammu and Kashmir desperately want peace. The sovereignty issue remains, as in 1947–1948 and 1989–1990, the heart of the matter. A peace process based on a framework capable of addressing the multiple but interrelated local and international dimensions that make up this conflict is a critical, urgent necessity.

5

PATHWAYS TO PEACE

Whenever things threatened to fall apart during our negotiations—and they did on many occasions—we would stand
back and remind ourselves that if negotiations broke down
the outcome would be a bloodbath of unimaginable pro-
portions, and that after the bloodbath we would have to sit
down again and negotiate with each other. The thought always sobered us up and we persisted, despite many setbacks. You negotiate with your enemies, not your friends.

—NELSON MANDELA,
reflecting on the transition to a
multiracial democracy in South Africa, 1997

IN HIS ADDRESS to the United Nations General Assembly in the autumn of 2002, Secretary-General Kofi Annan
identified hostility between India and Pakistan as one of the most
"perilous" threats to global peace and security. "In South Asia,"
he noted, "the world has recently come closer than for many

years past to a direct conflict between two nuclear weapon–capable states." "The underlying causes" of the conflict "must be addressed," he argued, "gladly" acknowledging and "strongly" welcoming efforts made by "well-placed" U.N. member-states to persuade the two countries to reduce the tension (in June 2002 apprehension about an imminent India-Pakistan war had eased after a visit by Richard Armitage, a U.S. deputy secretary of state, to the capitals of both countries). If another confrontation between the two countries threatened to ignite war, Annan warned, "the international community might have a role to play." The next day it was reported, citing "a top U.S. official" as the source, that during discussions in New York, Annan and U.S. President George W. Bush "had agreed on their hope to move beyond crisis management to real solutions on Kashmir."[1]

Around the time the dangers of festering conflict in and over Kashmir were being discussed in the corridors of global politics and diplomacy, a controversy arose in India over an advertisement by Cadbury India Limited, the Indian branch of a leading international confectionery manufacturer. Seeking to sell a new brand of chocolates called Temptations, the advertisement depicted a map of Jammu and Kashmir along with a caption: "I'm good. I'm tempting. I'm too good to share. What am I? Cadbury's Temptations or Kashmir?" A minor furor ensued. The head of the Hindu nationalist Bharatiya Janata Party (BJP) in the city of Mumbai (Bombay), India's commercial and financial center, pointed out that "Kashmir is a very sensitive issue and thousands of [Indian] soldiers have sacrificed their lives for it . . . such ads just trivialize the issue." "How can an ad campaign, in the name of creativity, even imply that Kashmir is a state to be shared with anyone?" he asked, "threatening national protests" to force the withdrawal of the advertisement. The firm relented immediately. "The press advertisement for Cadbury's Temptations," a statement clarified, "was issued entirely in good faith, with no intention whatsoever to offend the sentiments of the public. We offer our sincere apology to any section of the public that may have been offended."[2]

Meanwhile, a different drama was dominating public attention in Indian-controlled Jammu and Kashmir (IJK). This related to the case of a woman named Shehnaz Kausar, a Pakistani citizen from a village in Mirpur, a district in Pakistani-controlled "Azad" Jammu and Kashmir (AJK). In October 1995 Shehnaz, then a recent bride aged twenty-five, jumped into the Jhelum River to commit suicide after being physically and mentally tortured by her in-laws. As fate would have it, she did not drown but was washed up by the river's currents on the Indian side of the Line of Control (LOC), and was arrested by the Indian army. After interrogating her for three days, Indian military intelligence concluded that she was not a spy, and handed her over to local police authorities. She was then charged under clause 2, section 3 of IJK's Ingress and Internal Movement (Control) Ordinance, and subsequently sentenced to fifteen months' imprisonment and a fine of 500 Indian rupees for illegal breach of the LOC.

Shehnaz was sent to a district jail in the IJK town of Poonch, close to the de facto border with AJK, to serve her sentence. There she was repeatedly raped by Mohammed Din, a prison guard. After enduring several weeks of violence she complained to senior jail staff, who transferred her in late January 1996 to the region's central jail in the city of Jammu, 250 kilometers south of Poonch. There it was discovered that she had become pregnant. In October 1996 Shehnaz gave birth in prison to a daughter, whom she named Mobeen. In February 1997 her jail term ended but the woman was not released. Instead she was kept in prison, along with her baby, pending repatriation to Pakistan. A "no-objection" certificate needed for her repatriation took Indian authorities four years to process, and was issued only in June 2001. In the interim, Shehnaz started to earn a basic living stitching clothes in prison, and Mobeen started going to nursery school with a daily police escort.

In June 2001 the mother and daughter were taken to a border post at Attari/Wagah, on the India-Pakistan frontier in the Punjab. Pakistani border guards, known as Rangers, agreed to take Shehnaz back but refused to accept Mobeen, on the grounds that the little girl was not a Pakistani citizen but an Indian. Shehnaz refused to return to Pakistan without her daughter, and was driven back to prison in Jammu. There, to provide a legal basis for her continued detention, she was arrested under the Jammu and Kashmir Public Safety Act (PSA), a draconian IJK law which is normally used against suspected terrorists and others accused of subversive and "anti-national" activity and provides for two years of incommunicado detention without any formal charge, court appearance, or trial.

Shehnaz Kausar's case was taken up before the IJK high court by a Jammu lawyer, A. K. Sawhney (incidentally a Hindu) and his son Aseem Sawhney. In August 2002 a two-judge Jammu bench of the court, consisting of Justice Tejinder Singh Doabia and Justice Sudesh Kumar Gupta (a Sikh and a Hindu, respectively) issued a nineteen-page ruling. The ruling quashed Shehnaz's detention under the PSA as "unconvincing," observed that the woman had already served her sentence for violating the LOC, and noted that a small child was being forced to grow up in prison for no fault of her own. "Under normal circumstances," the judges wrote, "a minor is to have the same domicile as his or her father." But this being a case where the paternity of the child had not yet been definitively ascertained, the court directed that as a child "conceived and born in the state [of IJK]" Mobeen would be treated as domiciled in IJK. (Mohammed Din, suspended from his job, was being tried at the time for rape in a district court, and DNA samples had been taken from him and Mobeen to establish paternity. Din was apparently inclined to acknowledge paternity, but only if Shehnaz first withdrew the rape charge.) As such, the judgment stipulated, Mobeen was entitled to claim and receive citizenship of the Republic of India, and was free to stay on in IJK indefinitely, or until she was accepted by Pakistani authorities and wished of her own accord to go to Pakistan.

The court also ruled that "as the minor cannot stay without her mother, who is her legal guardian, the consequential order of releasing her [Shehnaz] is also being passed." The court further ordered the IJK government, which it noted was the accused rapist's employer, to pay Shehnaz compensation of 300,000 Indian rupees for wrongful imprisonment, which would be deposited in Mobeen's name and used to fund her education, and to arrange housing facilities for the mother and daughter. The IJK government did not follow up on these orders with any urgency, and a few weeks after their release, Shehnaz and Mobeen, the latter approaching her sixth birthday, were living temporarily in their lawyers' home. Sawhney then filed a contempt petition against the IJK government, and "the high court issued notices to the state [IJK] chief secretary and director-general of police for alleged deliberate and intentional delay in implementing the court orders."

But the worst of Shehnaz's seven-year ordeal was clearly over. The case and the verdict aroused great interest throughout IJK, especially since under the provisions of IJK's Resettlement Act (whose operation is temporarily suspended under an order from India's Supreme Court in response to a plea from the government of India, which fears its potentially destabilizing implications), Shehnaz, as a resident of "Pakistan-occupied Kashmir," over which India claims rightful sovereignty, is automatically entitled to resettle in IJK. "A Child without a Father Gets a Country in Jammu & Kashmir" was the headline of one front-page story, datelined Jammu, in a major Indian newspaper based in Delhi, while another report, datelined Srinagar, carried in Indian Jammu and Kashmir's top English daily, was headlined: "Shehnaz Symbolizes Tragedy of the Two Kashmirs."[3]

Conceptualizing Peace

Kashmir is one of the world's great frontier regions. This is not just in the geographical sense, although the territory is wedged between Pakistan, India, China (Xinjiang province and Tibet), and, in one northwestern corner, Afghanistan. It is also, and more significantly, a frontier in the political and ideological sense—where Indian and Pakistani state nationalisms (and their respective followings within Kashmir) collide with each other and clash with a third quasi-nationalism, a "homeland" identity centered on but not limited to the Valley of Kashmir, which spawns a popular conception of sovereignty at odds with the claims of both states.

This intractable and intricate conflict presents an extraordinarily daunting challenge for any peace-building process. The analysis and argument I have developed in this book suggest that any such process needs to be based on the following principles:

- The contending nation-state perspectives on Kashmir are stalemated. The intrinsic character of the dispute calls for a *multinational* framework of peace-building—a framework that acknowledges and accommodates *all* of the competing national (and quasi-national) identities and agendas, and negates and rejects *none*. This need not—in-

deed for practical reasons perhaps *should* not be the explicitly stated basis of any peace process. A tacit, implicit
understanding and commitment will more than suffice.

• The Kashmir conflict has multiple dimensions and is defined by a complex intersection of an international dispute with sources of conflict internal to the disputed territory and its Indian- and Pakistani-controlled parts. Any
approach to resolving this multi-layered conflict must
necessarily involve multiple, but connected and mutually
reinforcing, tracks or axes of engagement and dialogue.

• The de facto Indian and Pakistani sovereignties over their
respective areas of Kashmir cannot, should not, and need
not be changed. As I have shown, especially in Chapter 4,
ideas of either erasing or redrawing the border currently
known as the LOC are both infeasible and potentially extremely dangerous, risking sharp escalation of the conflict. Fortunately, eliminating or shifting existing de facto
borders and jurisdictions is not at all necessary for a viable peace process. The substance of the Kashmir problem can be adequately addressed without altering the territorial status quo, and ways exist of transcending the
limitations imposed by those frontiers without abolishing them.

• The maintenance of existing de facto sovereign jurisdictions and the territorial status quo between states must
be complemented, and balanced, by recognition and redress of the grievances and aspirations of the large proportion of the population of J&K—particularly of IJK—
who see themselves as victims of the stance and policies

of one or both states. The term *azaadi* (freedom), the driving force of movements for self-determination in Kashmir for over six decades, has multiple meanings and a fluidity that can potentially become an asset, if rigid meanings premised on territory give way to an interpretation that foregrounds democratic rights to participation, representation, and self-government. Unless and until state power comes to an honorable accommodation and compromise with such a subtly reframed, non-maximalist yet substantial meaning of *azaadi*, Kashmir will remain a zone of intractable, recurrent conflict.

An approach premised on these basic principles does not necessitate that any of the contending states and non-state political actors in Kashmir formally renounce or repudiate their established positions and declaratory ideological stances. It requires only a willingness to engage with other points of view in a civilized manner and the negotiating skills to craft a strategic compromise between opposed perspectives.

Of contemporary conflicts involving disputes over the legitimate locus and unit of sovereignty and clashing visions of national self-determination on the same territory, Northern Ireland's conflict bears a striking resemblance to that of Kashmir. As in Kashmir, the origins of the problem are to be found in the circumstances of imperial Britain's withdrawal from its colony, Ireland, in the early 1920s, when twenty-six of Ireland's thirty-two counties were constituted as an "Irish Free State" (which became a republic in 1937) while six northern counties were retained under British sovereignty. The population of this six-county unit, comprising the major part of the historic region of Ulster, was more than two-thirds Protestant, a community that considered its national identity to be British, not Irish, and whose leaders were implacably opposed to becoming citizens of any kind of Irish state. However, almost one-third of the population consisted of Catholics, who regarded their national identity as Irish and became a minority "stranded" on the wrong side of the border created by Ireland's partition. Their plight was compounded when Northern Ireland's Protestant elite, with London's tolerance if not active encouragement, erected a regime systematically repressive and discriminatory toward the Catholic population, who were seen as a disloyal minority and a Trojan horse for the overwhelmingly Catholic Irish Republic south of the border, which regarded Northern Ireland as a temporarily separated part of the national territory. Northern Ireland's Catholics endured the status of third-class citizens for almost fifty years, until a major civil rights movement developed in the late 1960s. The Protestant regime responded with severe police repression, and the long-simmering conflict of aspirations and allegiances in Northern Ireland rapidly boiled over into a major crisis.

In the early 1970s Northern Ireland descended into a situation approximating civil war, as a resurgent Irish Republican Army (IRA) emerged from decades of hibernation to confront the forces of the Protestant regime, and "loyalist" (extreme pro-British) armed groups appeared in the Protestant community to counter the IRA. Large numbers of British troops were sent to Northern Ireland to restore order and keep the warring groups apart. Although some sections of the Catholic community initially welcomed the soldiers as protection from Protestant police and mobs, relations deteriorated precipitously, and in a matter of months British soldiers became targets of the IRA, whose republi-

can ideology saw British control of Northern Ireland as the source
of the entire problem.

In 1972 the authorities in London dissolved the Protestant regime and Northern Ireland entered a lengthy period of direct
rule from the British capital. On the ground, a protracted, ugly
war of attrition ensued involving the IRA, armed loyalist groups,
the overwhelmingly Protestant Northern Ireland police force, and
the British army. During three decades of "the Troubles," some
thirty-five hundred persons were killed in political violence and
thirty-six thousand injured (of a population of 1.5 million). Tens
of thousands were driven out of their homes, and thousands
served prison time for perpetrating violence, including grisly sectarian murders, and for being members of illegal paramilitary organizations. Northern Ireland acquired a well-deserved reputation
as the site of an extremely bitter, intractable conflict and as one of
the most divided, polarized societies on earth. In the early 1980s a
historian of Ireland wrote the following words: "History is indeed
a difficult prison to escape from and the history of Ireland [is] as
difficult as any . . . Yet change is the business of history and the
historian has a vested interest in seeing change come about. Having traced the foundations on which the prison of Irish history
was built he can only wait and hope to see British and Irish alike
one day walk away."[4]

Because of the structural similarities between the conflicts in
Northern Ireland and Kashmir—an inter-state sovereignty dispute
(a legacy of imperial withdrawal and partition) over a territory,
paralleled by polarization of the territory's population between
groups with different national identities and incompatible notions
of self-determination—the path to troubled peace in Northern
Ireland is of interest and relevance. Like that in Northern Ireland,
the Kashmir conflict has multiple dimensions and is defined by

the intersection of "internal" conflict caused by clashing preferences on identity and allegiance with a long-standing international contest over legitimate sovereignty. The Northern Ireland
peace process, which resulted in the landmark "Good Friday"
Agreement of April 1998, marked a moment when the countries
and factions involved made, in the words of the Republic of Ireland's prime minister, "enormous moves that they had dared not
dream about for the previous seventy years," that is, since the inception of the Northern Ireland question.[5] The Agreement has
three "strands," each corresponding to one dimension of the
problem:

Strand 1 relates to the internal political setup and governmen-
tal structure of Northern Ireland. The institutional design is
premised on the notion that the "Unionist" (British) and "Nationalist" (Irish) identities in Northern Ireland, and the rival political
aspirations and preferences that flow from them, are "equally legitimate" and must both be accommodated in the institutional
framework on the basis of equality, mutual recognition, and tolerance (however reluctantly given by some). The legislature is the
108-member Northern Ireland Assembly, in which the Unionist
and Nationalist segments of the population are represented, along
with a small minority of others who reject being pigeonholed in
either category, in proportion to their strengths in the population.
Catholics have gained from demographic change and are now at
least 43 percent of Northern Ireland's population, so the first post-
Agreement Assembly has 58 declared Unionists, split between pro-
Agreement moderates and rejectionist hardliners, 42 declared Nationalists, divided between a slight majority of 24 moderate Nationalists and 18 pro-IRA republicans, and 8 members unaffiliated
with either bloc. This Assembly can make decisions and pass legislation on major political issues only by cross-community consent,

that is, by *concurrent majorities* in the Unionist and Nationalist blocs (on other matters, the same cross-community voting procedure can be triggered at the request of 30 deputies).

The executive arm of government, the cabinet, consists of an equal number of ministers from the Unionist and Nationalist communities, and the major parties of both communities are represented in this cabinet. This broadly based, power-sharing executive is jointly headed by a "first minister" and a "deputy first minister" elected by means of the cross-community consent procedure. This is intended to ensure that the first minister is a moderate Unionist and his deputy a moderate Nationalist, who should be able to work together. The Northern Ireland institutions enjoy jurisdiction over a wide range of powers devolved from the center (the British Parliament in Westminster), with the possibility of further expansion of autonomy "with the consent of the [British] secretary of state [for Northern Ireland affairs] and the approval of Westminster"; "maximum autonomy while remaining within the Union is feasible, provided there is agreement to that within the Northern Ireland Assembly."[6] The overall structure of government is a model of *consociation:* power-sharing between representatives of the fundamental political segments in a divided society. This structure and its procedures lend themselves to deadlock and blackmail, but they also provide a vital guarantee of inclusiveness, sharing of political power, and a barrier against the hegemony— let alone a monopoly of political authority and office—of any one segment or school of opinion.

Strand 2 of the Agreement deals with the cross-border dimension of the Northern Ireland question. Under the terms of the Agreement, the Republic of Ireland has significantly modified its claim to Northern Ireland and accepts that British sovereignty over Northern Ireland can yield to Irish sovereignty—that is, unification of the island of Ireland—only if and when a majority of Northern Ireland's people vote in favor of such a change. As I pointed out in Chapter 4, this effectively postpones the issue, since Unionists will continue to be a thin majority of Northern Ireland's population for at least another decade—but in the event of a future Catholic majority, this plebiscitary provision may have deeply inflammatory implications. However, two facts remain: Northern Ireland is a part of the Irish Isle; and it contains a very large (and growing) minority that considers its national identity to be Irish, not British, and probably supports a united Ireland (although moderate Nationalists, unlike republicans, are typically willing to soft-pedal this issue in deference to Protestant opinion). Strand 2 of the 1998 Agreement thus establishes an institution of cross-border linkage and cooperation—the North-South Ministerial Council (NSMC).

As its name suggests, this body consists of ministers from Northern Ireland's autonomous, power-sharing government and their counterparts from the Republic of Ireland's sovereign government. Its broad mandate is to develop cooperation between the two governments in areas where there is judged to be significant "mutual cross-border and all-island benefit" in doing so. During negotiations leading to the Agreement, Unionists tried to minimize the scope and authority of this cross-border council, while Nationalists emphasized its importance. In the end, a rapprochement was reached whereby the NSMC was empowered to implement policy for the entire island in a few relatively uncontroversial spheres—inland waterways, food safety, trade and business development, European Union programs, the Irish/Gaelic and Ulster/Scottish languages, and aquaculture and marine matters. It was charged with the task of gradually developing cross-border links and cooperation on a broader and more significant range of subjects, including aspects of transport, agriculture, education, health, environmental protection, and promotion of tourism. It was made compulsory for all Northern Ireland ministers—Unionists as well as Nationalists—to participate in the NSMC, and the NSMC and the Northern Ireland Assembly were made codependent, meaning that one cannot survive and function without the other. The NSMC is supposed to meet twice a year in plenary format, and ministers can also meet individually on a "regular and frequent basis" with their counterparts to discuss links and cooperation in their fields of responsibility. The overall effect of Strand 2 is to introduce a limited, north-south confederal element into relations between Northern Ireland and the Republic of Ireland.

Strand 3 of the Agreement provides the foundation for the ambitious institutional architecture established by Strands 1 and 2. It aims to promote the "harmonious and mutually beneficial development of the totality of relationships" between all the governments and peoples of the British and Irish Isles. One institution that works to this end is the British-Irish Council, a deliberative forum jointly chaired by the prime ministers of Britain and the Republic of Ireland, which brings together not only ministers in the two sovereign governments and members of the British and Irish parliaments but also executive members (ministers) from all of the United Kingdom's devolved, autonomous regional governments—Scotland and Wales in addition to Northern Ireland. A much more significant institution for practical purposes is the British-Irish Inter-Governmental Conference, which is chaired by the Republic of Ireland's foreign minister and the British government's secretary of state for Northern Ireland affairs, and is supported by a standing secretariat. This intergovernmental institution gives the Republic of Ireland consultative access to all British policy formulation on Northern Ireland matters that have not been devolved to the competency of the autonomous Northern Ireland institutions (and perhaps also the cross-border NSMC), and that thus remain under the jurisdiction of the British government (that is, on the equivalent of a Union List of subjects). There is provision for members of the Northern Ireland Assembly to be involved in these intergovernmental consultations, but not on the same footing as the representatives of the governments of the two sovereign states.

In May 1998 this multidimensional agreement was put to parallel referenda, conducted separately, in Northern Ireland and the Republic of Ireland. It was approved by an overwhelming majority of 96 percent in the Republic. In Northern Ireland, 71 percent of those voting supported the framework, including the vast majority of Catholic voters but only a very slender majority of Protestant voters.

The point of this survey of Northern Ireland's peace-building framework is not to suggest that it is a model than can be readily replicated or transplanted to any other location of conflict, including Kashmir. Every case has its own specific context, features, and dynamics. But specificity does not equal uniqueness. No two situations of conflict are ever identical, but they are often *comparable:* although there are important differences, there may also be significant, even striking similarities. Among major contemporary conflicts, that in Northern Ireland, with its configuration of internal and international sources and local and external dimensions, provides the most meaningful comparison to Kashmir. The approach and framework for moving from intractable, perennial conflict to peaceable accommodation in Northern Ireland may hold interesting and relevant clues, perhaps even lessons, for peacemaking in Kashmir. The substance, content, and sequencing of a peace process will certainly vary, because of differences in contexts and specific attributes, but the basic principles and essential elements defining such a process may not be significantly dissimilar.

Protracted violence marked by brutality engenders radicalization and deepens divides, but over time it also releases an opposite dynamic in a war-torn society: war-weariness, a desperate yearning for the return of a peaceful, normal climate, and delegitimation of violent methods among all but a hard core of sectarian extremists on all sides. A quarter-century of the Troubles produced such a situation in Northern Ireland, where most ordinary people, regardless of sharp differences in allegiances and sympathies, wished the gun to be taken out of politics. This public sentiment had a gradual, subtle, but ultimately powerful effect on the thinking of political forces on both sides of the divide, and it remains a vital asset of the Northern Ireland peace process, which is undergoing a difficult implementation. Apart from fringe extremists, nobody wants the peace process there to collapse entirely, because the prospect of a return to violent polarization is unacceptable to most. As the fate of the Palestinian-Israeli process in the Middle East demonstrates, the aftermath of a failed peace process is likely to be even worse, and more destabilizing, than no peace process at all.

After more than thirteen years of unrelenting violence, the "gun culture" evokes revulsion among the vast majority of people in Jammu and Kashmir, particularly in the theater of armed conflict in IJK—regardless of differences in political persuasions and allegiances. Protracted armed conflict has not only inflicted terrible human loss and suffering but also had a deeply adverse impact on infrastructures and the environment, which are basic to the

quality of life. This ultimately affects almost all people in the pop
ulation, whether they identify with the pro-India, pro-Pakistan, or
pro-independence segments. War-weariness also affects the Indian
military, paramilitary, and police forces deployed in Kashmir, most
of whom would welcome a respite, leading optimistically to permanent liberation, from the thankless, life-endangering task of
ensuring security and combating guerrillas (although it needs to
be mentioned that some elements of the counterinsurgency
apparatus have a vested interest in conflict because they reap significant material benefits from it—fat financial rewards for killing
insurgents, ransom extorted from families of citizens detained, often fraudulently, as militant supporters, and profits secured from
smuggling Kashmir's natural resources such as timber).

This war-weariness presents a genuine if in itself slight opportunity to work toward peace. However, as in Northern Ireland,
that opportunity can bear fruit only if a serious accommodation
and compromise can be fashioned between polarized views and
contending positions. That in turn can occur only if and when
the principal protagonists-cum-adversaries realize that the conflict
is a harmful and burdensome stalemate, which none can hope to
"win" unequivocally and permanently. It is only then that the
logic of mutual destruction can yield to the logic of mutual accommodation, a turning point reached in another protracted and
vicious South Asian conflict, the ethnic war in Sri Lanka, after
twenty years of bloodletting, belligerence, and confrontation.

The limits to comparing Northern Ireland with Kashmir are ob-
vious. Three salient points of difference, in particular, suggest that
the road to peace in Kashmir and the subcontinent may be considerably more tortuous than that in Northern Ireland.

First, the peace process in Northern Ireland was, and remains,
driven by the shared determination of the British and Irish states

to find a viable and durable formula for peace. This joint endeavor and resolve—evident since the 1985 Anglo-Irish Agreement between the two governments, in retrospect an important precursor to the much more comprehensive Good Friday Agreement reached thirteen years later—has sought to set aside a centuries-old history of bitter animosity between British and Irish. It has been facilitated by the fact that the majority of people in mainland Britain do not regard Northern Ireland as an absolutely integral part of the British state and that leaders of the Republic of Ireland, while sympathetic to the grievances and aspirations of the Nationalist population in Northern Ireland, have generally rejected the ideology and methods of violent Irish republicanism as both immoral and self-defeating to the cause of Irish nationalism. Even so, the shared agenda of making peace has been severely tested before and after the landmark 1998 agreement by internal (intersegmental) antagonisms in Northern Ireland as well as by the continuing appeal of a hard-line rejectionist position among a large section of the Unionist population (which suggests that in addition to intersegmental antagonism, *intra*segmental disagreements, as for example among the Sinhalese-Buddhist majority of Sri Lanka, may be obstacles to peace agreements and their lasting stabilization).

In Jammu and Kashmir (especially in IJK), the internal divisions between segments with conflicting notions of self-determination are real, but the major obstacle to a peace process is the abysmal relations between India and Pakistan. The governments of the two countries are usually inclined almost reflexively to a stance of zero-sum confrontation on the Kashmir dispute, and make a habit of promoting and articulating maximalist stances and uncompromising rhetoric on the question. Both have formidable pressure groups resistant to the subtle, tacit change of direction necessary for a peace process. In Pakistan, influential elements of the military elite may not be disposed to make peace with India, and may favor the policy established since the late 1980s—threatened after 11 September 2001 by the changed geopolitical context and American pressure—of bleeding India by supporting insurgency. In India's diverse political spectrum, flexibility on Kashmir, based on a genuine, realistic acknowledgment of deeply rooted grievances in IJK *and* of the necessity of working with Pakistan if the problem is to be meaningfully tackled, is the exception rather than the norm. There are indications in particular that right-wing Hindu sectarian elements, which have become a major influence on policymaking at the heart of the BJP-led coalition governing in New Delhi, favor exploiting a continuing conflict in and over Kashmir for their own domestic political purposes.

A second difference between J&K and Northern Ireland is that British-Irish intergovernmental cooperation on Northern Ireland was greatly facilitated by the two countries' common membership in a dynamic regional organization of integration and cooperation—the European Community (EC), known since 1992 as the European Union (EU)—which both nations joined in 1972. It is substantially easier for countries embroiled in a contentious bilateral dispute to cooperate on settling the problem under an overarching regional framework of cooperation and integration, which links the countries through supra-state institutions and reduces the salience of rigid national-sovereignty discourses and state borders. Such regional blocs help open up the discursive / ideological and institutional space for the fashioning of compromise solutions on even the most intractable disputes over territory and identity. The process of cooperation under the auspices of the EC/EU, the steadily increasing integration of the European political space, and the growing legitimacy and autonomous role of sub-state regions across Europe (as well as emerging trans-frontier links between such regions) under that framework have been especially helpful to the progressive improvement of British-Irish relations, and to the fashioning of an imaginative, multidimensional peace process in Northern Ireland.[7] No comparable regional body exists in South Asia, where the South Asian Association for Regional Cooperation (SAARC) remains in a largely embryonic stage, its potential stunted above all by the hostile relations between India and Pakistan.

The third difference is that the Northern Ireland peace process benefited at crucial junctures from the constructive involvement of a third party. This was the United States. The Clinton administration developed a keen interest in the nascent moves toward peace and a negotiated compromise on Northern Ireland as early as 1994. The respected political veteran the U.S. president sent to frequently frustrating peace talks between 1995 and 1998, the former Senate majority leader George J. Mitchell, made useful contributions to the peace process.[8] Indeed, Mitchell was not just instrumental in the making of the Good Friday accords, but returned to Northern Ireland in late 1999 to help salvage the peace agreement from the threat of breakdown.

With regard to Kashmir, any third-party role is flatly rejected by India, the status quo power in the conflict, which insists on the bilateral character of the dispute but whose elite appears reluctant to engage in a substantive intergovernmental process with Pakistan. There is no doubt that any Kashmir peace process must be driven primarily by the initiative and commitment of the principals, New Delhi and Islamabad. But given the hostility between the two capitals, the unpromising track record of purely bilateral dialogue on Kashmir, and the threat the Kashmir conflict poses to regional security and global peace, low-key, indirect, and discreet facilitation by credible third parties—which is *not* styled as intrusive mediation—may be both necessary and potentially efficacious.

Even in Sri Lanka, a third-party role played unobtrusively but effectively by Norway has proved invaluable to the peace process. With regard to Kashmir, any such role would probably be most effectively played by an informally constituted consortium of influential countries, possibly in collaboration with important multilateral organizations, which does not preclude a country or countries with particular influence with one or both principals playing a more substantial behind-the-scenes role.

This identification of differences between contexts and prospects in Northern Ireland and Kashmir is not only a sobering reminder of the challenges to moving from conflict to peace in the latter case but also an instructive illumination of key points at which a subcontinental peace process would require reinforcement in order to be minimally viable. In addition, three lessons of the experience of building peace in Northern Ireland may be relevant to Kashmir.

First, the process should be structured to be in principle as broadly based and inclusive as possible. The idea is to give the maximum number of players a stake in the process, while minimizing the number of potential spoilers and wreckers. Of course, in practice not all players would be of equal or even significant weight and influence, and one should also beware of players who may be intent on sabotaging a process from within, but the *principle* of broadly based participation is nonetheless vital. The inclusive principle applies not only but particularly to political representatives of erstwhile or even current "militants" and "terrorists" who are prepared to give dialogue, negotiations, and peace a chance. In Northern Ireland, the participation in the peace process of Sinn Fein, the political wing of the Provisional IRA, was anathema to many Unionists, but it was absolutely essential. The participation of small political parties closely linked to loyalist militants in the Protestant community was also crucial.

Second, any process that seeks to deescalate protracted conflicts and then craft broadly acceptable compromises on issues of fundamental disagreement is necessarily a gradual, time-consuming endeavor, incremental in nature. It is impractical and can be dangerous to expect decisive results and "solutions" to emerge virtually overnight. This is not to say that peace processes should be indefinitely prolonged and open-ended. It is important to set reasonable, mutually agreed upon time frames for step-by-step progress, but deadlines should not be an overriding priority.

Third, recurrent crises and even breakdowns are an integral part of such processes. There are numerous pitfalls, ambushes, and setbacks on the path to peace in Kashmir, and this is entirely normal. Indeed, the rocky experience of implementing the April 1998 agreement for Northern Ireland demonstrates that nothing can be taken for granted even after apparently milestone agreements have been reached. Compromise agreements that attempt to reconcile conflicting claims to sovereignty and self-determination are difficult not only to reach but also to sustain. As experts on Northern Ireland have written, it cannot be predicted "that multinational political settlements always succeed"; "in an ethnonationally divided territory over which there are rival claims to sovereignty, polarized party and paramilitary blocs, and no reasonable prospects of peaceful integration within one nationalist identity . . . such agreements are precarious, but they are infinitely better than the alternatives—fighting to the finish, or the panaceas proposed by partisan or naïve integrationists."[9] However, fundamentally unsound and unequal peace processes such as that between the Palestinians and the Israelis can collapse completely and defy salvage or repair, and this is a contingency that needs to be guarded against from the outset.[10]

Track 1: The New Delhi–Islamabad Axis

The key to breaking the deadlock in Kashmir lies in the metropolitan capitals of India and Pakistan. Concerted, sustained intergovernmental cooperation between India and Pakistan is the essential basis of any Kashmir peace process. If such intergovernmental cooperation were to occur, the other dimensions of the Kashmir problem might turn out to be surprisingly tractable. In its absence, however, no lasting, substantial progress is possible on those other fronts, and the Kashmir question will continue to be a prime source of international tension, regional instability, and violent internal conflict.

In order to promote a sustained and fruitful peace process, the intergovernmental framework needs to take an *institutionalized* form. It cannot remain ad hoc, limited to periodic, high-profile *events*—such as meetings between leaders of the two countries or between career officers of the two foreign services. Such encounters, and discussions, must be part of a sustained *process* and a coherent, institutionalized intergovernmental framework of peace-building. An institution such as a permanent intergovernmental council needs to be constituted.

The official Pakistani position has generally been to insist that Kashmir is "the core issue" in India-Pakistan relations, to which the Indians have usually responded that Pakistan suffers from a Kashmir fixation and that Kashmir is only one of a number of issues between the two countries. The Indians have instead called for an intergovernmental dialogue to be broadly conceived and structured—a so-called composite process aimed at overall normalization of bilateral ties—and have sometimes preferred to call Kashmir simply an "issue" rather than a "dispute." These are relatively minor divergences of perspective that are often deliberately exaggerated to forestall prospects of intergovernmental dialogue, and they can be easily reconciled. The focus and mandate of a permanent India-Pakistan intergovernmental council should probably be comprehensive, rather than focused solely on the Kashmir dispute, but with an understanding that Kashmir is the most important of a range of bilateral issues and the main focus of efforts.

Such an intergovernmental council should be chaired by the prime ministers of India and Pakistan, with the foreign ministers of the two countries possibly functioning as working chairs. The membership should include, in addition, the president of Pakistan, the president of India (if constitutionally permitted; this office is largely titular but carries symbolic clout), the interior and defense ministers of both countries, the top professional civil servants in both interior and foreign ministries, the chiefs of military staff of both countries, and selected parliamentarians from the two sides. Of course, the institutional structures of India and Pakistan differ significantly. India has a stable model of parliamentary supremacy and cabinet government and a nonpolitical military, while Pakistan is yet to work out a balance in presidential-parliamentary and civil-military relations. The fact that key decisionmaking lies in different domains in India and Pakistan needs to be kept in mind but does not in itself pose an obstacle to effective intergovernmentalism. Two categories of persons could be given invitee status to such an intergovernmental body (but without membership): eminent citizens of both countries who have shown a commitment to resolving their antagonism through peaceful means; and, at an appropriate point, top ministers of inclusive and autonomous governments in IJK and AJK.

Far from being a pie in the sky, a joint coordinating body such as a permanent India-Pakistan intergovernmental council not only is practically indispensable for initiating and taking forward a serious peace process on Kashmir, but would represent the realization in concrete, institutional terms of the vision and agenda expressed in the two most important intergovernmental declarations of the last thirty years—the Simla Agreement of July 1972 and the Lahore Declaration of February 1999. Both these documents constitute forward-looking declarations of principles and concise statements of purpose, agreed at the highest political level after negotiations on successive drafts presented by the two sides.

During the summer of 1972 in the hill resort of Simla, India, "the Government of India and the Government of Pakistan . . . resolved that the two countries put an end to the conflict and confrontation that have hitherto marred their relations and work for the promotion of a friendly and harmonious relationship and the establishment of durable peace on the subcontinent . . . reconciliation [and] good neighborliness." The two governments further resolved that "the basic issues and causes of conflicts which have bedeviled relations between the two countries for the last 25 years shall be resolved by peaceful means . . . through bilateral negotiations or by other peaceful means mutually agreed upon between them." With regard to the Kashmir conflict, the agreement stipulated that "in Jammu and Kashmir, the Line of Control resulting from the ceasefire of December 17, 1971 shall be respected by both sides without prejudice to the recognized position of either side. Neither side shall seek to alter it unilaterally, irrespective of mutual differences and legal interpretations. Both sides further undertake to refrain from the threat or use of force in violation of this Line." It was further specified that "this Agreement will be subject to ratification by both countries in accordance with their respective constitutional procedures," and the concluding clause stated that "both Governments agree that their respective Heads will meet again at a mutually convenient time in the future and that, in the meanwhile, the representatives of the two sides will meet to discuss further the modalities and arrangements for the establishment of durable peace and normalization of relations."[11] The promise of that Simla summer was squandered—or more correctly, never systematically pursued—in part because of the absence of effective intergovernmental mechanisms that could build and direct the process visualized by the agreement.

The threads were picked up twenty-six years later, in February 1999 in Lahore, Pakistan, in the context of a Jammu and Kashmir (especially IJK) transformed since 1990, and in the aftermath of nuclear tests conducted by both countries in the summer of 1998. The Lahore Declaration issued that winter by the prime ministers of India and Pakistan is if anything even clearer, and more ambitious, than the Simla Agreement. It bluntly asserts that "an environment of peace and security is in the supreme national interest of both countries and the resolution of all outstanding issues, including Jammu and Kashmir, is essential for this purpose." It is "convinced that durable peace and development of harmonious relations and friendly cooperation will serve the vital interests of the peoples" of both countries. "Recognizing that the nuclear dimension of the security environment of the two countries adds to their responsibility for avoidance of conflict," and "reiterating the determination of both countries to implement the Simla Agreement in letter and in spirit," the "respective Governments" agreed to "intensify their efforts to resolve all issues, including the issue of Jammu and Kashmir," and to "intensify their composite and integrated dialogue process" (that is, not restricted solely to Kashmir but with Kashmir as a central issue) on the basis of an "agreed bilateral agenda." Two other principles are significantly mentioned: the governments "affirm their commitment to the goals and objectives of SAARC . . . with a view to promoting the welfare of the peoples of South Asia," and undertake to "promote and protect all human rights and fundamental freedoms."[12]

The thaw of Lahore lasted only until the summer of 1999, when elements of the Pakistani military decided to provoke a border conflict with India along the LOC in the Kargil sector of Ladakh, in a misguided and counterproductive attempt to "internationalize" the Kashmir conflict. That did not prevent India's "moderate" Hindu nationalist prime minister from inviting the person allegedly responsible for the Kargil intrusion, the chief of the Pakistani army, General Pervez Musharraf—who subsequently deposed the discredited civilian prime minister Nawaz Sharif in October 1999 and appointed himself president of Pakistan in 2001—to a summit meeting held in Agra, India, home to the Taj Mahal, in July 2001. The meeting proved inconclusive. Two months later, on 11 September, the World Trade Center and Pentagon attacks shook the world, and in an altered geopolitical environment Musharraf's regime was embraced as a key ally by the United States, which had until then shunned him as a dictator. This development offended India, which had been steadily improving its own relationship with the only global superpower during the 1990s, partly at the expense of the traditional U.S. relationship with Pakistan. The spate of *fidayeen* strikes by Islamist militant commandos against high-profile targets in IJK—which began immediately after Pakistan withdrew from Kargil under U.S. pressure—and the deadly strike on India's parliament in New Delhi in December 2001 further strained relations, and India reverted to a hard-line stance of demanding that the Pakistani government ensure that "cross-border terrorism" cease before any resumption of dialogue with Pakistan could be contemplated.

The Indian government has a valid point with regard to "cross-border terrorism," which further destabilizes precarious intergovernmental relations. The Pakistani government also has a partially plausible case that it cannot prevent all such attacks, that hawks in India use these attacks as a pretext to destroy the prospect of constructive intergovernmentalism that could jointly address the roots of radicalism and terrorism, and that continuous abuses of the human rights of people in IJK have played a major role in such radicalization. In the autumn of 2002 the *fidayeen* tactics well known in IJK since 1999 reached the largest city of India's western Gujarat province, when two young men armed with assault rifles and grenades stormed a Hindu temple and cultural complex, killing at least thirty visiting civilians and several police personnel and Indian commandos before being killed after a twelve-hour battle. The trigger for this macabre incident was a pogrom against Gujarat's Muslim minority earlier in 2002—after the murder of sixty Hindu nationalist activists on a train by a Muslim mob in a small Gujarat town—in which more than a thousand Muslim men, women, and children were killed, often in savage circumstances, by organized groups of far-right Hindus in Gujarat's cities and villages.

The road to peace between India and Pakistan passes through Srinagar. Simla 1972 and Lahore 1999 provide important, abidingly relevant signposts for that difficult, tortuous road. One of the conditions for a viable subcontinental peace process is, of course, a cessation of armed hostilities (or something approximating such a cessation) in IJK. With an India-Pakistan intergovernmental mechanism, an institutional expression of a shared commitment to dialogue and cooperation, in place, the United (Muttahida) Jihad Council, the coordinating body for all guerrilla groups operating in Kashmir except Lashkar-e-Taiba (LeT), would find it extremely difficult to reject a ceasefire if they wished to retain any credibility that theirs is a "freedom struggle" and not "terrorism." In such a situation, the Pakistani government and military would be under strong international pressure to ensure a halt to guerrilla activity, and it is doubtful how long maverick groups like LeT could continue on a violent path if isolated.

All members of the "international community" with an interest in the Kashmir conflict should therefore invest their efforts and leverage in the development of an India-Pakistan intergovernmental axis in the form just outlined. Intergovernmental cooperation, and its institutionalization, is not only vital for such short-term goals as a cessation or near-cessation of violence. In the longer term, a permanent intergovernmental council can provide the mechanism for giving the government of each country a reciprocal, consultative role in the governance of the part of Jammu and Kashmir that is under the effective sovereignty of the other country. That could be an important element in the overall structure of a settlement, along with Tracks 2 and 3 outlined below.

Track 2: The New Delhi–Srinagar Axis

If cooperation on the international dimension of the Kashmir conflict is the essential foundation for any peace process, the "internal" dimension of relations between IJK and the center of power in New Delhi is also vital. The democratization of IJK's political and institutional space in a way that can enable lasting peace is a complex challenge.

In the autumn of 2002 the government of India organized elections, condemned by Pakistan and boycotted by almost all independentist and Pakistan-oriented groups in IJK, to constitute a new IJK legislature and government for a term of six years. The first phase of polling, in the northern Valley districts of Baramulla and Kupwara, the Jammu districts of Rajouri and Poonch, and the Ladakh district of Kargil, was described in Chapter 4. In the second phase, the Valley's capital city, Srinagar, the city's rural hinterland, the adjoining Valley district of Badgam, and the district of Jammu (which includes Jammu city) elected their representatives. Participation averaged 59 percent in Jammu district, a predominantly Hindu area, ranging from a high of 70 percent in Chhamb, a pocket on the LOC which has been the site of fierce fighting in all India-Pakistan wars, to a low of 40 percent in the urban Jammu West constituency. In the Valley, "many came willingly [to vote], some were forced to come [by Indian security forces], and a majority stayed away. [There was] a genuine urge to vote in parts of Badgam district, especially in Shia-dominated areas, Ganderbal and Kangan assembly segments [rural pockets of Srinagar district], army coercion in the Sunni areas of Badgam, especially in Beerwah and parts of Chadoora [segments], and a near-total boycott in the city of Srinagar."[13]

This synopsis tellingly captures the local complexity of politics. About 35–40 percent of Badgam district's electorate consists of Shia Muslims. This community and its leaders are split between pro-India and pro-*azaadi* positions, but overall the pro-India element is stronger and the pro-*azaadi* stance weaker among the Shias than among the Valley's dominant Sunni population, partly because of sectarian Shia-Sunni violence in Pakistan, where the Shia minority has been targeted by radical Sunni groups, some of which are also active in the war against India in Kashmir. However, 60–65 percent of Badgam's population consists of Sunni Muslims, and most of their areas are "a separatist and militant bastion," which includes such villages as Soibugh, home of the Hizb-ul Mujahideen (HM) commander Syed Salahuddin. Residents of many villages in these areas told of being forced to vote after threats and beatings by the ubiquitous Indian soldiers and special police forces. Kangan, a rural pocket north of Srinagar, is an area dominated by ethnic Gujjars and a stronghold of Mian Altaf, a prominent Gujjar National Conference (NC) politician and former government minister, who has a strong local following. Ganderbal, also north of Srinagar, is a Kashmiri-speaking area which produced Maulana Masoodi, a legendary NC and Plebiscite Front leader between the 1940s and the 1960s, and in the 1990s produced numerous guerrilla fighters and "martyrs." Parts of this area have a strong HM guerrilla presence, but some people voted nonetheless with the sole motive of defeating the NC candidate, party president Omar Abdullah (Sheikh Mohammad Abdullah's grandson). Abdullah suffered a humiliating defeat by a candidate sponsored by the People's Democratic Party (PDP), whose populist campaign against repression and human rights violations struck a chord with the electorate. Indeed, reporting on the elections, an independent monitoring group called the Coalition for Civil Society, an alliance of local and Indian human and civil rights groups, observed that most of "those who went to cast their votes voluntarily said that they were doing so either to defeat the NC or to back a candidate who they believed would address long-standing issues."[14]

In the capital city of Srinagar, only 3 percent of the registered electorate voted, according to India's election commission. Throughout the day, "a deathly silence hung over the city, and there was hardly any activity in the city's 578 polling stations."[15] Virtually the only sign of activity, apart from police and paramilitary forces omnipresent on the streets, was provided by a few mobile squads of men owing allegiance to the pro-India NC, who traveled across the city casting bogus votes at some polling stations. In contrast to 1990–1995, the peak period of the insurrection, there is no longer any overt guerrilla presence or activity in most parts of the city; however, it is much more difficult to round up residents and force them to vote in congested neighborhoods of a city of 1.5 million people than in remote villages in rural areas saturated with Indian troops. In old Srinagar's Eidgah district, where Kashmir's largest martyrs' graveyard is located, a citizen pointed to two thousand graves of *shaheed* who have fallen since 1990 fighting for the cause of self-determination and said: "We cannot vote. They stand between us and India's elections." Ironically, this mass boycott ensured candidates of the deeply unpopular NC a default "victory" over their PDP and other rivals in most Srinagar constituencies.

During the campaign for these elections, the NC's father-son leadership, the incumbent chief minister Farooq Abdullah and his son Omar, the party's declared choice for the chief minister's post, had trouble mustering an audience at most of their scheduled public meetings. Some meetings had to be canceled, while at others "security personnel heavily outnumbered the audience," which consisted of the same group of party activists trucked from one site to the next across the Valley. At one such rally, held in the Badgam town of Charar-e-Sharief, site of Kashmir's most revered Muslim shrine, a disgusted citizen observing the proceedings said: "Enough of this *tamasha* [farce]. These politicians, especially this Abdullah family, only want to take from us, never to give anything. Now we have nothing left to give them anyway."[16]

When Sheikh Abdullah's son and grandson arrived to campaign in the town of Anantnag, the political nerve center of the southern Kashmir Valley, they found the entire town shut down by a spontaneous *hartal* (strike) to protest their visit. As the two southern Valley districts of Anantnag and Pulwama prepared for their date with Indian democracy in the third round of the staggered elections, Indian media reported that "there is hardly any place here where any poll fervor is visible." This was partly because of "fear . . . amid a massive militant [guerrilla] presence," but "there is another reason for the lack of poll fervor here. Participation in the elections remains an act of treachery against 'the cause' [of *azaadi*], the anti-incumbent factor and the wretched [living] conditions of the people notwithstanding." As a result, there was "little support for either" the NC or its main challenger, the PDP.[17] In the town of Bijbehara, a PDP stronghold just north of Anantnag, "people said they would resist any coercion [to vote] by the [Indian] security forces. 'Look at this old man, Ghulam Rasool, whose son Hilal [a HM guerrilla] was killed just last week. Can we betray his blood,' said a youth. He said boycott is the first option for most people and the second option is to see the NC defeated." There were some, however, "who want to vote to get some respite from routine problems. 'We are definitely for *azaadi* but until it is achieved we want some redress of our grievances,' said a villager in Posh Kreeri village" near Bijbehara.

The town of Anantnag was in an uncompromising mood, however. "We can have peace only if the Kashmir issue is resolved permanently," one citizen observed, while another asserted that "we are for *azaadi* and nobody will come out to vote here." In Pahalgam, a predominantly rural constituency of Anantnag district, "Mubashir Hasan of Srigufwara village said: 'So many have sacrificed their lives [for *azaadi*]. Last time [in 1996] we were dragged out to vote [by Indian forces] and it may be done this time as well. Our only interest is to survive the election day in peace.'" In the nearby village of Baktoor, Lal Khan, a resident, queried: "What are these elections for? We had expectations that something might happen at the Agra summit and there would be an end to bloodshed, but it did not happen." In Kulgam, another constituency in Anantnag district, "for most people, staying away from the polls is the first priority. 'If it is inevitable [at gunpoint], the vote will go against NC,'" a citizen predicted.[18]

On 1 October 2002 the southern Kashmir Valley voted during the designated polling hours of 7 A.M. to 4 P.M. As of 1 P.M., with only three more hours of polling to go, the voter turnout in sixteen constituencies in Anantnag and Pulwama districts, reported on the basis of Indian election commission statistics in an Indian newspaper, ranged from a high of 14.88 percent in Rajpora to a low of 0.85 percent in the town of Anantnag.

In Pahalgam, which recorded a relatively high participation rate of 13.34 percent at 1 P.M., "when mediamen reached [the] polling station . . . at 11 A.M., National Conference candidate Rafi Ahmad Mir was seen repeatedly punching the buttons of the EVM [electronic voting machine] himself. The village has 1029 votes and 258 had been cast until 11 A.M. The mediamen were [then] forced out of the station by policemen and election officials." Mir was pitted in a high-profile contest against the PDP's popular woman leader Mehbooba Mufti in Pahalgam. Elsewhere, "security personnel were seen coercing people to vote in Shopian town," and "Pulwama witnessed huge anti-election demonstrations," as "Srinagar city and the other districts of the Valley remained totally shut down following a *hartal* call given by the Hurriyat Conference and backed by almost all separatist organizations."[19] By the end of polling at 4 P.M., according to India's election commission, 26 percent had voted in Pulwama district and 24 percent in Anantnag district (including a "high" of 33 percent in Pahalgam constituency), plus 59 and 56 percent, respectively, in the Hindu-majority Jammu districts of Kathua and Udhampur. The aggregate turnout claimed for the four districts was 41 percent; an Indian newspaper report published on the eve of polling had noted that "on Tuesday, Pulwama and Anantnag in the Kashmir

Valley, and Kathua and Udhampur in Jammu go to the polls.
Sources said the Government [of India] 'expects' 40 percent–plus
attendance."[20] On the morning of polling day, a terrorist squad
opened fire and lobbed grenades in the town of Hiranagar in
Kathua district, close to the border with Pakistani Punjab, killing
nine people.

In the Kashmir Valley, eyewitness reports in the Indian media
confirmed that "the towns of Shopian, Anantnag, Bijbehara, Tral,
Pampore and Pulwama altogether boycotted polling [while] villages in the two districts witnessed low to moderate polling."
However, the "low to moderate polling" in rural areas came at
a price:

> People in Shopian appeared defiant and took out sev-
> eral processions shouting anti-election and pro-*azaadi*
> slogans. A mob of 300 protested when [Indian] army
> men tried to herd them into polling booths at Bunagam
> [village]. Residents of Batapora too said army men
> ordered them to vote. In the neighboring villages of
> Gagrin, Memandhar, Chanpora, Kanipora and
> Alyalpora, too, security forces were coercing people to
> vote. Residents of Alyalpora said they were brutally
> beaten when they refused to vote. Residents of
> Anantnag, Bijbehara and Pampore [towns] complained
> that security forces had seized their identity cards [es-
> sential for everyday movement] and told them they
> would only get them back after they cast their votes.[21]

Other eyewitness accounts in Indian media also spoke of "ghost
towns" and rampant coercion of unwilling, protesting voters
"herded" to polling stations in many villages by Indian soldiers after house-to-house visits, threats, beatings, and orders to vote

broadcast over mosque loudspeakers. Most such "people said boycott was their first option," but under duress, they were casting
votes for anti-NC candidates to bring about "change." Even so,
the bulk of polling centers wore a deserted look, with negligible
to zero voting, while only a trickle of voluntary voters were discernible in most of the rest. There was uncoerced voting, motivated by local loyalties or animosities, in only a small minority of
polling stations, while in a few, small groups of veiled women or
NC men were being allowed to vote repeatedly. "At one booth"
in Bijbehara, "the only vote was cast . . . by a candidate." "Scores
of people were massacred by security forces outside this booth
[in 1993]," a young man named Arshad remembered. "Since I was
born, I have come across only one aspiration, and that's *azaadi*."
In the town of Qazigund, Naseema, a woman from an adjacent
village who had been "herded" to vote along with the men,
termed the elections "a divine curse." The Coalition for Civil Society, whose four teams of monitors visited one hundred polling
centers, concluded that the third phase of voting "stands out for
the spread and extent of violent coercion in most of the sixteen
constituencies in the two districts." Regarding guerrilla threats
to enforce a boycott, "barring two places where people reported
that the local commander of a militant outfit [HM] had issued
posters that warned those casting their vote of dire consequences,
we did not come across any other form of coercion by militants.
Strangely, in Chandigam [village] people said they would have
boycotted the poll anyway so the poster was redundant."[22]

Near Awantipora, a town in Pulwama district, seven Border Security Force (BSF) soldiers returning from guarding a polling station were killed when their vehicle hit a land mine. In Srinagar,
the NC leader Omar Abdullah told a press conference that "for
settling the Kashmir issue, initiation of a dialogue with Pakistan is

necessary" and added that "these polls are only to elect representatives to set up a government in the state [IJK]" and "whatever settlement you are talking about is the domain of Islamabad and New Delhi, and the extent to which elected representatives [of IJK] will be part of that dialogue is something the Government of India will have to decide once dialogue starts with Islamabad." In New Delhi, meanwhile, an unnamed "key government functionary" asserted that "for decades Kashmiris have complained that they never got a free and fair election. Now they have it . . . This has been the most violent election [ever] in Kashmir. Pakistan tried its best to prevent it, but Kashmiris turned out to vote in unprecedented numbers. It only proves our point that Kashmiris believe in India." The morning after the Valley's southern districts voted, five more BSF soldiers were killed near Tral, a stronghold of HM guerrillas, when their patrol vehicle was blasted by a roadside bomb. In IJK's south, two civilians were killed and nineteen were injured by an explosive device planted in the fuel tank of a passenger bus near the city of Jammu. IJK's chief of police, who is not from IJK, attributed escalation of violence to "desperation among terrorist outfits since [public] response to the elections has been spectacularly good."[23]

As discussed in Chapter 2, IJK has a history of being ruled by compliant cliques, usually of limited representative character or none, installed at New Delhi's behest. It also has a history of its autonomous regime being eroded and virtually destroyed by authoritarian central intervention, operating in collusion with those compliant local elites. What is needed in IJK is the establishment of a genuinely competitive, representative, and accountable political framework. This is needed first of all to ensure a minimum quality of governance. Most of IJK's governments have known that their position, and hence their survival, has depended not on the will of IJK's people but on the sufferance of New Delhi. Indeed, on the rare occasions that favored cliques have shown inclinations to chart their own course, they have been summarily deposed by actions orchestrated from New Delhi and replaced by less popularly based and more subservient clients—this is what happened to Sheikh Abdullah's government in 1953 and to his son Farooq Abdullah's government three decades later in 1984. Members of IJK governments, fully aware of this political reality, have typically spent their time in office accumulating personal wealth, by looting development resources and the exchequer, and persecuting political opponents, aggravating problems of misgovernance and corruption. These governments have had the paradoxical traits of being highly predatory and utterly powerless at the same time.

There is a more important reason, however, why IJK needs a representative and consequently accountable political framework. Narrowly based governments which have New Delhi's patronage but limited or negligible popular sanction have effectively been crippled because they have suffered from a chronic legitimacy problem. Eventually, opposition to such governments, denied normal institutional outlets, became radicalized and assumed an anti-systemic form. This was the root cause of the uprising and guerrilla war that erupted in 1990, when the puppet theater disintegrated and the puppeteer, in a tragically self-fulfilling prophecy, found itself confronting exactly the kind of self-determination movement it had always feared.

Given IJK's political circumstances, a framework of government which has broadly based popular legitimacy is essential but also extremely difficult to achieve. As matters stand, two of the three segments of political allegiance and opinion in IJK—pro-independence and pro-Pakistan are excluded from institutional politics and have no recourse except the street (where, until Mufti Sayeed's liberalizing government assumed office in November 2002, their protests were invariably disrupted and broken up by the police or military) or the gun. Prior to the 2002 IJK elections, the government of India made significant attempts to co-opt pliable elements of the Hurriyat Conference—the conglomerate of parties and groups espousing self-determination—into its electoral process. Indian media reported that defectors from the Hurriyat fold and any others willing to renounce the self-determination agenda would "be guaranteed electoral victories. At least 17 of the 87 seats in the [IJK] assembly would be kept aside as 'safe seats'" for such elements.[24] The tactic of co-optation was combined with repression directed against Hurriyat Conference elements identified as intransigent. Thus three of the seven members of the coalition's executive committee—the defiantly independentist Jammu and Kashmir Liberation Front (JKLF) leader Yasin Malik and the pro-Pakistan veterans Syed Ali Shah Geelani and Sheikh Abdul Aziz—were jailed under draconian laws during the months leading up to the elections.

The twin tactics of co-optation of those willing to play the game and repression of the rest have been recurrent features of Indian policy toward IJK for decades. In the 2002 election, consistent with the historical pattern, these tactics failed. Moderate advocates of self-determination like the Hurriyat leader Mirwaiz Umer Farooq, a young and articulate political-religious figure, and other seasoned activists such as Shabbir Shah and the purged HM commander Abdul Majid Dar declined to be co-opted. The only candidates affiliated with the Hurriyat Conference who eventually contested elections were five members of the People's Conference (PC) party who stood as independent candidates in the PC's home base in the Valley district of Kupwara (and four of them were defeated by their NC rivals, in an outcome against the overall anti-NC trend). As explained in Chapter 4, they participated at all largely with the limited, tactical motive of gaining the upper hand over the NC in local politics, and they insisted that they had not renounced the cause of *azaadi*. Their decision reflected a pragmatic quest among a section of IJK's pro-*azaadi* population to elect candidates, even if to Indian institutions, who promise to give voice to the demand for a comprehensive peace process that will engage the internal and international dimensions of the Kashmir conflict. In other areas of the Valley, the PDP was the vehicle of choice for the expression of this tendency.

As a tactic, this approach makes more sense than holding out in eternal *intezaar* (waiting and longing) for a plebiscite that will never happen. However, it also has serious limitations, and in itself can never achieve a broadly based, inclusive political space in IJK. In fact, a decisive majority of the Valley's population heeded the boycott stance of the Hurriyat Conference and guerrilla organizations such as HM and refused to participate in elections intended to lend "democratic" legitimacy to Indian-sponsored institutions, while many others participated only under severe duress, essentially at gunpoint. The Indian government's invitation to anti-India groups to take part in these elections amounted to this: We will decriminalize you and include you in the sphere of "legitimate" politics, constituted on our terms, if you capitulate to our power and our perspective on the Kashmir conflict. Criminalization, repression, and exclusion of "unacceptable" and "treasonous" points of view must indeed yield to decriminalization, recognition, and inclusion in IJK's political life. But the change cannot happen on these terms, which represent a crude attempt to resurrect the pre-1990 puppet theater with the same puppeteer and a somewhat diversified collection of puppets. It can happen only in the context of a broader peace process committed to engaging and meaningfully addressing these other dimensions of the conflict:

- a role for Pakistan as a party to the dispute

- the question of self-rule for IJK

- the question of the "other" Kashmir under Pakistani control across the LOC and its future relationship to IJK.

In Northern Ireland, Sinn Fein and its leaders Gerry Adams and Martin McGuinness, both former IRA commanders, have neither abandoned their Irish national identity nor renounced their core political belief, the ideology of united Ireland. Had advance surrender been demanded or expected, there would have been no Northern Ireland peace process. Similarly, no Unionists have compromised their British national identity or their preference for remaining part of the United Kingdom of Great Britain and Northern Ireland. As noted earlier, the Northern Ireland peace process has been based on the premise that both sets of identities are "equally legitimate," and this principle opened up the space for the crafting of a skillful political compromise—with internal and external dimensions—between aspirations that had for decades been mutually exclusive. A tacit acceptance of the same sort of principle is necessary in Kashmir. The path to troubled peace in Northern Ireland was strewn not just with obstacles and setbacks, including recurrent killings and bombings, but with bitter distrust and recrimination during negotiations.[25] Indeed, Gerry Adams and the Ulster Unionist Party (UUP) leader David Trimble shook hands with each other—and that too perfunctorily—for the first time only *after* the Good Friday Agreement had been signed.

When George Mitchell returned to Northern Ireland in late 1999 to help untangle disagreements that threatened the Agreement's implementation, he noted that "not long ago, the Ulster Unionists and Sinn Fein did not speak to each other directly [even when in the same room]. In the early weeks of the [1999] review [of the Agreement] their exchanges were harsh and filled with recrimination." But gradually a "reluctant camaraderie" developed, and "discussions became serious and meaningful."[26]

In the 1970s the republican movement in Northern Ireland emphasized armed struggle over political participation; a young Martin McGuinness first became known as the commander of the Provisional IRA in Catholic-dominated Derry, the province's second-largest city after Belfast. By the 1980s, as the limitations of maximalist rhetoric and armed struggle became apparent, nonviolent political activity assumed greater importance in the movement's strategy and Sinn Fein, the IRA's political wing, began to organize among the working-class Catholic population. The slogan of the movement during that decade was "The Armalite [an assault rifle] and the Ballot Box," that is, a dual strategy of armed struggle and political mobilization. The advent of the peace process in the 1990s strengthened the movement's emphasis on nonviolent politics, as did a long series of talks during 1988–1994 between Adams and John Hume, the widely respected leader of the Social Democratic and Labor Party, a moderate Nationalist party based among the Catholic middle class. In 2000 McGuinness became Northern Ireland's minister of education, a key post in a cabinet headed by the UUP's Trimble. Like other ministers, Unionist and Nationalist, he took an oath of office that pledged to uphold peaceful politics and to discharge ministerial responsibilities in a nonsectarian manner, working for all citizens of Northern Ireland irrespective of community and political allegiance.

The moderating effect of a genuine, substantive peace process on the "hard men" of the IRA was gradual but eventually remarkable. The IRA had been identified with grim warnings that "Not a Single Bullet, Not an Ounce of Semtex [explosive]" in its arsenal would ever be turned over to anyone. In 2002 the organization "decommissioned" some of its weapons and apologized to the families of civilians killed during the previous three decades.

On the other side of the divide, among the Protestant community, small political parties led by former loyalist (extreme pro-British) terrorists turned out to be among the most dedicated supporters of the peace process. One such figure, David Ervine, who was elected to the inclusive Northern Ireland Assembly in 1998, "while passionately committed to the [British] union . . . had no hesitation about talking with Sinn Fein or anyone else in the search for a society of peace and equality." In 1997 Ervine, a working-class Protestant who has served six years in jail for loyalist terrorism, responded to statements against the peace process made by the rejectionist Unionists Ian Paisley and Robert McCartney: "That's easy for you to say, safe as you and your family are in the [upper-class] suburbs. If there's war [again] it's we and our sons who will do the fighting and dying. We want this process because it's our only hope for peace."[27]

Violence has a radicalizing effect but it can also have a powerful moderating effect, especially on erstwhile perpetrators. Yasin Malik, the leader of the independentist JKLF, one of the pioneers of the armed campaign against Indian rule that erupted in 1989–1990, permanently renounced the gun in 1994. The JKLF, viewed in the early 1990s as a deadly, fanatical terrorist group, had become a "moderate" if still "separatist" organization by the middle of the decade, and it is no longer even formally banned by the Indian government. By the mid-1990s the pro-Pakistan HM, led in the

Valley by a ruthless commander called Abdul Majid Dar, known to be a favorite of the Pakistani military's Inter-Services Intelligence, had supplanted the JKLF as the fountainhead of allegedly irreconcilable, irrational terrorism. But in August 2000 Dar declared: "Even if this violence continues for another ten years, ultimately the concerned parties will have to sit around a table and find a solution through talks. So it is better that a serious and meaningful dialogue begin now, so that further bloodshed is stopped."[28] The Martin McGuinnesses and David Ervines of Kashmir are waiting in the wings, but, like McGuinness and Ervine, they cannot and will not renounce the core convictions that motivated their struggle.

The core issue in the New Delhi–Srinagar relationship can be summarized in one word: *khudmukhtari* (self-rule). In the Valley and some other parts of IJK, such is the historical legitimacy and popular appeal of the idea of self-government, free of malign control and interference from New Delhi, that even the NC, a subordinate satellite of New Delhi, raises the issue periodically. Prior to the 1996 elections that restored it to office in Srinagar, the NC demanded the reinstatement of IJK's "pre-1953" autonomous regime—that is, the regime in which New Delhi had exclusive jurisdiction only over matters relating to foreign policy, defense, currency, and communications. This was the division of powers confirmed after negotiations between the prime ministers of IJK and India, Sheikh Abdullah and Jawaharlal Nehru, in the Delhi Agreement of July 1952 (see Chapter 2). In June 2000 the IJK assembly, dominated by NC members, passed an autonomy resolution on the same lines. The proposal was received unfavorably in India's Parliament, although a few members spoke in support of the principle of autonomy as an essential, central component of any settlement.[29] Prior to IJK elections in the autumn of 2002, the beleaguered NC once again dangled autonomy before a skeptical public. Campaigning in the Valley, the party president Omar Abdullah declared that "the day is not far when the Central Government will be compelled to restore the autonomy of the State" in order to meet the "aspirations of the people."[30]

The autonomy issue raises complex constitutional questions pertaining to center-state relations in India, and is a sensitive issue in both IJK and Indian politics. It is arguably correct that IJK benefits from some of the economic, financial, and legal aspects of its "integration," even if largely involuntary, with the Indian Union effected post-1953, and it is neither necessary nor desirable that these aspects be reversed. However, if a rapprochement between New Delhi and Srinagar is to be achieved, the 1952 Delhi Agreement's central principle—"maximum autonomy for the local organs of state power, while discharging [IJK's] obligations as a unit of the [Indian] Union"—will have to be revived. This principle should be the guiding spirit of the New Delhi–Srinagar dimension of a Kashmir peace process, while the precise content and substantive detail of the design and reinstitutionalization of an autonomous regime in IJK would be matters for negotiation. This would inevitably prompt chauvinist cries in India about capitulation to fundamentalist secessionists. Nonetheless, a democratically negotiated and reconstituted relationship between New Delhi and Srinagar, based on the principle of maximum devolution of decisionmaking powers from the center, is entirely consistent with India's democratic, quasi-federal structure and with the provisions of India's own constitution relating to IJK, and is not in conflict with a unanimous resolution passed in India's Parliament in 1994 proclaiming IJK to be an "integral part" of the Union.

A carefully crafted compromise between the Indian state's sovereignty over IJK and "maximum autonomy" for IJK institutions would probably approximate the pre-1953 division of powers—a delicate balance destroyed after 1953 by Indian governments intervening through blatantly unilateral, authoritarian, and undemocratic means—in important respects. If in the process IJK's autonomy became greater in some symbolic and substantive ways than the typical status of a unit of the Indian Union, that would be because no other unit of the Indian Union has such a large segment of its population estranged from the authority of the Indian state. The peculiar internal context of IJK and the constitutional history of its relationship with the Indian Union would justify a degree of such "asymmetry." Indeed, IJK has its own constitution from the 1950s, framed by its own constituent assembly. This is unique because India's states do not have individual constitutions.

In Chapter 4 I explained why the independentist conception of self-determination is untenable given realpolitik, the entrenched interests of states, and the internal social and political diversity of IJK and of J&K as a whole. *Azaadi* in a maximalist version is unrealizable, as well as potentially undemocratic because its territorial fixation and plebiscitary basis are insensitive to the views of large numbers of people in J&K who prefer to live under Indian or Pakistani sovereignty. However, *azaadi* subtly redefined as *khudmukhtari*—substantial and real self-rule short of sovereignty, the striking of an honorable balance between the realities of state power and aspirations to "freedom"—is a *sine qua non* of any Kashmir peace process and any settlement. This is especially true of IJK, but also, secondarily, of AJK.

In the peace process currently under way to end another bloody, protracted, and stalemated subcontinental conflict, the ethnic war in Sri Lanka, the Liberation Tigers of Tamil Eelam

(LTTE), one of the most violent and radical self-determination movements in the world, have redefined their maximalist stance. At the first round of peace talks, held in Thailand in September 2002, Anton Balasingham, the Tigers' chief negotiator, said that "over and above the intricate questions of conflict resolution and power sharing" that need to be negotiated, "the deepest aspiration of our people is peace, a peace with justice and freedom, a permanent peace in which our people enjoy their right to self-determination and to co-exist with others." According to Balasingham, who has been the LTTE's ideologue for three decades, the Tigers aim to negotiate a restructuring of Sri Lanka's unitary and centralized political framework in a way that will guarantee "substantial autonomy" for "northeastern Sri Lanka, the homeland of the Tamils and Muslims." (It is a significant reformulation of the Tamil nationalist "homeland" concept to admit that the "homeland" does not belong to Tamils alone but is shared with the Muslims.)

Balasingham added that "to fight for political independence and statehood" would be "the last resort under the principle of self-determination if our demand for regional autonomy and self-government is rejected." In response, the Sinhalese-led Sri Lankan government's chief negotiator, G. L. Peiris, a constitutional expert and cabinet minister, asserted that he viewed all aspects of the peace process as "a partnership between the Government of Sri Lanka and the LTTE."[31] In December 2002, after another round of peace talks, the LTTE announced that it had reached agreement with the government to pursue "internal self-determination" for the Tamil people based on "regional self-government" and "a system of self-rule" for Tamil-majority northeastern Sri Lanka "within a federal structure" for the country. The LTTE's supreme leader, Velupillai Prabhakaran, publicly confirmed what the Tigers called "a radical move to clarify the policy orientation of his organization."[32]

A self-rule framework for IJK can be devised only through an all-party forum of talks—held in conjunction with an India-Pakistan intergovernmental process—which includes representatives of all pro-India, pro-Pakistan, and pro-independence parties and groups, from all regions of IJK, who wish to participate. Almost all independentist and pro-Pakistan factions in IJK would be willing to participate in such a forum, provided it was part of a wider, substantive peace process addressing the multiple dimensions of the Kashmir problem. Most factions in IJK who stand for self-determination are moderate in their approach and know that a compromise is inevitable. The occasionally overblown rhetoric of some of their leaders and their demonization as "separatists" in India do not detract from this reality. Indeed, many independentist and pro-Pakistan leaders and groups might even be prepared to moderate their rhetoric, replacing controversial terms such as self-determination with more innocuous expressions. Of major IJK-specific parties of a pro-India orientation, a forward-looking party such as PDP would participate with enthusiasm in such a forum, while NC would be unable to oppose the goal of a broadly agreed-upon self-rule framework if it wished to retain any political base and credibility. It would be important that at least one of the two major all-India parties, Congress and BJP (the former of which has significant support among Hindus in the Jammu region), be supportive of the talks and of the overall peace process.

The consultations would probably be lengthy, but some time frame should be set for agreement on a framework. To prevent such talks getting bogged down in speeches and disagreements, they would need to be chaired—gently and at times robustly guided—by persons acceptable to a wide range of participants, selected perhaps from among eminent Indian citizens with a deep engagement with the Kashmir conflict. Once broadly agreed upon, the proposed framework for self-rule could be placed before India's Parliament for discussion and consideration. During a period of post-conflict normalization and political transition, lasting several years, IJK would probably require a *broadly based, power-sharing transitional government* including representatives from each of the three basic political segments of IJK's population and all regions, ethnicities, and faiths. The experience of peace processes in other divided societies, such as South Africa, suggests the strong necessity of such an interim period and inclusive transitional regime before normal patterns of competitive politics can be contemplated.

Opposition to a negotiated self-rule framework would probably come, with external instigation, from fringe groups in IJK active in a few Hindu-majority parts of the Jammu region and possibly the Buddhist-dominated Leh district of Ladakh, plus some migrant Kashmiri Pandit groups, who are the local standard-bearers for authoritarian central control of IJK and/or the kinds of internal partition schemes, "trifurcation" or worse, that I analyzed and rejected in Chapter 4. Although these positions are bankrupt, such fringe groups would need to be taken seriously for two reasons. First, they seek to exploit and inflame genuine fears and legitimate concerns of sections of the population in the Jammu and Ladakh regions—especially Jammu Hindus and other groups like Sikhs and Ladakhi Buddhists who, it must be remembered, are all minorities in IJK—regarding their status, future, and rights. Second, it is likely that powerful political forces in India, closely linked as sponsors and backers to otherwise minuscule rejectionist groups in IJK, would attempt to foster such opposition to sabotage a peace process.

TRACK 2A: THE SRINAGAR-JAMMU AXIS

The most important imperative is to secure broadly based agreement on a self-rule framework between the Kashmir Valley and Jammu regions, whose population sizes are almost equal (roughly 5 million and 4.5 million, respectively) and which together account for about 97.5 percent of IJK's people (Ladakh has the remaining 2.5 percent). In the Jammu region, especially but not only among its non-Muslim, mainly Hindu majority, a perception that IJK's political life and structure are overly Valley-centric has long been a source of latent discontent. This resentment has its origins in J&K's 1846–1947 dispensation, when a Jammu-based Dogra Hindu elite held the Valley's Muslim population in virtual servitude (see Chapter 1). Allegations of discrimination against Jammu in the allocation of political representation and office, government employment, and development resources are often exaggerated, but the question of equitable interregional relations is nonetheless valid. I have shown why proposals for internal partition (such as "trifurcation") advanced by sectarian groups in Jammu and Ladakh who seek to cynically exploit interregional differences, are fatally flawed. However, there is one very important variation between the political contexts of IJK's two populous regions: unlike the population of the Valley, a resilient stronghold of pro-*azaadi* sentiment, the bulk of the Jammu region's population belongs to the pro-India stream of political opinion. The more mature political figures identified with self-determination politics in the Valley, such as Shabbir Shah, have long been conscious of this basic variance and have worked to promote interregional dialogue with Jammu.

The issue of interregional variation would inevitably, and justly, be important in any process of consultation and negotiation in-

tended to devise a self-rule framework for IJK as a whole. The solution to the problem lies in a framework of self-rule that is *multi-
tiered* and based on a concept of *cascading* devolution. It is instructive that some of the most tenacious advocates of varying forms
of self-rule (independence, or autonomy under existing de facto
sovereignties) have been sensitive to the distinct political circumstances and dynamics of different regions. The maximalist vision
of self-determination was presented in 1970 by a veteran independentist ideologue, the JKLF leader Amanullah Khan, who was
born in Gilgit in Pakistan's Northern Areas, lives in Rawalpindi,
Pakistan, and has been active in AJK politics for decades. Khan argued for "a united, neutral, secular, federal republic" of Jammu
and Kashmir encompassing the Indian- and Pakistani-controlled
parts of the former princely state. He noted that "justice and eq-
uity demand that the State be a federal one to afford full opportunities to the people of its different regions to administer their own
areas and eliminate risks of domination, economic and political,
of any region over others."

To this end, Khan suggested that the reunified, sovereign state
be a union of three regions—Kashmir Valley, Jammu, and a "frontier region" comprising Gilgit and Baltistan (under Pakistani control since 1947) along with Ladakh (which is largely under Indian
control)—corresponding to pre-1948 administrative demarcations.
In a classic federalist argument, he contended that each constituent region should have "maximum internal autonomy": "Each
province [region] is sub-divided into districts and these districts
should have their own internal arrangements. At the center, there
should be a bicameral parliament with the lower house having
representation on the basis of population of different provinces
and the upper house equal representation for each province."[33]

In 1968 Balraj Puri, a veteran writer, journalist, and political activist who lives in Jammu city, presented a working paper to an all-party forum called the Jammu and Kashmir State People's Convention, convened at the initiative of Sheikh Mohammad Abdullah during one of his brief spells out of Indian prisons. Puri proposed a five-tiered decentralized institutional structure for IJK, leading to "a federation [IJK] within a federation [the Indian Union]." The tiers would be village, block, district, region, and state. Puri advised that each of the three constituent regions of IJK—Kashmir Valley, Jammu, and Ladakh—should have its own elected legislature, with authority over matters devolved from the IJK level of government, and an executive accountable to the legislature. He also argued that the upper chamber of a bicameral IJK legislature, constituted on the basis of equal representation for each region, should "specifically be entrusted with promoting inter-regional understanding and resolution of inter-regional disputes," and that "any legislation intended to amend the constitution of the state [IJK], alter inter-regional relations or change the overall status of the state, must first be referred to the upper house for its opinion." He counseled that the government bureaucracy and development agencies also be decentralized as much as possible, to regional and subregional levels.[34]

The *matryoshka*-doll complexity of IJK's society and politics poses special but not insurmountable challenges for the engineering of political structures that can accommodate, even if uneasily, a multitude of conflicting allegiances and competing aspirations. Sound ways exist of narrowing interregional differences, and the Srinagar-Jammu dimension (as well as the Srinagar-Leh dimension) of IJK's internal tensions can and should be constructively tackled as subsidiary to the democratic reconstruction and reconstitution of the New Delhi–Srinagar relationship. By long-established practice in IJK, Srinagar is the summer capital, where the government and administration are based for half the year, while the city of Jammu functions as the winter capital. (This necessitates a so-called *durbar* or royal court move, a term that reflects J&K's past as a princely principality, twice a year.)

A framework of multi-tiered devolution can potentially mitigate not only interregional differences but also *intra*regional differences such as those between the Jammu region's three Hindu-majority and three Muslim-majority districts, and those between the Muslim-dominated Kargil and Buddhist-dominated Leh districts of Ladakh. In fact, the embryo of such a framework already exists in IJK. A Ladakh Autonomous Hill Development Council (LAHDC) was established in 1995 in response to Buddhist demands for local self-government. In late 2002 Mufti Mohammad Sayeed's PDP-led IJK government expanded the status and competencies of this autonomous body and announced that a similar council would be established for the Kargil district by 30 June 2003. There are also plans to set up an umbrella regional authority for both Ladakh districts, whose chair will rotate between representatives of Leh and Kargil. As noted in Chapter 4, Leh Buddhists had resumed agitation in 2002, with backing from extreme right-wing Hindu groups in India, particularly the Rashtriya Swayamsevak Sangh, for separation of the whole Ladakh region from IJK and its conversion into a protectorate directly administered from New Delhi—a move strongly opposed by Muslim-dominated Kargil. But in late 2002 the leaders of the LAHDC, "praising the PDP-led government's decision to further empower it as 'historic' . . . said that it will go a long way towards development of the area and in meeting the aspirations of its people."[35]

The dispute over Kashmir is a multi-layered problem defined by multiple contentious relationships at "internal" and international levels, and it requires a multi-track approach geared toward a multidimensional settlement with interlocking parts.

TRACK 2B:THE ISLAMABAD-MUZAFFARABAD AXIS

The relationship between the Pakistani state and "Azad" Jammu and Kashmir is another "internal" dimension of the Kashmir problem. It is far less critical than the New Delhi–Srinagar dimension: AJK is a much smaller, less populous, and less diverse area than IJK, and there is no armed conflict between the Pakistani state and AJK residents. However, as noted in Chapter 2, repression and restrictions on political freedoms and participatory rights are a serious problem in AJK. Thus:

> While criticizing India's [2002] election [in IJK] some people in AJK are unhappy with the version of democracy they are served up on their own side of the Line of Control dividing the territory. Zahid Sheikh [a resident of Muzaffarabad, AJK's capital] sought to stand as a candidate of the [independentist] Jammu & Kashmir Liberation Front in elections to AJK's 48-member legislative assembly in July 2001. His nomination papers and those of other party colleagues were rejected on the grounds that they had not signed a declaration stating that they support the accession of disputed Kashmir to Pakistan. Sheikh said that elections in AJK are not conducted according to democratic norms. "They are not free and fair. Election laws bar pro-independence people from taking part."[36]

Like its Indian counterpart in IJK, the Pakistani state is deeply fearful of the underlying popularity of independentist, unifica-

tionist ideas among sections of AJK's population.[37] Hence the exclusion of one of the two basic strands of political belief in AJK
from the arena of institutional politics, which is consequently monopolized by AJK affiliates of Pakistani parties and local political
formations, such as the Muslim Conference party, whose loyalty
to Pakistan is beyond suspicion. In order to rectify this situation,
an end to such exclusion needs to be negotiated between Pakistani authorities and the pro-independence groups, coupled with
an end to the use of police methods against activists of pro-independence groups such as JKLF, the Jammu and Kashmir People's
National Party, and their youth and student wings. Power-sharing
in AJK's government between pro-Pakistan and pro-independence
parties should be considered, to foster an inclusive and representative political system. In addition, although AJK has acquired a pan-
oply of "autonomous" institutions—including its own constitution and an elected president, legislature, prime minister, supreme
court, high court, election commission, and public service commission—the operation of this self-government is subject to various forms of intervention and manipulation by Pakistani authorities. Such intervention and manipulation need to be minimized.
As part of an overall, multi-dimensional settlement, it is desirable
that there should be a rough symmetry between the autonomy of
IJK from the federal center in India and the autonomy of AJK
from the center in Pakistan.

NORMALIZATION AS A PRELUDE TO DEMOCRATIZATION

The democratization of IJK's political space involves knotty, substantive, long-term issues and would, even in a best-case scenario,
take several years. To build and sustain momentum for the long
haul, tangible normalization measures need to be delivered as rapidly as possible in IJK, a society deeply scarred by continuous

guerrilla warfare and counterinsurgency. These measures relate to three interconnected areas:

- human rights

- policing arrangements

- political prisoners.

The human rights crisis which gripped the Valley from January 1990 on was described in Chapter 3. After thirteen years and many twists and turns, ups and downs in insurgency and the war against insurgency, the situation remains grave, volatile in some areas and simply grim in others. Some parts of the Valley, including most towns, are more peaceful than they were during the first six years of the fighting, but deeply insecure conditions persist in much of the Valley, exacting a daily toll of civilians, soldiers and police officers, and insurgents in guerrilla attacks and counterinsurgency operations. For example, in late November 2002 seven Indian army personnel, three women and two children, and two policemen were killed when the bus transporting them from Srinagar to Jammu hit a land mine planted by HM guerrillas at the southern end of the Kashmir Valley. Twenty-three others were seriously injured.[38] During the 1990s most of the Jammu region also experienced the spreading of guerrilla war, and some of the worst zones of armed conflict are located in Jammu, in the districts of Doda, Rajouri, and Poonch, and parts of Udhampur. Much of IJK resembles a huge prison camp, swarming with military and paramilitary camps, bunkers, checkpoints, and patrols, and citizens feel harassed and oppressed in this environment. The problem is severely compounded by the fact that the vast majority of India's army and paramilitary personnel deployed in the Valley and the war zones of Jammu consist of men, mostly non-Muslims, from outside IJK.

As a ceasefire or a very significant reduction of violence leading toward cessation is achieved, the Indian security presence should rapidly become as inoffensive and unobtrusive as possible toward local populations. This means a drastic reduction in bunkers, checkpoints, aggressive patrolling, and cordon-and-search operations (crackdowns), and redeployment of most army and paramilitary units away from population centers, either to barracks in IJK, bases outside IJK, or traditional duties of border security. The longer-term goal must be to strengthen the capacity of ordinary police forces made up of local residents to carry out routine tasks of maintaining public order and security with fairness and efficiency, and to marginalize counterterrorism police such as the Special Operations Group (SOG), drawn from among IJK residents including turncoat guerrillas, whose reputation for brutality and criminality has surpassed even the unsavory record of army and paramilitary forces composed overwhelmingly of non-IJK personnel.

Effective mechanisms for monitoring and enforcing compliance with human rights standards among Indian security forces are essential. India's National Human Rights Commission, which under the leadership of J. S. Verma, a former chief justice of the country's supreme court, has built a credible reputation as a human rights defender, can play a major role in this if allowed to do so, as can IJK's own state human rights commission and its judiciary (the high court), most of whose rulings and directives on human rights cases and standards have simply been ignored by the counterinsurgency apparatus for more than a decade. International humanitarian agencies such as the International Committee of the Red Cross, which has been playing a limited role in IJK since late

1995, and IJK-based, Indian, and international human rights watchdog groups can also help in improving the human rights environment. An acknowledgment by the government of India that large-scale abuses have occurred, and that these are regretted, would help heal deep psychological wounds. Nongovernmental groups trying to help widows, orphans, and other victims of the conflict can operate much more effectively after violence ends or is reduced to negligible levels. Special attention should also be paid to the needs of all persons displaced by the conflict, including members of the Valley's Pandit community, so that all who wish to do so can return to their homes and localities and live with security and dignity.

The release of political prisoners and an end to abuse of emergency regulations would be an especially important confidence-building step. During 2002 three of the Hurriyat Conference's seven executive committee members (the first-tier leadership) languished in Indian jails, detained under draconian laws such as India's Prevention of Terrorism Act (POTA) and IJK's Public Safety Act (PSA) primarily to prevent them from mobilizing public opinion against the Indian-sponsored elections. One of the three, the religious conservative Syed Ali Shah Geelani, known for his pro-Pakistan views, is a cardiac patient in his seventies who was elected thrice to the IJK legislature during the 1970s and 1980s. Another, the independentist JKLF's Yasin Malik, was first arrested under POTA and severely assaulted by SOG men while in custody. When the POTA case against him disintegrated as witnesses who had allegedly incriminated him in money-laundering recanted, he was rearrested under the PSA, which allows incommunicado detention for two years without any legal process, and denied medical attention needed for urgent health problems.[39] Malik was freed in November 2002 by the new PDP-led government of IJK. These are the best-known cases, but hundreds of second- and third-tier activists of parties and groups favoring self-determination, including known "moderates," are also in prison without having committed or commissioned any act of violence. Some other prisoners who participated in the guerrilla war in its early phase, such as Showkat Bakshi of the JKLF (also released by the PDP-led government in November 2002) and Mushtaq-ul Islam of Hizbullah, have been incarcerated since 1990 or 1991, even though their organizations have long forsaken violence (JKLF) or become defunct (Hizbullah).

The Northern Ireland peace process not only developed the three-strand framework that tackles the fundamentals of the conflict in all its dimensions. It also established two key subcommittees, one to deal with the issue of "decommissioning" the arsenals of republican and loyalist militant groups, the other to address the issues of reform of the police system, fair and impartial administration of justice, the status of political prisoners, observance of human rights standards, and socioeconomic aspects of post-conflict reconstruction. Any transition from war toward peace in Kashmir needs to be supported by parallel moves to establish a degree of normalization, rule of law, and a minimally civil state-society relationship not based simply on *zulm* (repression). This is precisely the agenda of the PDP leadership, which "in its [election] manifesto . . . promised to repeal POTA, the Disturbed Areas Act, the Armed Forces Special Powers Act, disband the SOG, set up a commission to probe disappearances, release detainees, and work for the final settlement of the Kashmir dispute."[40] The first point of the thirty-one-point common minimum program of the PDP-led coalition government states:

> The goal of the coalition government is to heal the
> physical, psychological and emotional wounds inflicted
> by fourteen years of militancy, to restore the rule of

law in Jammu & Kashmir state, to complete the revival
of the political process begun by the recently concluded
[IJK] elections, and to request the Government of India
to initiate and hold sincerely and seriously, wide-rang-
ing consultations and dialogue, without conditions,
with the members of the [IJK] legislature and other segments of public opinion in all three regions of the state
to evolve a broad-based consensus on the restoration of
peace with honor in the state.[41]

This is a positive and promising statement of purpose, which
clearly sees liberalizing reforms and normalizing measures—
known as the PDP's "healing touch" policy—as steps toward a serious, sustained, and multidimensional peace process (although
PDP leaders are careful not to be publicly drawn, as yet, on either
self-rule for IJK or Pakistan's role in a peace process, both highly
sensitive topics in India). But even the near-term part of the
agenda—implementation of the "healing touch" initiatives—faces
scarcely disguised hostility from Hindu hard-liners leading India's
coalition government in New Delhi, especially from the home (interior) ministry headed by L. K. Advani, India's deputy prime minister. The extent to which the top leaders of the Congress party,
whose IJK wing is the PDP's main coalition partner in Srinagar/
Jammu, understand the history, gravity, and complexity of the
Kashmir conflict is also questionable, as is the commitment of the
Congress to the PDP's clear, bold, and feasible vision of a peace
process. There is also the threat of violence from hard-line militant groups. In December 2002 one of the sixteen PDP deputies in
the IJK legislative assembly, elected in October from the Valley
constituency of Pampore, was assassinated as he stepped out of
his local mosque after offering Friday prayers.[42] Mufti Mohammad

Sayeed and his top party colleagues like his daughter Mehbooba and Muzaffar H. Beigh, IJK's finance and law minister, face a situation which is daunting to say the least. But they deserve credit for attempting to initiate the first halting steps in the long journey toward peace in Kashmir.

Track 3: The Srinagar-Muzaffarabad Axis

In November 2000 a delegation of citizens from the IJK city of Jammu visited AJK. Comprised mostly of Hindus, the delegation included IJK's most senior journalist, Ved Bhasin, and Krishan Deo Sethi, a veteran political activist, both seventy years old. Bhasin's family is from an AJK town called Bhimbar, and Sethi grew up in another AJK town, Mirpur. Neither had visited the Pakistani-controlled zone of Jammu and Kashmir since late 1947. As the delegation crossed the LOC and entered AJK, its members were mobbed by joyous crowds out to give the visitors from across the border the warmest possible welcome. Almost buried under garlands, the visitors were escorted from one town to another, and from one emotional public reception to the next. Throughout, they heard one slogan being chanted over and over again: *"Is paar bhi azaadi, us paar bhi azaadi"* (Freedom on this side, freedom on that side).[43]

I have argued that erasing *or* redrawing the Line of Control in Kashmir is neither feasible nor desirable. It is not feasible because it would violate the bottom-line position on sovereignty and territorial integrity of one or both states involved in the Kashmir dispute. Feasibility constraints aside, it is not desirable because shifting or eliminating the border represented by the LOC not only cannot provide a solution to the fundamental disagreements over legitimate sovereignty internal to J&K, but risks a grave exacerbation of local and inter-state conflict arising from those disagreements. At the same time, I have argued that the "cross-border" dimension of the Kashmir conflict is inevitable because history, international law, regional geopolitics, and local religious, ethnic, and political ties all spill across the boundary called the LOC.

Fortunately, ways exist of substantively tackling the dilemma represented by the LOC—the frontier drawn in blood through Jammu and Kashmir in 1947–1948—which do not require any change in existing, de facto territorial jurisdictions of states in Kashmir. A well-known American policymaker and intellectual, Strobe Talbott, has spelled out an approach based on three key principles to conflicts over sovereignty and self-determination in the contemporary world. First, existing international borders, however contested and contestable, should generally "not be changed by force, either by wars of aggression or wars of secession," as creating "small, fractious states" out of "large, repressive or failed states" may aggravate the problem instead of resolving it. Second, states "have a responsibility . . . to ensure that all who live within the boundaries of the state can consider themselves fully respected and enfranchised citizens of that state." In some cases, of which Kashmir would surely qualify as one, a third, crucial element is needed to ensure that "self-determination can flourish without requiring the proliferation of micro-states or encouraging irredentist conflict." The way "to make a virtue out of porous borders and intertwined economies and cultures" is through institutionalization of "cross-border economic development and political cooperation"—whether between states or parts of states, or both—an opportunity opened up by "globalization and its sub-phenomenon, regionalization." "The most successful states" of the early twenty-first century, in Talbott's convincing prognosis, will be the countries "that harness these forces and facts of life rather than deny them."[44]

A longer-term Kashmir settlement necessitates that the LOC be transformed—from an iron curtain of barbed wire, bunkers, trenches, and hostile militaries to a linen curtain between self-governing Indian and Pakistani regions of Jammu and Kashmir. Realpolitik dictates that the border will be permanent (albeit probably under a different name), but it must be transcended without being abolished in order to meet the aspirations of those, on both sides of the line, who do not like the LOC, either in principle or in its present trajectory. This means that self-rule frameworks in IJK and AJK must be complemented by cross-border institutional links between the regions under Indian and Pakistani sovereignty. This will connect the large pro-independence population in areas under Indian sovereignty with their compatriots across the internal and international frontier (and vice versa), and the smaller but still sizeable pro-Pakistan segment to their preferred state, and vice versa (had a pro-India segment existed in Pakistani-controlled Kashmir, it would also have had the effect of connecting them to their preferred state, and vice versa). In the longer run, such cross-border linkages are the solution to the problem of "cross-border terrorism."

In concrete terms, this might mean the establishment of a cross-border Jammu and Kashmir ministerial council that brings together ministers from IJK and AJK governments to develop co-operation in areas where it makes sense to do so. (These governments must, to reiterate, have a broadly based inclusive character during a transitional phase, including representatives of all three strands of basic political orientation on the Indian side of the LOC and both on the Pakistani side, probably requiring that these governments be based on internal power-sharing arrangements.) Such matters, selected from devolved subjects under the competency of these governments, could include aspects of intra-J&K

trade and commerce, intra-J&K waterways, cross-border transport, environmental protection and preservation, agriculture, cultural matters, and tourism. To begin with, such cross-border cooperation would be modest, with the potential to expand over
time. An inter-entity legislators' group could also be established to
provide a cross-border forum for communication and consultation between members of elected IJK and AJK assemblies. Such
institutional links between the two Kashmirs, along with a soft
border that permits the legal, legitimate movement of citizens,
would be the final element of the institutional architecture of an
overall settlement.

Foreign affairs, external defense, currency and macroeconomic
policy, and some aspects of communications would be likely to remain the exclusive prerogatives of the sovereign governments of
India and Pakistan under such a settlement. On other matters that
remain under the purview of central governments, a permanent
India-Pakistan intergovernmental council can provide the mechanism for each sovereign government to give the other consultative
access to formulation and implementation of policies that relate
to their respective territorial jurisdictions in Jammu and Kashmir.

The framework for peace proposed in this chapter is ambitious,
given entrenched positions and antagonisms. Yet this is the only
viable framework on the basis of which a durable peace can be
built in Kashmir and the subcontinent. It takes full account of the
core concerns of states regarding sovereignty and territorial integrity, and it points to the way in which a modus vivendi can be con-
structed between the status quo Indian and the revisionist Pakistani perspectives on the conflict. At the same time, it argues for
an honorable compromise between state power and popular aspi-

rations to *azaadi* as essential for a serious peace process and a genuine settlement. And it points to practical ways of reconciling conflicting aspirations and allegiances within Jammu and Kashmir. This strategic roadmap to peace addresses all dimensions of the Kashmir conflict and shows the way to move beyond the present impasse with a skillfully crafted accommodation that respects all stances on the conflict and rejects none.

A framework such as this would be opposed neither by a relatively moderate regime in Pakistan which happens to be strongly influenced by its relationship with the United States, nor by the vast majority of political groups favoring self-determination nor, indeed, by some of the most influential insurgent formations (such as HM) active in Kashmir. For India, the status quo power in the conflict, negotiating a compromise settlement would liberate enormous financial and human resources now invested in a protracted war of pacification and control that cannot be won militarily, prove India's maturity and confidence as the world's largest and most diverse democracy, and significantly advance India's well-founded aspiration to be an economic and political player of global stature. In the event of a military escalation of the Kashmir conflict, India, a huge country of enormous economic potential, has much more to lose than Pakistan does.

Any agreement on Kashmir should be ratified by the parliaments of India and Pakistan, as well as by any other relevant bodies in the two countries. It should also be put to popular referenda, conducted separately, in the Indian and Pakistani parts of Jammu and Kashmir. Until the logic of mutually destructive conflict is superseded by an alternative logic of a peace process framed in terms of the universal values of *insaaniyat* (humanity) and *insaaf* (justice), Kashmir will remain a flashpoint of global concern in a militarized and nuclearized subcontinent.

NOTES

Introduction

1. The official Indian inquiry into the 1999 conflict has been published as *From Surprise to Reckoning: The Kargil Review Committee Report* (New Delhi: Sage, 2000). For a different perspective, see All Parties Hurriyat Conference, *Kargil Crisis: Need for Introspection* (New Delhi: Kashmir Awareness Bureau, 1999).

2. Paula R. Newberg, *Double Betrayal: Repression and Insurgency in Kashmir* (Washington: Carnegie Endowment for International Peace, 1995), 74.

3. Information from my interviews with surviving JKLF activists from the early phase of the uprising.

4. "16,000 Terrorists Killed over Thirteen Years," *Kashmir Times*, 5 Dec. 2002, 1; see also "J&K Arms Haul Enough for Two Small Wars," *Times of India*, 7 Apr. 2002 (internet ed.).

5. These works are excerpted in Muzamil Jaleel, "Dead Poets' Society: People in Kashmir Valley Resort to Poetry to Express Their Pain and Document Trauma and Tragedy," *Indian Express*, 13 July 2002 (internet ed.).

6. Sir Albion Bannerji, quoted in Mohammad Ishaq Khan, *History of*

Srinagar, 1846–1947: A Study in Socio-Cultural Change (Srinagar: Cosmos, 1999), 191.

7. Prem Nath Bazaz, *Kashmir in Crucible* (New Delhi: Pamposh, 1967), 128.

8. C. E. Tyndale Biscoe, *Kashmir in Sunlight and Shade* (London: Seeley, Service and Co., 1922), 77.

9. Frederick Whelan, "Democratic Theory and the Boundary Problem," in J. Roland Pennock and John Chapman, eds., *Liberal Democracy*, NOMOS XXV (New York: New York University Press, 1983), 13–47. Robert Dahl, *Democracy and Its Critics* (New Haven: Yale University Press, 1989), 207.

10. The broad assessments in this paragraph are based on my extensive field research throughout the Jammu, Kashmir Valley, and Ladakh regions of IJK between 1995 and 2002, and on my interviews with JKLF activists from Mirpur and Poonch, AJK.

11. William Wallace, "Reconciliation in Cyprus: A Window of Opportunity" (discussion paper, European University Institute, 2002), 9, 12.

1. Origins of the Conflict

1. See Ian Copland, *The Princes of India in the Endgame of Empire, 1917–1947* (Cambridge: Cambridge University Press, 1997).

2. For the text of the Treaty of Amritsar, see Jyoti Bhushan Dasgupta, *Jammu and Kashmir* (The Hague: Martinus Nijhoff, 1968), 387–388.

3. Prem Nath Bazaz, *Inside Kashmir* (Srinagar, 1941; Mirpur: Verinag, 1987), 252–253.

4. C. E. Tyndale Biscoe, *Kashmir in Sunlight and Shade* (London: Seeley, Service and Co., 1922), 79–80. Kashmir's most famous king, Zain-ul-Abidin, ruled from 1420 to 1470 and is remembered as an intelligent and enlightened monarch. The mass conversion of the Valley's people from Hinduism to Islam occurred largely in the fourteenth century, and Sufi mystics played a major role in the process. The patron saint of the Kashmir Valley is the main Sufi preacher of that period, Sheikh Nooruddin Noorani. His discourse combined Sufi Islam with Hindu Shaivite elements; he is traditionally referred to as Nund Rishi by Val-

ley Hindus. See Mohammad Ishaq Khan, *Kashmir's Transition to Islam: The Role of Muslim Rishis* (Delhi: Manohar, 1994). Noorani's shrine and mausoleum, located in a town thirty kilometers from Srinagar, was gutted by arson in 1995, sparking outrage in the Valley. The Kashmir Valley was captured by the Mughals in 1586, whose rulers treated it as a summer resort and laid out the beautiful Mughal gardens of Srinagar. In 1752 the Valley was overrun by Afghans (Pashtuns), who held it until 1819, when the forces of Ranjit Singh's expanding Sikh kingdom captured the region.

5. Mohammad Ishaq Khan, *History of Srinagar, 1846–1947* (Srinagar: Cosmos, 1999), 193.

6. Alastair Lamb, *Crisis in Kashmir, 1947 to 1966* (London: Routledge and Kegan Paul, 1966), 28.

7. Khan, *History of Srinagar*, 192. Rita Manchanda, "Guns and *Burqa*: Women in the Kashmir Conflict," in Rita Manchanda, ed., *Women, War and Peace in South Asia: From Victimhood to Agency* (New Delhi: Sage Publications, 2001), 55.

8. Dasgupta, *Jammu and Kashmir*, 61.

9. Lamb, *Crisis in Kashmir*, 31.

10. Prem Nath Bazaz, *Kashmir in Crucible* (New Delhi: Pamposh, 1967), 135. Dasgupta, *Jammu and Kashmir*, 61–62.

11. Dasgupta, *Jammu and Kashmir*, 66.

12. Josef Korbel, *Danger in Kashmir* (Princeton: Princeton University Press, 1954), 149.

13. Control of Hazratbal passed into the hands of independentist JKLF guerrillas from 1990 until 1996, when they were evicted by Indian security forces amid a bloodbath.

14. Khan, *History of Srinagar*, 198. In the early 1990s the aged Masoodi was murdered in his Srinagar home by pro-Pakistan Kashmiri militants young enough to be his grandchildren, who regarded any Kashmiri figure who had had any sort of association with India in the past as a traitor. Also in the 1990s, Sheikh Abdullah's grave and mausoleum in Srinagar—he died in 1982—had to be placed under the guard of Indian

security forces to prevent its desecration, in a society that had once re-garded him as a deliverer of near-divine stature.

15. When the NC became the de facto government in Srinagar in late 1947, one of its first decisions was to name Srinagar's central square Lal Chowk (Red Square) in honor of the Moscow original and the So-viet Union. The decision reflected the presence of a sizeable pro-com-munist segment in the party leadership.

16. Dasgupta, *Jammu and Kashmir,* 66–68, 189. For the text of the charter of women's rights, see Urvashi Butalia, ed., *Speaking Peace: Women's Voices from Kashmir* (Delhi: Kali for Women, 2002), 313–315.

17. "Where Is Sheikh's Naya Kashmir?" *Indian Express,* 24 June 2002, 1.

18. Quoted in M. J. Akbar, *India, the Siege Within: Challenges to a Nation's Unity* (Harmondsworth: Penguin, 1985), 227–228.

19. Dasgupta, *Jammu and Kashmir,* 189, 188.

20. Daniel Thorner, *The Agrarian Prospect in India* (Bombay: Allied Pub-lishers, 1976), 50. Wolf Ladjensky, "Land Reform: Observations in Kashmir," in L. J. Walinsky, ed., *Agrarian Reforms as Unfinished Business* (Oxford: Oxford University Press, 1977), 179–180.

21. Dasgupta, *Jammu and Kashmir,* 190.

22. Ibid., 70.

23. Richard Symonds, reporting on the Poonch uprising in *The Statesman* (Calcutta), 4 Feb. 1948.

24. Liaquat Ali Khan in a radio broadcast on 4 Nov. 1947, quoted in Dasgupta, *Jammu and Kashmir,* 107.

25. Ibid., 95. Some of the commanders were professional military officers who had served first in Britain's Indian army and subsequently in the anti-colonial Indian National Army, formed in Southeast Asia from the ranks of prisoners of war captured by the Japanese, and led by the In-dian nationalist leader Subhas Chandra Bose between 1943 and 1945. The trucks and some weapons were supplied by the government of Pakistan's NWFP.

26. Balraj Puri, "Kashmiriyat: The Vitality of Kashmiri Identity," *Contempo-rary South Asia* 4, 1 (March 1995), 57.

27. Dasgupta, *Jammu and Kashmir*, 113.
28. Ibid., 109. Lamb, *Crisis in Kashmir*, 46–48. A. G. Noorani, *The Kashmir Question* (Bombay: Manaktalas, 1964), 61.
29. For the text of this resolution, passed on 21 April 1948, see Dasgupta, *Jammu and Kashmir*, 395–398.
30. Ibid., 401.
31. For the text of this resolution, see ibid., 402–403.
32. Noorani, *The Kashmir Question*, 68.
33. See Dasgupta, *Jammu and Kashmir*, 220.
34. "We have fought four wars over the LOC," Musharraf said in January 2002. He was presumably referring to 1947–1948, 1965, 1971, and 1999. "Pakistan Cannot Accept LOC as Border: Musharraf," *Indian Express*, 18 Jan. 2002 (internet ed.). In August 1965 several thousand Pakistani military personnel, mostly from AJK, supported by some civilian volunteers from the same area, infiltrated into IJK to engage in sabotage and foment an uprising. Pakistani military planners hoped to take advantage of two factors: perceived demoralization in the Indian military after defeat in a border conflict with China in late 1962, and serious political unrest in IJK between late 1963 and 1965. The operation failed; no anti-India uprising occurred in any part of IJK, while many infiltrators were apprehended by Indian security forces on the basis of information given by locals. The attempt backfired further when India decided in September 1965 not to limit hostilities to J&K alone but instead to broaden the conflict to encompass the entire India-Pakistan border, meaning a full-fledged war. In the Kargil sector of Ladakh in 1999, the infiltrators were mostly professional soldiers and officers of the Pakistani army's Northern Light Infantry, which is recruited from AJK and the Northern Areas, supported by some units of *mujahideen* fighters. The world community, including major countries like the United States and China, fearing an escalation beyond limited war, responded by calling for strict non-violation of the LOC. The operation stiffened Indian resolve instead of compelling India to open negotiations with Pakistan on Kashmir, and it was Pakistan that faced interna-

tional pressure to withdraw its forces. There were two differences from the 1965 situation, however. First, the Indians did not opt to widen the conflict to a general war, and this change was attributed by Pakistanis to their nuclear deterrent against an Indian conventional attack on Pakistan. Second, although India fought its battles on the Kargil heights in the name of protecting the "territorial integrity" of the country and reaffirming Kashmir's status as an "integral part" of the Indian Union, most people in IJK felt thoroughly estranged from the battles being waged with such fervor in their name. On the reaction in the Valley, see Muzamil Jaleel, "It Was Not Our War," in Sankarshan Thakur et al., *Guns and Yellow Roses: Essays on the Kargil War* (New Delhi: Viking, 1999), 63–94. For a synopsis of the Kargil crisis, see Sumantra Bose, "Kashmir: Sources of Conflict, Dimensions of Peace," *Survival* 41, 3 (Autumn 1999), 149–153.

2. The Kashmir-India Debacle

1. Quoted in Prem Nath Bazaz, *Kashmir in Crucible* (New Delhi: Pamposh, 1967), 136–137.

2. For the text of this address see Saifuddin Soz, *Why Autonomy for Kashmir?* (New Delhi: Indian Center for Asian Studies, 1995), 121–139.

3. See A. G. Noorani, *The Kashmir Question* (Bombay: Manaktalas, 1964), 101.

4. *Speeches and Interviews of Sher-é-Kashmir Sheikh Mohammad Abdullah* (Srinagar: Jammu and Kashmir Plebiscite Front, 1968), vol. 2, 13; vol. 1, 15–16.

5. Benedict Anderson, *Imagined Communities: Reflections on the Origins and Spread of Nationalism* (London: Verso, 1991), 145–146.

6. *India Today*, 31 Mar. 1987, 26. Khemlata Wakhloo, *Kashmir: Behind the White Curtain, 1972–1991* (Delhi: Konark, 1992), 321.

7. *India Today*, 15 Apr. 1987, 40–43. According to the prearranged division of spoils, NC got thirty-eight seats, mostly in the Valley, and Congress twenty-four, mostly in the Jammu region.

8. *Illustrated Weekly of India*, 10–16 Oct. 1992, 4.

9. "Kashmir: Valley of Tears," *India Today,* 31 May 1989.

10. See Muzamil Jaleel, "Kashmir Town Shows the Way: Polls Free and Very Unfair," *Indian Express,* 27 May 2002 (internet ed.).

11. For the text of the resolution, see Jyoti Bhushan Dasgupta, *Jammu and Kashmir* (The Hague: Martinus Nijhoff, 1968), 406–407.

12. Balraj Puri, *Kashmir: Towards Insurgency* (Delhi: Orient Longman, 1993), 45–49. Noorani, *The Kashmir Question,* 59.

13. Balraj Madhok, a founder of Praja Parishad and later all-India president of the Bharatiya Jan Sangh, India's Hindu nationalist party now known as Bharatiya Janata Party (BJP), quoted in Dasgupta, *Jammu and Kashmir,* 195.

14. In India's quasi-federal system, there are three lists of subjects: an extensive Union List under the purview of the central government in New Delhi, a State List reserved for legislation at the level of the units of the Indian Union (states), which includes such subjects as policing and education, and a Concurrent List, a gray area of shared jurisdiction.

15. See Dasgupta, *Jammu and Kashmir,* 194.

16. Ibid., 196.

17. Soz, *Why Autonomy for Kashmir,* 128.

18. Bazaz, *Kashmir in Crucible,* 151. Since 1948 the district of Poonch has been divided between Indian and Pakistani zones. The town of Poonch and a considerable slice of rural Poonch lie in IJK, the rest across the LOC in AJK. India's Poonch district has a Muslim majority of 90 percent, while the district of Rajouri to its south has a Muslim majority of 65 percent. Most of the Muslims of Poonch and Rajouri are ethnic Rajputs or Gujjars and Bakerwals, non-Kashmiri speakers ethno-culturally distinct from the Kashmiri-speaking Muslims who dominate the Valley and most of Doda. The *towns* of Poonch and Rajouri, however, have Hindu/Sikh majorities. While most Rajouri-Poonch Muslims (like their AJK neighbors across the LOC) are divided from Kashmir Valley/Doda Muslims by ethnicity and language, they are also divided from their Hindu compatriots in Jammu by communal cleavages.

19. See R. K. Jain, ed., *Soviet-South Asian Relations*, vol. 1: *1947–1978* (Atlantic Highlands, N.J.: Humanities Press, 1979), 3–4.

20. Syed Mir Qasim, *My Life and Times* (Delhi: Allied Publishers, 1992), 68–70.

21. Josef Korbel, *Danger in Kashmir* (Princeton: Princeton University Press, 1954), 246. Dasgupta, *Jammu and Kashmir*, 212–213.

22. Dasgupta, *Jammu and Kashmir*, 212–213.

23. See Jain, ed., *Soviet-South Asian Relations*, 15–20.

24. Dasgupta, *Jammu and Kashmir*, 223–224, 222, 224.

25. Puri, *Kashmir: Towards Insurgency*, 45–49.

26. Dasgupta, *Jammu and Kashmir*, 227, 228.

27. Ibid., 226. Noorani, *The Kashmir Question*, 73.

28. Dasgupta, *Jammu and Kashmir*, 226.

29. For the text of this resolution, see ibid., 408.

30. See Tapan Bose et al., "India's Kashmir War," in Asghar Ali Engineer, ed., *Secular Crown on Fire: The Kashmir Problem* (Delhi: Ajanta, 1991), 262–267.

31. See Neville Maxwell, *India's China War* (London: Jonathan Cape, 1970).

32. For the text of this agreement, see Dasgupta, *Jammu and Kashmir*, 389–391.

33. Ibid., 269–270.

34. Puri, *Kashmir: Towards Insurgency*, 45–49. M. J. Akbar, *India, The Siege Within: Challenges to a Nation's Unity* (Harmondsworth: Penguin, 1985), 258.

35. Dasgupta, *Jammu and Kashmir*, 308–309.

36. Bazaz, *Kashmir in Crucible*, 100.

37. Dasgupta, *Jammu and Kashmir*, 323, quoting Indian newspaper reports of the time.

38. Reeta C. Tremblay, "Jammu: Autonomy within an Autonomous Kashmir?" in Raju G. C. Thomas, ed., *Perspectives on Kashmir* (Boulder: Westview, 1992), 164. Puri, *Kashmir: Towards Insurgency*, 89.

39. Ibid., 31–32. Dasgupta, *Jammu and Kashmir*, 333.

40. Bazaz, *Kashmir in Crucible*, 100–104.

41. Ibid., 99–100. Donald Horowitz, *Ethnic Groups in Conflict* (Berkeley: University of California Press, 1985), 243–249.

42. Akbar, *India, The Siege Within*, 267. Bazaz, *Kashmir in Crucible*, 157.

43. Shaheen Akhtar, "Elections in Indian-held Kashmir, 1951–1999," *Regional Studies* 18, 3 (Summer 2000), 37.

44. Puri, *Kashmir: Towards Insurgency*, 49. Alastair Lamb, *Kashmir: A Disputed Legacy, 1946–1990* (Karachi: Oxford University Press, 1992), 209–210.

45. Qasim, *My Life and Times*, 106, 132.

46. Akhtar, "Elections in Indian-held Kashmir," 87, citing Keesing's Contemporary Archives (1968).

47. Ibid., 38–39.

48. Balraj Puri, *Jammu and Kashmir: Triumph and Tragedy of Indian Federalism* (Delhi: Sterling, 1981), 151. For the text of the 1975 Delhi Accord, see Qasim, *My Life and Times*, 138–140.

49. This applies to India, Pakistan, and Sri Lanka. For thirty-eight of Indian democracy's first forty-two years (1947–1989), the country was governed by Congress prime ministers belonging to three generations of the Nehru family—Nehru himself, Indira Gandhi, and her son Rajiv Gandhi. In Pakistan, Benazir Bhutto, the Pakistan People's Party (PPP) prime minister on two occasions, is the daughter of Zulfiqar Ali Bhutto, former foreign and prime minister. In Sri Lanka, Sirimavo Bandaranaike succeeded her husband, Solomon Bandaranaike, as prime minister in 1960; their daughter, Chandrika Kumaratunga, became prime minister in 1994 and later president.

50. For more on this critical phase in Indian politics, which directly facilitated the rise of Hindu majoritarian nationalism in India in the 1990s, see Sumantra Bose, "Hindu Nationalism and the Crisis of the Indian State: A Theoretical Perspective," in Sugata Bose and Ayesha Jalal, eds., *Nationalism, Democracy and Development: State and Politics in India* (Delhi: Oxford University Press, 1997), 119–124.

51. Achin Vanaik, "The Kashmir Problem," *Times of India*, 18 Apr. 1990, op-ed page.

52. Farooq Abdullah, *My Dismissal* (Delhi: Vikas, 1985), 1-2.

53. Akhtar, "Elections in Indian-held Kashmir," 32.

54. Interviewed in *India Today*, 30 Nov. 1986.

55. M. J. Akbar, quoted in Engineer, ed., *Secular Crown on Fire*, 291.

56. *India Today*, 15 Apr. 1987, 40-43.

57. *India Today*, 15 Nov. 1986, 43, and 30 Apr. 1990, 10.

58. Personal information from JKLF sources.

59. Puri, *Kashmir: Towards Insurgency*, 56-57; "Kashmir: Valley of Tears," *India Today*, 31 May 1989.

60. Philippe Schmitter and Terry Lynn Karl, "What Democracy Is . . . and Is Not," in Larry Diamond and Marc Plattner, eds., *The Global Resurgence of Democracy* (Baltimore: Johns Hopkins University Press, 1993), 39-52.

61. Courtney Jung and Ian Shapiro, "South Africa's Negotiated Transition: Democracy, Opposition and the New Constitutional Order," *Politics and Society* 23, 3 (Sept. 1995), 271-273.

62. Juan Linz, *The Breakdown of Democratic Regimes: Crisis, Breakdown and Re-equilibration* (Baltimore: Johns Hopkins University Press, 1978), 28-33.

63. Interview with Amanullah Khan in *The Statesman* (Calcutta), 28 Apr. 2002. Leo Rose, "The Politics of Azad Kashmir," in Thomas, ed., *Perspectives on Kashmir*, 238. For a survey of AJK's politics between 1947 and 1965, see Dasgupta, *Jammu and Kashmir*, 231-248. Dasgupta's account highlights two features: endemic factionalism within AJK's semi-feudal elite, and the Pakistani state's strict control of AJK politics. Rose covers more recent developments.

64. On these concepts, see Eric Nordlinger, *Soldiers in Politics: Military Coups and Governments* (New Jersey: Prentice-Hall, 1977), 21-29.

3. The War in Kashmir

1. *Times of India* (Delhi), 6 May 1990.

2. Muzamil Jaleel, "I Am Going at the Call of Allah and Doing What Allah Has Made Our Farz," *Indian Express*, 25 Nov. 2001 (internet ed.).

3. See Tapan Bose et al., "India's Kashmir War," in Asghar Ali Engineer, ed., *Secular Crown on Fire: The Kashmir Problem* (Delhi: Ajanta, 1991), 161.

4. Ibid., 229-230.

5. Hameeda Bano, speaking in April 1994, quoted in Victoria Schofield, *Kashmir in Conflict* (London: Tauris, 1996), 231.

6. *India Today*, 30 Apr. 1990, 13.

7. Ayesha Kagal, "Accidental Terrorists," *Times of India*, 29 Apr. 1990.

8. *India Week* (Delhi), 24 Aug. 1990.

9. Edward Desmond, "The Insurgency in Kashmir, 1989-91," *Contemporary South Asia* 4, 1 (Mar. 1995), 13. "Militancy in Kashmir Valley Completes Fourteen Years," *Kashmir Times*, 1 Aug. 2002 (internet ed.); Amnesty International, *"If They Are Dead Tell Us": Disappearances in Jammu and Kashmir* (London: Amnesty International, Feb. 1999).

10. Muzamil Jaleel, "BSF's Men Gang-Rape 17-Year-Old in Valley, Family Made to Watch," *Indian Express*, 20 Apr. 2002, 1. The victim was a Gujjar girl in a mountain hamlet near Pahalgam, in the southern part of the Valley.

11. For documentation of the human rights crisis during the *intifada* phase, see Amnesty International, *India: Torture and Deaths in Custody in Jammu and Kashmir* (London: Amnesty International, Jan. 1995), which details 715 cases of summary executions and deaths under torture since 1990; Asia Watch, *Kashmir under Siege* (New York: Human Rights Watch, May 1991); Asia Watch–Physicians for Human Rights, *Rape in Kashmir: A Crime of War* (New York: Human Rights Watch, June 1993); Asia Watch–Physicians for Human Rights, *The Human Rights Crisis in Kashmir: A Pattern of Impunity* (New York: Human Rights Watch, June 1993); Fédération Internationale des Ligues des Droits de l'Homme, *Kashmir: A People Terrorized* (Paris, Aug. 1993); Committee for Initiative on Kashmir, *Kashmir: A Land Ruled by the Gun* (Delhi, Dec. 1991); Saqina Hasan, Primila Lewis, Nandita Haksar, and Suhasini Mulay, *Kashmir Imprisoned* (Delhi: Committee for Initiative on Kashmir, July 1990), an investigation into conditions for women in the Valley; Bose et al., "India's Kashmir War," 224-270; and People's Union for Civil

Liberties, "Report on Kashmir Situation," ibid., 210–223. A useful compilation of reports that appeared during 1990 in newspapers and magazines worldwide is A. R. Minhas and Mustahsan Aqil, *Kashmir: Cry Freedom* (Mirpur: Kashmir Record and Research Cell, 1991).

12. *India Today*, 31 Jan. 1990. *Illustrated Weekly of India*, 10–16 Oct. 1992, 6.

13. *Hindustan Times*, 29 Aug. 2001 (internet ed.).

14. "Hizb-ul Mujahideen behind Army Convoy Ambush," *Times of India*, 25 Nov. 2001 (internet ed.); "Army Commanding Officer, Bodyguards Killed in Blast," *Kashmir Times*, 20 Aug. 2002 (internet ed.); "Securitymen Retaliate with Vengeance: 130 Houses Torched, Villagers Tortured, Scores Missing," *Kashmir Times*, 23 Aug. 2002 (internet ed.). Shakeel Ansari's brother Farooq Ansari, also a militant, was killed in a shootout with Indian forces in 2000. Shakeel was injured in that encounter but escaped.

15. Bose et al., "India's Kashmir War," 261.

16. See Sumantra Bose, *The Challenge in Kashmir: Democracy, Self-Determination and a Just Peace* (New Delhi: Sage, 1997), 78–79.

17. Amitabh Mattoo, writing in the *Illustrated Weekly of India*, 10–16 Oct. 1992, 10. Mattoo's parents, eminent citizens of Srinagar, have continued to live there throughout the troubles.

18. Khemlata Wakhloo and O. N. Wakhloo, *Kidnapped: 45 Days with Militants in Kashmir* (Delhi: Konark, 1993), 396.

19. For such allegations see Rashtriya Swayamsevak Sangh, *Genocide of Hindus in Kashmir* (Delhi: Suruchi Prakashan, 1991).

20. *India Today*, 28 Feb. 1993, 22–25.

21. "15,000 Pandits Throng Khir Bhawani Temple: Muslims Greet Pilgrims, Serve Eatables," *Kashmir Times*, 18 June 2002 (internet ed.); "Kashmiri Pandits Throng Ramji Temple after 13 Years," *Hindustan Times*, 21 Apr. 2002 (internet ed.).

22. See Amanullah Khan, *Free Kashmir* (Karachi: Central Printing Press, 1970).

23. Zargar was captured by Indian forces in 1992. In December 1999 he was one of three jailed militants released by the Indian government in exchange for the freedom of 160 hostages after a group of Pakistani

religious radicals hijacked an Indian Airlines plane flying from Kathmandu to Delhi to Kandahar, then the nerve center of the Taliban regime in Afghanistan. The others released were Ahmed Omar Saeed Sheikh, a British citizen of Pakistani origin, who in 2002 was sentenced to death in Pakistan for his role in the January 2002 kidnapping and murder of the *Wall Street Journal* reporter Daniel Pearl in Karachi, and Maulana Masood Azhar, a radical Pakistani cleric captured by Indian forces in the Kashmir Valley in 1994.

24. This sequence of events is reconstructed on the basis of my interviews with leading JKLF activists from IJK and AJK, supported by my own field research in IJK.

25. See note 23.

26. John Rettie and Ghulam Nabi Khayal, "Kashmiris Round on Pro-Pakistan Groups," *Guardian* (London), 22 June 1994, 11.

27. An Institute of Kashmir Studies report, *Catch and Kill* (Srinagar, 1993) details 118 such cases. IKS is affiliated with the conservative religious party Jama'at-I-Islami, which in turn is the political affiliate of the guerrilla organization Hizb-ul Mujahideen.

28. A. G. Noorani, "The Tortured and the Damned: Human Rights in Kashmir," *Frontline*, 28 Jan. 1994, 44–48.

29. My information from reliable sources.

30. See *India Today*, 29 Feb. 1992, 15; 15 Mar. 1992, 31–32.

31. *India Today*, 31 May 1993, 27.

32. Ved Bhasin, editor-in-chief of the *Kashmir Times*, a daily newspaper published in Jammu.

33. Conclusions based on my research and personal information.

34. Rettie and Khayal, "Kashmiris Round on Pro-Pakistan Groups."

35. Desmond, "Insurgency in Kashmir," 11–12. Paula R. Newberg, *Double Betrayal: Repression and Insurgency in Kashmir* (Washington: Carnegie Endowment for International Peace, 1995), 73.

36. See Human Rights Watch, *India's Secret Army in Kashmir* (New York: HRW, 1996).

37. Four RR formations of approximately ten thousand soldiers each op-

erate in designated zones of responsibility in northern Valley districts (Kilo Force), southern Valley districts (Victor Force), Doda-Kishtwar in Jammu (Delta Force), and Rajouri-Poonch in Jammu (Romeo Force).

38. Commentary in *Greater Kashmir*, Apr. 28, 2002.

39. See Bose, *The Challenge in Kashmir*, 152–170, and Shaheen Akhtar, "Elections in Indian-held Kashmir, 1951–1999," *Regional Studies* 18, 3 (Summer 2000), 49–61.

40. "Three Cops, Hizb Terrorist Killed in J&K Encounter," *Hindustan Times*, 9 Sept. 2002.

41. For the text of the Lahore Declaration, see *www.indianembassy.org/South_Asia/Pakistan/lahoredeclaration.html*. For Indian and Pakistani perspectives on the nuclear dimension, see Raju G. C. Thomas and Amit Gupta, eds., *India's Nuclear Security* (Boulder and London: Lynne Rienner, 2000); Lieutenant-General Kamal Matinuddin, *The Nuclearization of South Asia* (Karachi: Oxford University Press, 2001); and Rear Admiral Raja Menon, *A Nuclear Strategy for India* (New Delhi: Sage, 2000). For American perspectives, see George Perkovich, *India's Nuclear Bomb: The Impact on Global Proliferation* (Berkeley: University of California Press, 1999); and Ashley J. Tellis, *India's Emerging Nuclear Posture: Between Recessed Deterrent and Ready Arsenal* (Santa Monica: Rand, 2001).

42. On the reaction in the Valley, see Muzamil Jaleel, "It Was Not Our War," in Sankarshan Thakur et al., *Guns and Yellow Roses: Essays on the Kargil War* (Delhi: Viking, 1999). On the mood in the Kargil district immediately after the fighting, see Shujaat Bukhari, "The Battle Is a Non-Issue," *The Hindu*, 3 Sept. 1999. The 1965 and 1999 Pakistani incursions into IJK are compared in Chapter 1, note 34.

43. *Kashmir Times*, 1 Dec. 2002 (internet ed.).

44. JeM was launched under the leadership of Maulana Masood Azhar in early 2000, immediately after his release from Indian captivity in the circumstances described in note 23.

45. For analysis of the doctrinal roots of suicidal warfare in Kashmir and its parallels with historical and contemporary political movements, see Muzamil Jaleel's articles "Where Death Is the Weapon, and the Mes-

sage," "Martyrdom: The Prize for Taking One's Life," and "The Fight to the Finish," at *www.expressindia.com/kashmir/kashmirlive*. For an account of the development of *fidayeen* tactics in the Kashmir insurgency, see Masood Hussain, "Kashmir Separatists Remonstrate against Guest Militants," *Kashmir Times*, 23 Dec. 2001.

46. "Hizb Says Jammu Massacre Un-Islamic, Suspects Foreign Hand," United News of India (UNI) report carried in the *Kashmir Times*, 20 July 2002 (internet ed.).

47. For an analysis in historical and comparative perspective of the Tamil Tigers' conception of martyrdom and their practice of suicidal violence, see Sumantra Bose, *States, Nations, Sovereignty: Sri Lanka, India and the Tamil Eelam Movement* (New Delhi: Sage, 1994), 117–128.

48. "LeT Fidayeen Strike at CRPF Camp, Two Ultras Dead: Six Jawans Killed, Nine Hurt in Srinagar Attack," *Kashmir Times*, 23 Nov. 2002, 1.

49. "NC Caught in Gujjar Web in Rajouri, Poonch," *Kashmir Times*, 14 Aug. 2002 (internet ed.).

50. Prem Nath Bazaz, *Kashmir in Crucible* (New Delhi: Pamposh, 1967), 105–106.

51. *Daily Excelsior* (Jammu), 19 Sept. 2000, 1. "572 Ultras Killed in Rajouri-Poonch So Far This Year," *Hindustan Times*, 31 Oct. 2001 (internet ed.). "12 Ultras Killed in Rajouri-Poonch Encounters," *Kashmir Times*, 29 Apr. 2002, 1.

52. "LeT, JeM, HM Form Joint Panel in Jammu," *Kashmir Images* (Srinagar), 29 Apr. 2002, 1.

53. Pradeep Dutta, "At This School, It's To Sir with Love and Terror," *Indian Express*, 28 Nov. 2001 (internet ed.). "Militants Kill Judge, Three Others in Kashmir," *Indian Express*, 5 Dec. 2001 (internet ed.). "Nine Villagers Killed in Rajouri Encounter, Army Faces Public Rage," *Indian Express*, 22 Jan. 2002 (internet ed.). "Target Army HQ: Rajouri Police Recover Rocket Shells," *Kashmir Times*, 18 Feb. 2002 (internet ed.). "Army Captain, Four Terrorists Killed in Rajouri," *Hindustan Times*, 1 Aug. 2002 (internet ed.).

54. "Major, JCO among 11 Soldiers Killed in Surankote Encounter," *Kash-*

mir Times, 28 Nov. 2001 (internet ed.). "Seven Ultras, Major among Ten Killed in Surankote Encounters," *Kashmir Times*, 14 July 2002 (internet ed.). "Army Captain, Two Cops Killed in Militant Ambush," *Kashmir Times*, 31 July 2002 (internet ed.). "Two Civilians Killed in Surankote," *Kashmir Times*, 18 Aug. 2002. "Seven JeM Terrorists Gunned Down in Poonch," *Hindustan Times*, 8 Aug. 2002 (internet ed.).

55. *Kashmir Images*, 30 Apr. 2002, 1. "Militants Kill Four of Cop's Family in Jammu," *Indian Express*, 26 Aug. 2002 (internet ed.). "Terrorists Spray Bullets at J&K Bus Stand, Kill 12," *Hindustan Times*, 11 Sept. 2002 (internet ed.); "Three More BSF Men Dead, Surankote Toll 16," *Kashmir Times*, 13 Sept. 2002 (internet ed.).

56. "Two Priests among Nine Killed in J&K," *Times of India*, 29 Aug. 2001 (internet ed.). "Nine Killed in Jammu," *Times of India*, 18 May 2002 (internet ed.). "Four Civilians Killed in Ambush," *Kashmir Times*, 7 Nov. 2002, 1.

57. *Greater Kashmir*, 28 Apr. 2002.

58. "Top LeT Militant among Four Ultras Killed in Valley," *Hindustan Times* (J&K edition), 29 Apr. 2002.

59. "Five Policemen Injured as Militants Attack Kashmir Minister's House," *Hindustan Times*, 25 June 2002 (internet ed.). "Terrorists Kill J&K Minister," *Hindustan Times*, 11 Sept. 2002 (internet ed.).

60. Muzamil Jaleel, "Militants Spray Bullets at Funeral," *Indian Express*, 13 Sept. 2002 (internet ed.); Masood Hussain, "Lone's Burial Marked by Firing, Encounter in Lolab: Two Soldiers, Militant Killed in Battle," *Kashmir Times*, 13 Sept. 2002 (internet ed.).

61. "Nine Militants, Soldier Killed in Valley," *Kashmir Times*, 20 July 2002 (internet ed.). "Army Foils Fresh Infiltration Bid in Kupwara," *Hindustan Times*, 29 July 2002 (internet ed.). "Six Killed in Kashmir," *Kashmir Times*, 18 Aug. 2002 (internet ed.).

62. "1052 Terrorists Killed in 2002," *Kashmir Times*, 20 Aug. 2002.

63. "NC's Likely Poll Candidate Gunned Down," *Kashmir Times*, 1 Aug. 2002 (internet ed.). "NC Zonal President Shot Dead in Valley," *Kashmir Times*, 8 Aug. 2002.

64. *Statesman* (Calcutta), 7 Sept. 2000, 1.

65. "We Are in Danger: J&K Ultras," *Indian Express*, 10 Nov. 2001 (internet ed.).

66. "Musharraf Forced Us to Close Terror Camps in PoK: Militants," *Indian Express*, 29 July 2002. See also Zahid Hussain, "Pakistan's Link Man with Kashmir Militants Sacked," *Times* (London), 29 June 2002 (internet ed.). The purged officer was ISI's Brigadier Abdullah, head of the agency's Kashmir operations.

67. "Nobody Can Stop Us from Entering J-K: Militants," *Indian Express*, 27 Aug. 2002.

4. Sovereignty in Dispute

1. Statement of the External Affairs Ministry, Government of India, New Delhi, Jan. 1994.

2. "Mirpur Declaration" of JKLF, 5 Jan. 1995. The fifth of January is observed as "third option/right to independence day," the anniversary of a UNCIP statement of 1949 that resolved to establish a plebiscite administration in Jammu and Kashmir.

3. See Amanullah Khan, "India v/s India" (Rawalpindi: JKLF, 1991), 9–10. Khan is one of the founders of the JKLF movement. The same proposal for a three-way plebiscite, to be decided by a simple majority, was made in January 1994 by Raja Mohammad Muzaffar, then senior vice president of the AJK-based JKLF, to a meeting on Kashmir organized by the U.S. Institute for Peace in Washington.

4. Leo Rose, "The Politics of Azad Kashmir," in Raju G. C. Thomas, ed., *Perspectives on Kashmir* (Boulder: Westview, 1992), 251.

5. David Butler and Austin Ranney, *Referendums: A Comparative Study of Practice and Theory* (Washington: American Enterprise Institute, 1978), 36.

6. See Sumantra Bose, *Bosnia after Dayton: Nationalist Partition and International Intervention* (New York: Oxford University Press, 2002); Steven Burg and Paul Shoup, *The War in Bosnia-Herzegovina: Ethnic Conflict and International Intervention* (Armonk, N.Y.: M. E. Sharpe, 1999).

7. "Musharraf Rules out Conversion of LOC into Border," *Hindustan Times*, 12 Sept. 2002 (internet ed.).

8. "India to Welcome Proposal to Turn LOC into Border," *Statesman*, 7 Sept. 2002, 1.

9. "Pakistan Cannot Accept LOC as Border: Musharraf," *Indian Express*, 18 Jan. 2002 (internet ed.). Musharraf apparently put forward the same outline to Indian leaders during a visit to India in July 2001. He reiterated it during a talk show on the BBC's international television network, *Question Time Pakistan*, in September 2002.

10. For example, Gowher Rizvi, *South Asia in a Changing International Order* (New Delhi: Sage, 1993), 80–86. Rizvi suggests an independent state comprising the Valley and the "Azad" Kashmir districts which are under Pakistani control.

11. See John McGarry, "Orphans of Secession: National Pluralism in Secessionist Regions and Post-Secession States," in Margaret Moore, ed., *National Self-Determination and Secession* (New York: Oxford University Press, 1998), 215–232.

12. Kashmir Study Group, *Kashmir: A Way Forward* (Larchmont, N.Y., Jan. 2000).

13. "One Killed, Thirteen Injured in Kishtwar Grenade Attack," *Kashmir Times*, 19 Feb. 2002 (internet ed.).

14. See Sumantra Bose, "'Hindu Nationalism' and the Crisis of the Indian State: A Theoretical Perspective," in Sugata Bose and Ayesha Jalal, eds., *Nationalism, Democracy and Development: State and Politics in India* (Delhi: Oxford University Press, 1997), 104–164; and Thomas Blom Hansen, *The Saffron Wave: Democracy and Hindu Nationalism in Modern India* (Princeton: Princeton University Press, 1999).

15. "Divide J&K into Four Parts, Create Separate Enclave for Pandits: VHP," *Hindustan Times*, 23 June 2002 (internet ed.). The VHP rose to prominence in the 1990s as the spearhead of the Hindu sectarian movement's campaign to destroy a sixteenth-century mosque in the town of Ayodhya, northern India, and replace it with a Hindu temple. The mosque was razed by organized mobs of Hindu zealots in December 1992, sparking communal violence across India. The controversy is still an inflammatory and destabilizing issue in Indian politics.

See S. Gopal, ed., *Anatomy of a Confrontation: The Ramjanambhoomi-Babri Masjid Dispute* (Delhi: Penguin India, 1991).

16. Pradeep Kaushal, "Split J-K into Three Parts, Says RSS," *Indian Express*, 1 July 2002 (internet ed.).

17. "No Trifurcation of J&K: Advani," *Hindustan Times*, 3 July 2002 (internet ed.). The RSS is the parent organization of India's Hindu sectarian movement and deputes its members to lead all other organizations which constitute the movement, including the BJP (both Advani and the prime minister, Vajpayee, are RSS veterans).

18. Kaushal, "Split J-K into Three Parts." Pradeep Kaushal, "Split J&K: RSS Takes It Forward," *Indian Express*, 13 July 2002. Zafar Choudhary, "BJP Manifesto Reiterates Article 370 Abrogation," *Kashmir Times*, 14 Sept. 2002 (internet ed.).

19. Personal information from sources in Leh.

20. This group, which calls itself Pannun Kashmir, has reputedly been patronized since its formation in the early 1990s by elements of the Indian federal government's interior ministry, and receives considerable publicity in sections of the Indian media. See the report on its activities in *Sunday* (Calcutta), 23–29 Jan. 1994, 70–74.

21. Prem Nath Bazaz, *Kashmir in Crucible* (New Delhi: Pamposh, 1967), 151.

22. Muzaffar Raina, "All Parties in Kargil Oppose RSS Demand for Trifurcation," *Kashmir Times*, 13 Aug. 2002 (internet ed.).

23. Nicholas Sambanis, "Partition as a Solution to Ethnic War: An Empirical Critique of the Theoretical Literature," *World Politics* 52 (July 2000), 437–483. Bose, *Bosnia after Dayton*, ch. 4.

24. On the destabilizing and antidemocratic implications of the doctrine of self-determination in the contemporary, post-bipolar world, see Donald Horowitz, "Self-Determination: Politics, Philosophy and Law," in Moore, ed., *National Self-Determination*, 181–214.

25. "Polling amidst Mixed Reaction in Valley," *Kashmir Times*, 17 Sept. 2002 (internet ed.).

26. "J&K Voters Say They Were Forced to Vote," AFP dispatch, Srinagar, 16 Sept. 2002.

27. Mufti Islah, Tariq Mir, and Nazir Masoodi, "1st Day, 1st Show: No Hit but Surely Not a Flop," *Indian Express*, 17 Sept. 2002 (internet ed.). "Polling amidst Mixed Reaction," *Kashmir Times*.

28. Muzamil Jaleel, "Some Places Army Rushed in Where It Didn't Have to Tread," *Indian Express*, 17 Sept. 2002 (internet ed.).

29. "Protesters Burn Jeep of Ruling Party Candidate," *Indian Express*, 17 Sept. 2002 (internet ed.).

30. Only 2,546,913 citizens were registered to vote for these elections in the Kashmir Valley, whose population is over 5 million (all citizens aged eighteen and over are eligible to vote); 2,892,290 were registered in the Jammu region, which has a population of about 4.5 million. "Jammu Region Has More Voters Than Kashmir Valley," *Hindustan Times*, 25 Aug. 2002 (internet ed.). Voter registration did not pick up despite attempts by Indian security forces to intimidate citizens into acquiring voter cards; see Muzamil Jaleel, "Only the Voter ID Counts in Valley Now," *Indian Express*, 12 Aug. 2002 (internet ed.).

31. Muzamil Jaleel, "*Azaadi* and Election in Same Breath: Lone Associate to Contest, Gets Red Carpet," *Indian Express*, 30 Aug. 2002 (internet ed.). For more on Sofi's role and antecedents in Handwara politics, see Chapter 2.

32. Sayeed's other daughter, Rubaiya, was kidnapped by independentist JKLF militants in December 1989, when her father was India's interior minister; see Chapter 3.

33. Nazir Masoodi and Mufti Islah, "Four Villages and a Hurriyat Dove-Hawk Divide," *Indian Express*, 17 Sept. 2002 (internet ed.).

34. Tariq Mir, "22-Year-Old Votes for Peace," *Indian Express*, 17 Sept. 2002.

5. Pathways to Peace

1. "Indo-Pak Tension Major Threat to World Peace: Annan," *Hindustan Times*, 12 Sept. 2002 (internet ed.). "Bush, Annan Hold Talks on Kashmir Issue," AFP dispatch, New York, 13 Sept. 2002.

2. "Kashmir Chocolate Ad Angers BJP," AFP dispatch, New Delhi, 20 Aug. 2002.

3. Arun Sharma, "A Child without a Father Gets a Country in Jammu & Kashmir," *Indian Express*, 3 Aug. 2002, 1; "Shehnaz Symbolises Tragedy of the Two Kashmirs," *Kashmir Times*, 3 Aug. 2002, 1. See also Masood Hussain, "NC Government's Double-Standards on Mirpuri Woman's Case," *Kashmir Times*, 20 Aug. 2002, 1; Yamini Kaul, "Freedom Still Eludes Released Shehnaz," *Kashmir Times*, 8 Aug. 2002, 1; "Shehnaz-Mobeen Detention Case: Court Orders Release, Compensation, Stay in India of Pakistani Lady," *Kashmir Times*, 3 Aug. 2002, 1; and Irm Amin Beig, "Born in Jail, Question Mark on Mobeen's Nationality," *Kashmir Times*, 20 July 2002 (internet ed.).

4. Robert Kee, *Ireland: A History* (London: Weidenfeld and Nicholson, 1980), 248. For useful overviews of the Northern Ireland question, see Brendan O'Leary and John McGarry, *The Politics of Antagonism: Understanding Northern Ireland* (London: Athlone, 1996), and John Darby, *Scorpions in a Bottle: Conflicting Cultures in Northern Ireland* (London: Minority Rights Group, 1997). On the reemergence of the IRA and its political wing, Sinn Fein, see Patrick Bishop and Eamonn Mallie, *The Provisional IRA* (London: Heinemann, 1987).

5. Bertie Ahern, Prime Minister of the Republic of Ireland, speaking in January 2000, quoted in Padraig O'Malley, "Northern Ireland and South Africa: Hope and History at a Crossroads," in John McGarry, ed., *Northern Ireland and the Divided World: Post-Agreement Northern Ireland in Comparative Perspective* (Oxford: Oxford University Press, 2001), 301. For the text of the Good Friday Agreement, and reportage, commentary, and analysis on the peace process, see the *Irish Times* website, *www.ireland.com/special/peace*. For dissections of the historical context, structure, nuances, and implications of the peace-building framework, see Brendan O'Leary, "The Nature of the British-Irish Agreement," *New Left Review* (Jan.–Feb. 1999), 66–96; and Brendan O'Leary, "Comparative Political Science and the British-Irish Agreement," in John McGarry, ed., *Northern Ireland and the Divided World: Post-Agreement Northern Ireland in Comparative Perspective* (Oxford: Oxford University Press, 2001), 53–88.

6. O'Leary, "Comparative Political Science," 63.

7. See Antony Alcock, "From Conflict to Agreement in Northern Ireland: Lessons from Europe," in McGarry, ed., *Northern Ireland and the Divided World*, 159-180.

8. See George J. Mitchell, *Making Peace* (New York: Knopf, 1999).

9. John McGarry, "Northern Ireland, Civic Nationalism, and the Good Friday Agreement," 128; O'Leary, "Comparative Political Science," 53, 82.

10. See Edward W. Said, *The End of the Peace Process* (London: Granta Books, 2002).

11. For the text of the Agreement, see P. R. Chari and Pervaiz Iqbal Cheema, *The Simla Agreement, 1972: Its Wasted Promise* (Delhi: Manohar, 2001), 204-206.

12. For the text of the Lahore Declaration, see *www.indianembassy.org/South_Asia/Pakistan/lahoredeclaration.html.*

13. Muzamil Jaleel, "In Jammu and Valley, Phase 2," *Indian Express*, 25 Sept. 2002, 1.

14. Ibid.; "Voters' Ink Stains a Requirement in Badgam," *Indian Express*, 25 Sept. 2002 (internet ed.). "Coalition of Civil Society Report: Coercion, Bogus Polling Alleged," *Kashmir Times*, 25 Sept. 2002, 1.

15. Jaleel, "In Jammu and Valley, Phase 2," and "Voters' Ink Stains a Requirement in Badgam."

16. Sankarshan Thakur, "Farooq Abdullah Pulls Audience from Hat, Then Talks through It: Is Anybody Listening?" *Indian Express*, 21 Sept. 2002, 1; Tariq Mir and Mufti Islah, "Farooq Abdullah Owns Up, Says Sorry at His Flop Show: Declares Sops, Asks People to Vote without Fear," *Indian Express*, 21 Sept. 2002 (internet ed.).

17. Muzamil Jaleel, "South Kashmir Waits, Campaign Marred by Violence," *Indian Express*, 30 Sept. 2002 (internet ed.).

18. Muzaffar Raina, "It's PDP in Bijbehara, Boycott in Anantnag," *Kashmir Times*, 1 Oct. 2002 (internet ed.). Muzaffar Raina, "Pahalgam Becomes a Focus for NC, PDP," *Kashmir Times*, Sept. 30, 2002, 1. Masood Hussain, "In Kulgam, Marx and God Live Harmoniously," *Kashmir Times*, 30 Sept. 2002, 1.

19. *Indian Express*, 1 Oct. 2002 (internet ed.).

20. Udayan Namboodiri and Rashid Ahmad, "NC May Leave NDA after Polls: Omar," *Hindustan Times*, 1 Oct. 2002 (internet ed.).

21. Arun Joshi and Rashid Ahmad, "Blood-Spattered Third Round in J&K Elections," *Hindustan Times*, 1 Oct. 2002 (internet ed.).

22. "Mixed Trends in Valley: Boycott, Coercion, Willing Votes," and "Coercion Sparks Protests: Those Boycotting Had Second Option, Change," *Kashmir Times*, Oct. 2, 2002, 1. "Securitymen Responsible for Coercion in Phase III Polls: CCS," *Kashmir Times*, 2 Oct. 2002 (internet ed.).

23. Nazir Masoodi, "Polls No Solution: Omar Abdullah," *Indian Express*, 1 Oct. 2002, 1. Joshi and Ahmad, "NC May Leave NDA after Polls." "Fresh Wave of Terrorist Attacks Sweeps J-K," *Indian Express*, 2 Oct. 2002 (internet ed.).

24. Barkha Dutt, "Vajpayee Postpones Kashmir Visit," NDTV dispatch, Srinagar, 3 July 2002.

25. See Mitchell, *Making Peace.*

26. George Mitchell in the *Irish Times*, 18 and 19 Nov. 1999.

27. Mitchell, *Making Peace*, 185–186.

28. Quoted in *Kashmir Times*, 23 Aug. 2000, 1.

29. One such member was Krishna Bose, chair of the Parliament's standing committee on external (foreign) affairs.

30. "Centre Will Be Compelled to Restore Autonomy: Omar Abdullah," *Hindustan Times*, 18 Sept. 2002 (internet ed.).

31. Scott McDonald, "Tigers Say They Will Change Stripes, Give Up 'Eelam': 'Substantial Autonomy' Rather Than Statehood," *Indian Express*, 19 Sept. 2002, 1. See also Balasingham's statement at the opening session of the multi-stage peace talks at *www.eelam.com/talks2002/ab_thai160902.html.*

32. "LTTE Leader Calls for Autonomy and Self-Government for Tamil Homeland," LTTE press release, 27 Nov. 2002, accessed 5 Jan. 2003 at *www.eelam.com/leader_heroes_day_2002.html.* I had urged precisely such a reconstitution of Sri Lanka's state structure in 1994 in my book

States, Nations, Sovereignty: Sri Lanka, India and the Tamil Eelam Movement (New Delhi: Sage, 1994), ch. 5.

33. Amanullah Khan, *Free Kashmir* (Karachi: Central Printing Press, 1970), 139–149.

34. Balraj Puri, *Simmering Volcano: A Study of Jammu's Relations with Kashmir* (Delhi: Sterling, 1983), Annexure A.

35. "Mufti's Autonomy Sop for Ladakh," *Hindustan Times*, 30 Dec. 2002, 5.

36. "PoK Residents Sceptical about J-K Polls," *Indian Express*, 18 Sept. 2002 (internet ed.).

37. See Leo Rose, "The Politics of Azad Kashmir," in Raju G. C. Thomas, ed., *Perspectives on Kashmir* (Boulder: Westview, 1992).

38. "Sudden Upsurge of Violence in Kashmir Valley," *Kashmir Times*, 24 Nov. 2002, 1.

39. Committee for Initiative on Kashmir, *A Report on the Condition Of Mohd. Yasin Malik, A POTA Detainee* (New Delhi, Apr. 2002); "Yasin Malik Re-Arrested under PSA after Release on Bail by POTA Court," *Kashmir Times*, 21 July 2002, 1.

40. Nazir Masoodi, "The J&K Verdict: In Ganderbal, People Celebrate NC's Ouster," *Indian Express*, 10 Oct. 2002 (internet ed.).

41. See *Kashmir Times*, 28 Oct. 2002, 1.

42. Muzamil Jaleel, "Terror Strikes J&K Healing Touch: PDP Legislator Killed after Friday Prayers," *Indian Express*, 21 Dec. 2002, 1.

43. Author's personal information from Ved Bhasin and Krishan Deo Sethi.

44. Strobe Talbott, "Self-Determination in an Inter-Dependent World," *Foreign Policy* 118 (Spring 2000), 152–163.

GLOSSARY

Abdullah: Sheikh Mohammad Abdullah (1905–1982), Kashmir's most important political figure in the twentieth century. Founder of the NC. Cooperated with India against Pakistan in 1947–1948 and was prime minister of IJK from 1948 to 1953. Deposed by an internal coup supported by New Delhi in 1953, and spent most of the next twenty-two years in Indian prisons. Restored as chief minister of IJK in 1975 by India in exchange for dropping his self-determination agenda for Kashmir.

AJK: "Azad" (Free) Jammu and Kashmir. The more populous part of Pakistani-controlled J&K, with a population of approximately 2.5 million. AJK has six districts: Muzaffarabad, Mirpur, Bagh, Kotli, Rawalakot, and Poonch. Its capital is the town of Muzaffarabad. AJK has its own institutions, but its political life is heavily controlled by Pakistani authorities, especially the military.

APHC: All-Parties Hurriyat (Freedom) Conference. A coalition, based in Srinagar, of three dozen groups that stand for the "right to self-determination" in Kashmir. Some constituents have a pro-Pakistan orientation, some have a pro-independence stance, and the position of others is ambiguous. Formed in 1993, the APHC is ideologically descended from previous movements in IJK including the PF and the MUF. It advocates dialogue and negotiations involving India, Pakistan, and APHC representatives as the means to a settlement of the conflict.

Azaadi: Literally, "freedom." The rallying cry of supporters of self-determination in Kashmir.

BJP: Bharatiya Janata Party, "Indian People's Party." A party that calls itself Hindu nationalist and claims to speak for the identity and interests of India's Hindu majority. Accused by opponents of being sectarian and anti-Muslim, the BJP was a relatively minor opposition party until 1990, gained wider support in the 1990s, and has been the leading element of the coalition government in New Delhi since 1998.

BSF: Border Security Force. The largest component of the vast Indian paramilitary apparatus in IJK, extensively deployed in urban policing and counterinsurgency operations since 1990.

Congress: The party that led India's movement for independence from British colonial rule and dominated independent India's politics for four decades; now India's major opposition party. Congress has been closely identified with the Nehru-Gandhi family: Jawaharlal Nehru, prime minister 1947–1964; his daughter Indira Gandhi, prime minister 1966–1977 and 1980–1984; and her son Rajiv Gandhi, prime minister 1984–1989.

CRPF: Central Reserve Police Force. The second-largest Indian paramilitary force deployed in IJK, usually in a less active combat role than the BSF.

Dogras: An upper-caste Hindu community found in the plains and foothills of the Jammu region. A Dogra dynasty founded the princely state of J&K and ruled it from 1846 to 1947.

Gujjars: A Muslim community in J&K whose traditional occupation is farming and livestock-rearing in highland areas. There are sizeable Gujjar concentrations in some parts of both the Jammu region and the Kashmir Valley.

HM: Hizb-ul Mujahideen. The largest guerrilla organization active in IJK, and the only one still led by and largely composed of IJK residents. Formed in 1989, it has a pro-Pakistan orientation and has ideological and organizational links with the Jama'at-i-Islami, a conservative religious movement active in IJK, AJK, Pakistan, and Bangladesh.

IED: Improvised explosive device. A favorite weapon used by guerrillas against Indian forces in IJK. These makeshift bombs and mines are usually placed on roadsides to target foot patrols, vehicles, and convoys, and are often detonated by remote control.

IJK: Indian-controlled Jammu and Kashmir. The larger and more populous part of the former princely state. It has a population of slightly over 10 million, and comprises three regions: Kashmir Valley, Jammu, and Ladakh. The Valley and large tracts of the Jammu region have been sites of guerrilla warfare and Indian counterinsurgency operations since 1990.

ISI: Inter-Services Intelligence. The Pakistani military's premier intelligence and covert operations arm, which rose to prominence during General Zia-ul Haq's military dictatorship in Pakistan (1977–1988), primarily as the agency coordinating the U.S.-backed war against the Soviet Union and its allies in

Afghanistan. Deeply involved in supporting and controlling the insurgency in IJK since the late 1980s.

JeM: Jaish-e-Mohammad. A radical Islamic group centered in Pakistan and active in insurgency in IJK. Formed in early 2000 by Maulana Masood Azhar, a Pakistani cleric, JeM has been implicated in several major *fidayeen* (suicidal) attacks in IJK, as well as in the hijacking of an Indian airliner in 1999 and a suicidal raid on India's Parliament in 2001. Its members are also implicated in sectarian Sunni violence against minority Shia Muslims and Christians in Pakistan, and links with Al Qaeda are probable. JeM was formally banned in Pakistan in January 2002.

J&K: Jammu and Kashmir. The former princely state that is the subject of the Kashmir dispute. Besides IJK and AJK, it includes the sparsely populated "Northern Areas" of Gilgit and Baltistan, remote mountainous regions which are directly administered, unlike AJK, by the Pakistani central authorities, and some high-altitude uninhabitable tracts under Chinese control.

JKLF: Jammu and Kashmir Liberation Front. A movement founded in the mid-1960s in AJK with the declared aim of reuniting the entire territory of the former princely state as an independent state. It acquired support in IJK (especially in the Kashmir Valley) in the late 1980s, and its activists spearheaded the insurrection that began in 1990. By 1993 its dominance of the armed struggle was over, and it ceased guerrilla activity in IJK in 1994, but it continues to be the voice of independentist ideology in both IJK and AJK. In IJK it is led by Yasin Malik, a former guerrilla leader, and is one of the major constituents of the APHC.

LeT: Lashkar-e-Taiba. An insurgent group active in IJK since the
mid-1990s, spawned by a Pakistan-based movement professing an ultra-orthodox variant of Sunni Islam. Like JeM, LeT
is predominantly composed of Pakistani religious radicals;
its leader is Hafiz Muhammad Sayeed, a Pakistani academic
turned fundamentalist activist. LeT cadres have been responsible for the majority of *fidayeen* attacks in IJK since 1999,
and are the prime suspects in a number of massacres of non-
Muslim civilians. Along with JeM, LeT was formally banned
in Pakistan in January 2002.

LOC: Line of Control. The 740-kilometer dividing line between
IJK and AJK–Northern Areas. It originated in January 1949 as
a ceasefire line at the end of the first India-Pakistan war, was
slightly altered during the December 1971 war, and was renamed the Line of Control by intergovernmental agreement
in July 1972. To the south of the LOC lie another 200 kilometers of "working boundary" between Indian Jammu and Pakistan's Punjab province. At its northern end, the LOC ter-
minates at a point called NJ 9842 in the high Himalayas,
beyond which lies a glacial region, Siachen, contested between Indian and Pakistani forces and then Chinese territory.

MC: Muslim Conference. The All–Jammu and Kashmir Muslim
Conference was Kashmir's first political party, founded in
1932. It was absorbed into the NC in 1939, but was revived two
years later. It assumed a pro-Pakistan orientation during the
1940s, and since 1947 has been the major political formation
in AJK. Its best-known leader is Sardar Abdul Qayyum Khan,
who has been both prime minister and president of AJK.

MUF: Muslim United Front. An ad hoc coalition of disparate
groups, based mostly in the Kashmir Valley, formed to con-

test elections in IJK in 1987 in opposition to an alliance of the
NC and Congress. That election was massively rigged, and
many young men who worked as volunteers for MUF subsequently turned to guerrilla war against Indian authority with
Pakistani support.

NC: National Conference. The All–Jammu and Kashmir National
Conference, formed in 1939 under the leadership of Sheikh
Mohammad Abdullah, has historically been the dominant
party in the Kashmir Valley. It led the popular movement
against the Dogra rulers, and its first government (1948–1953)
implemented major land reforms in IJK. In 1953 the NC was
taken over by New Delhi–sponsored politicians, and
Abdullah's followers formed the PF. When Abdullah returned as IJK's chief minister in 1975, he reappropriated the
NC. In the 1980s its mass base was severely eroded under the
leadership of his son Farooq Abdullah, and it was further
marginalized after the guerrilla revolt began in 1990. The
party returned to head a government in IJK in 1996 after dubious elections, and it became identified with incompetence,
corruption, and brutal counterinsurgency tactics. In IJK's
late-2002 elections the NC suffered a humiliating defeat. It is
still the major opposition within IJK's spectrum of pro-India
parties, but it is only a shadow of the mass-based force it
once was.

Pandits: The Kashmir Valley's small (4 percent) Hindu minority. Most
Kashmiri Pandits left the Valley for Jammu city or Delhi after
insurrection gripped the Valley in 1990, although some
Pandits have continued to live in their Valley homeland.

PC: People's Conference. A political party formed in the Kashmir
Valley in the late 1970s, initially to provide an opposition to
the NC. The party was part of the MUF in 1987 and has

been a member of the Hurriyat Conference since the latter's formation in 1993. Its strength is largely confined to the Valley's northern Kupwara district. Its founder, the moderate self-determination advocate Abdul Ghani Lone, was assassinated in Srinagar, probably by pro-Pakistan militants, in 2002.

PDP: People's Democratic Party. A party formed in IJK in 1999 under the leadership of Mufti Mohammad Sayeed, formerly a leader of India's Congress party in the Kashmir Valley. The PDP presented itself as a reformist, pro-people party, occupying a middle ground between the APHC and the NC. It rapidly gained popularity, especially in the Valley, mainly because of Sayeed's daughter Mehbooba Mufti, an outspoken advocate of human and civil rights. In the late-2002 IJK elections the PDP won 16 of 46 electoral constituencies in the Valley and Sayeed became IJK's chief minister, heading an uneasy coalition government with Congress. The PDP's agenda is to implement liberalizing reforms and normalizing measures in IJK, in the hope of paving the way for an eventual peace process involving India, Pakistan, and all segments of political opinion in IJK.

PF: Plebiscite Front. An organization formed in Srinagar by Abdullah's supporters in 1955, after the sheikh was deposed and imprisoned for challenging New Delhi and the NC was taken over by India-supported politicians. The PF sought respect for civil liberties, an inclusive political system, and above all, a resolution of the self-determination question either through a referendum under U.N. auspices or through an India-Pakistan peace process with the participation of J&K's diverse political forces. Although harassed and occasionally outlawed by India and its client IJK governments, the PF was a mass-based movement in IJK between 1955 and 1975, especially in the Kashmir Valley.

RR: Rashtriya (National) Rifles. Regular Indian army troops deployed since the early 1990s on full-time counterinsurgency operations in IJK. Four RR formations of over 10,000 soldiers each operate in IJK, two in the Valley and two in the Jammu region.

RSS: Rashtriya Swayamsevak Sangh, "National Volunteer Organization." The ideological and organizational core of the group of organizations, including BJP, that make up India's Hindu nationalist movement. It has several million members across India.

SOG: Special Operations Group. A specialized counter-terrorism police force, consisting of IJK residents including former guerrillas, which became a byword for criminality and brutality during the term in office (1996–2002) of the NC government. One of the most popular campaign pledges of the PDP in the late-2002 elections was to disband the SOG, and after assuming office the PDP-led government moved to curtail its power and activities.

UJC: United (Muttahida) Jihad Council. An umbrella coalition of over a dozen *tanzeems* (guerrilla groups) active in IJK. It is based in Muzaffarabad, the capital of AJK.

VHP: Vishwa Hindu Parishad, "World Hindu Council." The most openly extreme of India's sectarian Hindu groups, motivated by a violently anti-Muslim agenda. It functions as a far-right pressure group in Indian politics, has dedicated cadres, and raises funds from its network of overseas supporters, particularly in the United States.

ACKNOWLEDGMENTS

I would like to thank a few people who have, directly or indirectly, helped my work on Kashmir over the years: Mr. Ved Bhasin, a true inspiration, and the Bhasin family of Jammu; Mr. Imtiyaz Ahmed Sofi and the Sofi family of Qamarwari, Srinagar, and Handwara, north Kashmir; Yasin, Amina, and the Malik family of Maisuma, Srinagar; and Mrs. Krishna Bose, MP, and the Bose family of Calcutta and Delhi.

INDEX

INDEX

304

Khan, Amanullah, 99–100, 126, 251
Khan, Ayub, 80
Khan, Khan Abdul Ghaffar, 22
Khan, Liaquat Ali, 34, 38, 42, 179
Khatib, Nadeem, 102, 104–107, 140, 146
Kishtwar, 63, 115, 118–119, 131, 148, 185–186, 191
Korbel, Josef, 23, 55
Kupwara, 51, 52, 104, 113, 115, 125, 131, 147, 158–160, 194–199, 230, 240

Ladakh, 15, 41, 55, 77, 85, 90, 93, 118, 138, 141, 181, 184, 227, 230; diversity of, 10, 191–193; agitation against Abdullah government, 57, 62, 63; India-China border clashes (1962), 76; Buddhist separatist agitation, 187, 188, 189; future position in IJK self-rule framework, 249–253
Ladakh Autonomous Hill Development Council, 253
Ladakh Buddhist Association, 192
Lahore, 15, 18, 140, 141, 142
Lahore declaration (1999), 140, 226–227, 228
Lamb, Alastair, 18
Lashkar-e-Taiba (LeT), 106, 142–144, 146–147, 150, 153, 158, 160, 228–229
Lawrence, Walter, 16
Leh, 41, 188–189, 191–193, 252–253
Line of Control (LOC), 2, 10, 11, 51, 63, 83, 95, 99, 103, 104, 105, 107, 111, 112, 113, 116, 117, 118, 125, 126, 129, 137, 141, 143, 147, 148–149, 151–152, 155–156, 158, 160, 163, 166, 172, 203, 204, 207, 227, 230, 241, 254, 271n34; origins, 41; conversion into international border, 178–180; redrawing, 180–183; status under Simla agreement, 225; transformation of, 261–264

Linz, Juan, 98
Lok Sabha, 82, 85, 92–93, 96–97
Lone, Abdul Ghani, 52, 53, 94, 197, 199

Malik, Yasin, 49–51, 99, 103, 128, 130, 135, 146, 171, 239, 243, 258. See also Jammu and Kashmir Liberation Front
Mandela, Nelson, 201
Masoodi, Maulana, 24, 64, 66, 79, 80, 231
Mir, Javed, 103, 129, 130
Mirpur, 12, 33, 40, 151, 169, 203, 261
Mirwaiz Farooq, 79, 132
Mirwaiz Umer Farooq, 239
Mitchell, George J., 220, 242
Mountbatten, Lord, 30, 36
Mufti, Mehbooba, 198, 234, 261
Mufti, Mohammad Sayeed, 93, 198, 239, 253, 260–261. See also People's Democratic Party
Musharraf, Pervez, 1, 42, 141, 143, 144, 145, 163, 168, 179, 181–182, 227
Muslim Conference (MC), 20, 21, 22, 29, 31, 55, 255
Muslim League, 21, 22, 29, 33
Muslim United Front (MUF), 48–49, 94, 98–99, 102, 132
Muzaffarabad, 32, 35, 40, 151, 163, 254, 261

Narayan, Jayaprakash, 84
National Conference (NC), 22, 23–29, 46, 52, 53, 54, 62, 64, 65, 74, 75–76, 78, 79, 85, 86, 89, 92, 96, 102–103, 108, 115, 117, 138, 159, 161, 169, 170, 192; formation of, 20–21; and Naya Kashmir manifesto (1944), 25–26; and land reform in Kashmir, 27–28; in 1947 Kashmir events, 31, 32, 33, 37, 38; in